AMORAL COMMUNITIES

Copyright © 2019 by Cornell University

All rights reserved. Except for brief quotations in a review, this book, or parts thereof, must not be reproduced in any form without permission in writing from the publisher. For information, address Cornell University Press, Sage House, 512 East State Street, Ithaca, New York 14850. Visit our website at cornellpress.cornell.edu.

First published 2019 by Cornell University Press

Library of Congress Cataloging-in-Publication Data

Names: Dragojevic, Mila, author.
Title: Amoral communities : collective crimes in time of war / Mila Dragojevic.
Description: Ithaca [New York] : Cornell University Press, 2019. | Includes bibliographical references and index.
Identifiers: LCCN 2019010038 (print) | LCCN 2019011863 (ebook) | ISBN 9781501739835 (e-book pdf) | ISBN 9781501739842 (e-book epub/mobi) | ISBN 9781501739828 | ISBN 9781501739828? (hardcover ; alk. paper)
Subjects: LCSH: War and crime—Croatia—History—20th century. | Civilians in war—Violence against—Croatia. | Political violence—Croatia—History—20th century. | Ethnic conflict—Croatia—History—20th century. | Yugoslav War, 1991–1995—Croatia. | War and crime—Uganda—History—20th century. | Civilians in war—Violence against—Uganda. | Political violence—Uganda—History—20th century. | War and crime—Guatemala—History—20th century. | Civilians in war—Violence against—Guatemala. | Political violence—Guatemala—History—20th century.
Classification: LCC HV6189 (ebook) | LCC HV6189 .D73 2019 (print) | DDC 364.1/38—dc23
LC record available at https://lccn.loc.gov/2019010038

AMORAL COMMUNITIES

Collective Crimes in Time of War

Mila Dragojević

CORNELL UNIVERSITY PRESS   ITHACA AND LONDON

To my brother
To the victims of violence

Contents

List of Illustrations	ix
Preface	xi
Abbreviations	xvii
Introduction: Civilians in Wars	1
1. The Making of Amoral Communities	22
2. Evidence of Amoral Communities	33
3. The Exclusion of Moderates	50
4. The Production of Borders	77
5. Memories and Violence	92
6. Violence against Civilians as a Political Strategy	117
Conclusion: Preventing Collective Crimes	142
Appendix: An Excerpt from the Field Notes by Helga Paškvan	147
Notes	155
References	179
Index	193

Illustrations

Table

1. Subnational variation of violence in World War II and the 1990s and case selection   17

Figures

1. Map of subnational variation in Croatia   xviii
2. Map of counties with mass violence against civilians in Croatia, 1991–1995   xix
3. Near the dividing line in Lipik and Pakrac, Western Slavonia   80–81
4. Memorial for victims of rocket attacks in Ivanovo Selo   102
5. Monument for victims of World War II and the violence in 1991 in Gornji Grahovljani   104
6. Monument for victims of Bleiburg, *Križni put*, and the Homeland War in Marino Selo   106

Preface

This book, the result of a personal journey, provides a scholarly study on wartime violence against civilians. It is an attempt to understand what conditions make such crimes possible, with the hope that somehow we can prevent them and avoid their long-lasting consequences. Just as Michel-Rolph Trouillot writes that "to condemn slavery alone is the easy way out" (1995, 148), in this work, I take a similar starting point with regard to violence against civilians. "What needs to be denounced here to restore authenticity," Trouillot writes, "is much less slavery than the racist present within which representations of slavery are produced" (148). If we apply this approach to the difficult topic of collective crimes, we are then tasked with recognizing the signs leading to such outcomes and confronting them in our present. But before we can recognize these signs in our contemporary society and in our everyday lives, we need to identify and understand them. Thus, one reason for writing this book was to understand how it is possible for a safe and peaceful community to transform itself, temporarily, into a violent and cruel place where a human life is suddenly valued less than a person's ethnicity or race. How could a person's unique set of interests, emotions, political views, and relationships, which develops over the course of one's lifetime, be reduced to the single dimension of ethnicity? In other words, what kind of a situation pushes intelligent, reasonable, and caring people to become angry or afraid, both willing to obey those calling for the death of fellow citizens perceived as ethnically different and unwilling to demonstrate the kind of compassion for them that used to be the norm?

The other reason for undertaking the writing of this book was that existing social science explanations did not fully address some questions about political violence that I developed as a result of learning about the real-life experiences of people who lived through a war, such as my own family. At the age of sixteen, I witnessed how my hometown in Eastern Slavonia became an amoral community in a very short time. Before the war, my twin brother and I had a happy childhood and youth, protected by loving and supportive parents and surrounded by friends in our neighborhood and school. Our parents always taught us to consider the other side of the story before forming opinions, to respect everyone regardless of their identity or wealth, and to act ethically in our lives. I remember daily family conversations about what to do when we began hearing about rising political instability in our city. During that time, I watched my parents think about how to protect us when they returned home from work. Once school finished in June, they decided to take my brother and me to my mother's parents in Vojvodina, my father returned to his work, and my mother used her leave to stay with us until we returned home, which we were supposed to do "in a few weeks." My father soon found out that he and my mother no longer had their jobs. On the urging of his parents, and with grenades already falling on our city from the Serb side of what was to become the wartime dividing line, he decided to join us, leaving behind his parents, who lived a bit further from the front lines and said that they would prefer to die in their own home than to be refugees. From that time, we were separated from our grandparents on my father's side by the wartime dividing line. In the fall of 1991, we were officially registered as refugees by the Red Cross. As the war intensified and my parents realized that they would not be returning to our hometown in the foreseeable future, my father tried unsuccessfully to find a job in Serbia. The only employment he was able to find at that time was on the territory of Croatia that was under the control of the Serb forces. In their attempt to save our lives, they would leave one amoral community only to end up in another one, a place where individuals were targeted or excluded solely on the basis of their ethnicity. These experiences represented for him for the rest of his life a direct challenge to his personal values of justice and peace. Everyone in my family survived the war, but my own memories of that period are profoundly sad, as I missed my grandparents, my home, and my childhood friends. One year after leaving my hometown, I came to the United States as a high school student, and from that point on, my host parents became my second parents and my immigrant experience the most prominent part of my identity.

In many ways, my family's dilemmas, and ultimately their choices, were comparable to those of many other parents and adults during times of war in their regions and countries, regardless of their personal identities. Yet my family's story is only one perspective, and each of the stories that follow in this book from Croatia, Uganda, and Guatemala offers a different and new perspective that needs to be taken into consideration in the study of political violence.

In this book, I rely primarily on the voices of people who experienced a war more or less directly. People with experiences of political violence, in the words of Veena Das, become "voiceless—not in the sense that one does not have words—but that these words become frozen, numb, without life" (2007, 8). Through this work, I attempt to return their voices to them. The participants in this study are witnesses of the time when violence happened, when violence could have been prevented, and when their lives were split into the "before" and the "after." Their perspective is that of the "after," and I find it even more valuable than the "before" or the "during" perspective because the experience is more complete, and the time that has passed since then has been a time of reflection and learning. For that reason, I consider the participants in this study not as research subjects but rather as our teachers.

Generous support for this research came from the Appalachian College Association Faculty Fellowship, the Harry Frank Guggenheim Foundation, the University of the South's Faculty Development Grants Fund, the Barclay Ward Faculty Research Fund, the James D. Kennedy III Fellowship, the University of the South's Summer Faculty Research Grant, and a sabbatical leave that allowed me to conduct fieldwork on three continents, write up my findings, and focus, above all, on the quality of the research. Over the course of the fieldwork, I encountered occasional and minor challenges in access to some respondents and materials, and I never insisted on participation, respecting personal reasons, whatever they may be. As the research for this book was conducted thoroughly and systematically over a period of several years, I was successful in gathering information from a comprehensive set of sources, including both state institutions and nongovernmental organizations, as well as, with help of local research assistants, recorded interviews of a diverse sample of respondents from all the regions that I chose to compare. I am deeply indebted to all interview participants who decided to share their personal experiences for this book. I am especially grateful to Sarah Marhevsky, who thoroughly read several versions of this manuscript and provided critical revision suggestions. I appreciate the critical editorial comments on the earlier versions of the manuscript from Roger Haydon, suggestions for improvement from the anonymous reviewers and the Cornell University Press editorial staff, and the excellent index by Sandy Aitken.

This project involved substantial fieldwork in three countries. This would have been impossible without the help and coordination of a great number of people. For support and research assistance in Croatia, I am especially grateful to my friends and colleagues Jasna Čapo and Vjeran Pavlaković, who generously helped me from the beginning to the end of this project with contacts and feedback. For help with interviews, I am thankful to Helga Paškvan and Mate Subašić, whose dedication and remarkable ethnographic skills were critical for the successful completion of most interviews for this book. I would also like to thank all the individuals in Croatia who gave me their time and helped me with contacts and interviews, and whose names I have decided not to mention in order to protect the identity of respondents. I am very indebted to each of you. Among many others in Croatia whom I have not included by name here, I am indebted to Tamara Banjeglav, Cody Brown, Vanni D'Alessio, Aco Džakula, Maja Povrzanović Frykman, Igor Graovac, Andjelka Grubišić-Čabo, Vesna Ivanović, Eugen Jakovčić, Nives Jozić, Jadran Kale, Hrvoje Klasić, Darija Marić, Dea Marić, Nikola Mokrović, Igor Mrkalj, Ante Nazor, Sofija Pejnović, Vjekoslav Perica, Antonija Petričušić, Tanja Petrović, Denis Pilić, Slaven Rašković, Drago Roksandić, Filip Škiljan,

Anamarija Starčević Štambuk, Ivica Šustić, and Vesna Teršelič, who helped at various stages of the research in Croatia and who were supportive of my work. I would also like to thank the staff of the Croatian National Archive in Zagreb; the Croatian National Archive offices in Slavonski Brod, Požega, Petrinja, Gospić, Split, and Rijeka; the Croatian Memorial Documentary Center for the Homeland War; Documenta; the Institute of Ethnology and Folklore Research; and the National and University Library, among others who helped generously with this research.

Amy Patterson and John Solomon, my colleagues at the University of the South, helped me with initial contacts in Uganda and Guatemala, respectively, and for these introductions I am very grateful to them. In Uganda, I am appreciative to Canon Gideon Byamugisha and his staff at the Friends of Canon Gideon Foundation for welcoming me and providing assistance during my stay. I would especially like to thank Grace Muwanguzi Kyeyune and James Claude Mutyaba for help with research, interviews, translations, and paperwork, as well as Andrew Mijumbi at the AIDS Support Organization in Uganda for guidance and assistance during the research approval phase. In Guatemala, I am deeply appreciative to Carlos Enrique Lainfiesta and Edna de Lainfiesta for their generous help with research, their hospitality, and their time. I also appreciate the information that Erin Beck and Christian Kroll shared with me as I prepared for my fieldwork in Guatemala.

For the critical and encouraging comments on draft versions of individual chapters and the book prospectus, I am grateful to my many colleagues at the University of the South, and especially in the Department of Politics and the International and Global Studies Program, who provided both intellectual and emotional support, as well as those who attended my panels of the Association for the Study of Nationalities; the Association for Slavic, East European, and Eurasian Studies; and the International Society for Ethnology and Folklore. In Sewanee, I would like to thank Christopher Van de Ven for help with maps and Samuel Helgeson for help with data collection in the initial stages of the book. Adam Dahl and Richard Ratzlaff helped with suggestions on how to reorganize the completed manuscript into the present form based on the first draft of the prospectus, and I am thankful to them. For the valuable support and advice at various stages of my work, I am grateful to Max Bergholz, Melani Cammett, Pauline Jones, Roger Petersen, and Susan Woodward (who also helped with the title).

I would also like to thank my former teacher and friend Helga Rist, who taught me that difficult personal experiences can give us strength and unique knowledge that we can convey to future generations, as well as friends and colleagues Kelly Bay-Mayer, Irm Haleem, Andrea Hatcher, Pradip Malde, and Donna Murdock for many inspiring conversations. My friends Ismaël Ghalimi, Oana Lauric, and Evrydiki Tasopoulou have been a continuous source of support for many years, and for that I am thankful to them. I am very grateful to all of my dear friends in Sewanee and all over the world whom I did not list by name here but who have been an important part of my life.

I am especially thankful to Manuel Chinchilla, who accompanied me, for his understanding and his generous spirit, which helped me bring this book to completion. For their love that sustained me, I am grateful to my biological and my American families, and especially to my mother, who encouraged me to pursue my dreams; my father, who was always proud of my intellectual work and who sadly did not live to see the completion of this book; and my brother Marko, who has been my support from far away throughout all these years.

Abbreviations

EGP	Guerrilla Army of the Poor (Ejército Guerrillero de los Pobres)
HDZ	Croatian Democratic Union (Hrvatska demokratska zajednica)
HKDS	Croatian Christian Democratic Party (Hrvatska kršćanska demokratska stranka)
HSP	Croatian Party of Rights (Hrvatska stranka prava)
ICJ	International Court of Justice
ICRC	International Committee of the Red Cross
ICTY	International Criminal Tribunal for the Former Yugoslavia
JNA	Yugoslav National Army (Jugoslavenska narodna armija)
NDH	Independent State of Croatia (Nezavisna Država Hrvatska)
NRA	National Resistance Army in Uganda
REMHI	Recovery of Historical Memory Project (Recuperación de la Memoria Histórica)
RSK	Serbian Republic of Krajina (Krajina or Republika srpska Krajina)
SAO	Serbian Autonomous Region of Krajina (Srpska autonomna oblast Krajina)
SDS	Serbian Democratic Party (Srpska demokratska stranka)
TO	Territorial Defense (Teritorijalna obrana)
UNLA	Uganda National Liberation Army
UPC	Uganda People's Congress

FIGURE 1. Map of subnational variation of missing persons in 2012 in Croatia

Sources: Natural Earth data; Esri data; International Committee of the Red Cross, Croatian Red Cross, and Ministarstvo branitelja Uprava za zatočene i nestale 2012. Created with the assistance of Christopher Van de Ven.

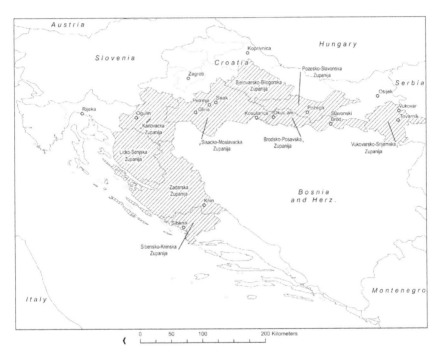

FIGURE 2. Map of counties with mass violence against civilians in Croatia, 1991–1995

Sources: Natural Earth data; Open Street Map data; Esri data; ICTY and Documenta. Created with the assistance of Christopher Van de Ven.

AMORAL COMMUNITIES

Introduction

CIVILIANS IN WARS

While I was doing fieldwork in Croatia in the spring of 2014, one of the topics reported in the media was the hearing of the lawsuit filed by the Republic of Croatia against Serbia at the International Court of Justice (ICJ) in The Hague regarding the genocide in the 1990s, during the Homeland War (Domovinski rat), the war's official name in Croatia.[1] While no official list of all civilian victims in the 1990s was published at the time of the hearing, one of the most prominent and contentious issues became the counting. This issue is not unique to Croatia, and it is characteristic of situations of mass violence in other contexts (Nelson 2015). The political stakes of the genocide trial were high for both states, and the officials were emphasizing a position in favor of the victims representing their respective state's dominant ethnicity, while downplaying or not even acknowledging the responsibility of their own state for other instances of targeted violence against civilians.[2] The states' and their respective political leaders' concerns for this trial was understandable given that the effects of the war were evident in Croatia, where almost everyone I would meet was more or less directly affected by it. Yet many of the individuals I talked to at that time were less concerned with the outcome of this hearing than with their other daily trials, such as the unemployment or the steady emigration of young people. The following statement of one of my respondents from the same period illustrates this well:

> If you watched last night's news, there was a report about emigration being the number one concern for the nation. We became a country in Europe with the greatest export of our young people and intellectuals.

But that was our politics. In order to enter into the EU, we talked about Europe how that was . . . they took what we educated. All the doctors, programmers, electrical engineers, they are going out and we are left on our own again as a country. We are paying the price of that politics. We took jobs from the young people. . . . I used to say that the whole time, "People, it is not a goal to enter into Europe in order to export the young people." The young people who finished the university . . . they thought they would work here. But there are no jobs here anymore.[3]

Encountering such disconnects between the interests of the state leaders and the perspectives of ordinary people was what motivated me to consider interviews as a method that may provide new understanding of the conditions under which targeted violence against civilians in wars takes place. Throughout this book, I consider individuals with divergent wartime experiences as teachers whose perspectives are incorporated productively into scholarly research.[4] The voices of those who experienced wars in their lives add depth, emotion, and, ultimately, more objectivity to a study of political violence.[5] Scholars of political violence who carry out fieldwork in postconflict areas know that one of the main challenges is the understandable lack of willingness of the people who have experienced wartime violence to open up to strangers and to trust them after they have faced, in some cases, violence from people they have known all their lives.[6] Yet many people who contributed to this study were courageous and ready to share their memories and insights because they trusted our intentions, not as researchers but as fellow human beings who wished both to hear and to feel with them what they have been through. As a result, many of our conversations started and ended in tears, and quite a few pages of this book were written in tears. I understood over the course of working on this project that empathy and learning go hand in hand. The success of field research depends on capturing the subtlety and introspection of those who have already done substantial analysis and processing of those difficult events personally over an extended period of time (Cammett 2013; Fujii 2009; Mosley 2013; Schatz 2009; Wedeen 2009). For that reason, the research would not have been as fruitful if it had been conducted in the immediate aftermath of the violence or once the generations that experienced violence firsthand were no longer alive. The following response illustrates well the type of retrospective analysis that individuals were performing in explaining how ethnicity, in some cases gradually and in others suddenly, became relevant during the period leading up to the war: "Look, I can tell you this. I was born here. My parents made their house here and we were always here. I didn't know my ethnicity until the war started. That was not important. I was brought up like that. My aunt, who was Catholic, watched me and taught me. My parents were not very religious, but I went to church. . . . It was a small town. Then, the time came when all of a sudden you were given this label on your head and you had to behave with friends accordingly."[7] Throughout this book, I consider voices such as this as the most critical evidence of the life and general conditions in which people lived in these communities both during and after wars (Arendt 1998).

Given this context within which I was conducting my fieldwork in Croatia, and the increasing focus on the micro-level analysis of violence in the contemporary political science literature, I joined the scholars who thought it was critical to bring politics back into the study of wartime violence against civilians, not to politicize the issues further but rather to understand both why and how this violence occurs in order to learn how it may be prevented (Balcells 2017; Straus 2015). For this reason, even though the focus of this book is on explaining the subnational variation of violence in the case of Croatia, it was necessary to place Croatia in a broader comparative context by including states with different historical conditions but comparable wartime targeted violence against civilians (Schatz 2009, 306). While cross-national comparisons are mostly based on secondary sources, I also rely on the interviews that I conducted along with my contacts and research assistants in Uganda and Guatemala for the purpose of this study.

This book seeks to address the following questions. First, under what conditions do ordinary people who have lived in peace for many years in the same communities turn against one another? My goal is to identify some causal mechanisms that link state-level political mobilization with the local-level recruitment of ordinary people who, in some cases, also perpetrate violence against members of their own communities. Here, the focus is more on the question of how rather than why, and on the process by which a community is transformed from a peaceful one to a violent one. Second, in this book, I also address the following question: What accounts for the subnational variation in the mass violence against civilians during the same war and in the same country?

The topic of violence against civilians is addressed by two sets of literature that are theoretically and methodologically disjointed—the interdisciplinary genocide scholarship and the civil wars and insurgency scholarship rooted primarily in the discipline of political science. My research builds on existing theoretical frameworks that bridge the gap between the literature on genocide and the research on insurgencies and civil wars in order to show how violence against civilians occurs.[8] The literature on genocide theorizes the association between state politics and genocide, and in this it is complementary to the work of scholars of nationalism who show that ideology and the struggle over political rule on the state level may be associated with ethnic violence, genocide, or collective crimes in time of war (Cederman, Gleditsch, and Buhaug 2013; Gurr 1969; Hechter 2000; Mamdani

2001; Straus 2015; Wimmer 2013). This scholarship traditionally focuses on a small number of salient cases without systematically incorporating cases in which genocide did not occur (Fein 1979; Goldhagen 1996; Hilberg 1992; I. Horowitz 1976; Kuper 1981; Staub 1989; Straus 2007; Valentino, Huth, and Balch-Lindsay 2004; Waller 2007; Weitz 2003). However, a number of scholars of nationalism and genocide carry out comparative cross-national analyses and include negative cases (Bulutgil 2016; Mamdani 2001; Mann 2005; Straus 2015; Wimmer 2001, 2013). For example, Scott Straus (2012, 2015) conducts a cross-national comparative analysis in addressing the question of why genocides happen during particular times in history in some African states but not in others. Furthermore, several scholars have carried out subnational comparative analyses of cases of genocide or targeted violence against civilians (Balcells 2017; Bergholz 2016; Fujii 2009). By including both a subnational and a cross-national comparative analysis, my book builds on this growing body of literature that attempts to understand the conditions associated with genocide and targeted violence against civilians in wars.

Recent political science literature on civil wars and insurgencies overcomes the problem of having too few cases or cases without variation in the outcome of interest by moving the analysis to the subnational level.[9] Most of this scholarship shows that mass violence against civilians is not the result of ancient hatreds, prejudice, deep social cleavages on the national level, or other, often referred to as irrational, motives of insurgents or state military forces. Rather, it shows that violence against civilians is frequently part of the participants' military strategy to gain greater control over the territory (Kalyvas 1999, 2005, 2006), the civilians (R. Wood 2010), or the adversary (Hultman 2007; Metelits 2010). Mass violence is also more likely to occur when territorial conflicts make ethnicity the most prominent political cleavage (Bulutgil 2016) and when insurgents have guaranteed access to local material resources (Weinstein 2007), as well as when external alliances exist that may provide military or economic support (Bulutgil 2010). While most political violence scholarship in the political science discipline focuses on military or economic factors, Lars-Erik Cederman, Kristian Skrede Gleditsch, and Halvard Buhaug (2013) reexamine political grievances as a cause of civil wars by using new data that incorporate the political and economic exclusion of ethnic groups in a state as a condition associated with the onset of civil wars. Furthermore, H. Zeynep Bulutgil (2016) incorporates both historical and political factors, such as dominant political cleavages and changes in the territorial borders of the states, in her cross-national analysis. These studies make an important contribution to the literature by showing that even seemingly illogical acts of violence, such as massacres of noncombatants, are in fact strategic acts aimed at gaining both military and political advantage over the course of a war. However, most of these studies overemphasize the national-level factors leading to violence while neglecting to show how national-level political or ethnic cleavages become relevant locally and make mass violence against civilians possible in certain communities.

Scholars of political violence have already started to acknowledge the new directions that research in this area may take. In the case of World War II violence in the Bosnian town of Kulen Vakuf, Max Bergholz (2016) shows when and how violence creates ethnicity as a relevant category of deep divisions in a community. Laia Balcells (2010, 2017) studies municipal-level violence in the Spanish Civil War and argues that factors other than military strategies, such as cleavages resulting from prewar political mobilization, may have different effects on the local level, and in some communities may be linked to violence against civilians.[10] In her work, Balcells (2017) brings politics back into the analysis by showing that political identities explain violence against civilians after military control is achieved in a given municipality. This book thus builds on the recent literature by showing how violence is used as a political strategy, as well as how state-level and micro-level cleavages become linked in some communities. More specifically, in my book, I show how communities where targeted violence against civilians becomes possible are created through certain local-level processes, such as the systematic exclusion of moderates through threats or violence and the division of a population that previously lived in one community along newly drawn dividing lines.

The Argument

I argue that *collective crimes*, or targeted violence against civilians in times of war, are acts with a political goal. The targeting of civilians on the basis of their ethnic or religious identity signals a certain political strategy of violence.[11] The concept of collective crimes combines elements of the definitions of both ethnocide (i.e., cultural genocide) and genocide (i.e., the killing of members of a particular group). The concept of collective crimes employed in this book further includes either the killing or harming (i.e., rape, injury, beating, torture, or arrest) of civilians who were not participating in the war at the time of the attack. Most studies of genocide or wartime crimes focus only on civilian victims and do not consider the destruction of the rival ethnic group's identity symbols, such as books, graveyards, property, or places of worship, which my use of the concept of collective crimes includes.

But why does targeted violence against civilians occur in some communities and not in others in time of war? This is because the process of *ethnicization* was triggered there first by two related mechanisms: the exclusion of moderates and the production of borders. I define *ethnicization* as the fusing of a political goal with ethnicity in order to secure political support. As a result, the range of political options becomes more limited, ambiguity of identification is artificially reduced, and defection from in-group is prevented. In some areas or communities, moderates, or those individuals who challenged the ethnicization process, were excluded through the use of targeted small-scale violence, threats, or social ostracism.[12] Additionally, the creation of new borders forced individuals to "choose" one of the two political ethnicities, and the population in those communities was divided and policed accordingly. As a result, in those communities, new identities, *political ethnicities*, formed and manifested themselves in ethnicity, becoming a shortcut for politically categorizing individuals. Over time, ethnicity became a dividing trait in relationships among family and friends, in the workplace, in neighborhoods, and even among children in schools and on playgrounds.

Thus, even before the war had started, some communities had already transformed into what I refer to throughout this study as *amoral communities*. In these communities, individuals were stripped of the freedom to express themselves or act on the basis of their personal views if those views did not align with one of the dominant and accepted political views. In those communities, eventually, the very definition of crime became altered by the wartime conditions described in the discourse of the local political leaders as the "state of exception," under which violence against civilians defined as the "enemy" on the other side of the newly drawn border was seen as a form of justified and preemptive self-defense against perceived threats, not to one's own biological existence but rather to the existence of one's ethnically defined state, seen as the extension of one's own life (Anderson 1983; Esposito 2011; Foucault [1978] 1990; Haleem 2012). In that sense, amoral communities were local-level contexts within which people perceived that their personal choices were severely limited to the options imposed on them by the conditions that created the context in which morality, or any decision-making ability based solely on one's own values, was absent altogether, as those who opposed their political leaders' calls for distrusting and turning against their neighbors or the process of ethnicization were silenced through violence or threats and eventually eliminated or removed from these communities. Once the distribution of the population into its respective political ethnicities was successfully carried out in those communities, following the production of borders, mass violence against civilians was used as a political strategy in order to further secure political power during the uncertain wartime period.[13]

I make a conceptual distinction between a *military* and a *political strategy* during wartime by defining *military strategy* as a set of tactics for eliminating threats during a battle and achieving military advancement and *political strategy* as a set of tactics for forming new political identities and securing political power over the desired territorially defined sovereign entities. In the first strategy, civilians are more likely to be harmed over the course of a bombing campaign or a military attack and are not singled out on the basis of their individual ethnicity, race, religion, or political views. In the second strategy, civilians who do not share the same ethnicity, race, religion, or political views as the occupying army are targeted for elimination. For example, in the case of Croatia, most massacres of civilians took place in the first year of the war while both sides in the conflict were trying to secure not only military but also political power over the territories and the population. In this context, the massacres that took place after military control was already established by the perpetrator, rather than during a battle or a military attack, would constitute the use of violence as a political strategy. Both strategies, however, may entail violence against civilians, and it may be difficult to distinguish the two empirically because they may overlap in wartime contexts.

Politics in Croatia before the Mass Violence

Before delving into the local conditions that made some communities more susceptible to targeted violence against civilians defined ethnically, it is critical to provide the historical context of the first political crises and instances of violence in the territory of Croatia. The Homeland War followed the formal dissolution of the Socialist Federal Republic of Yugoslavia when Slovenia and Croatia declared independence in the summer of 1991. The question of why Yugoslavia disintegrated has been addressed in the literature extensively.[14] While scholars disagree regarding whether the most critical factors are the general inflexibility and the failure of the Yugoslav political system to transition to a democratic political regime (Cohen 1993); the rise of nationalism across the entire region (Jović 2009; Ramet 1992); the role of churches in fomenting ethno-nationalism (Perica 2002); maneuvers among the political elite in competition for power that weakened the nonnationalist reformists through the use of threats and violence to incite fear, among other tactics (Gagnon 2004; Jović 2009; 2017, 57; Petersen 2002); or economic and international factors related to the post–Cold War global changes and the role of international actors and organizations (Cohen 2007; Glaurdić 2011; Lampe 1996; Shoup 2007; Woodward 1995), there is a general agreement that the primordial argument emphasizing "historical ethnic animosity" is a cause neither for the dissolution of Yugoslavia nor for the war that ensued (Dragović-Soso 2007). Before the mass violence, ethnic groups were highly heterogeneous in terms of political preferences and personal identification with a particular ethnicity or religion. Even during the rising nationalism in Serbia, Slovenia, and Croatia and the economic crisis and political uncertainties related to the processes of democratization and economic reforms that people across the entire former Yugoslavia faced in the late 1980s (Cohen 1993; Gagnon 2004; Woodward 1995), the populist-nationalist parties in Croatia and Serbia won in the first multiparty elections in 1990 without the absolute majority and continued to face strong opposition within their own respective republics (Gagnon 1995). Once in office, the winners gradually turned more nationalistic in their discourse and political orientation, as well as more authoritarian in their policies, in large part in response to the electoral threats that both the moderate opposition and the more extreme nationalist opposition (e.g., the Croatian Party of Rights [Hrvatska stranka prava] in Croatia and the Serbian Radical Party [Srpska radikalna stranka] in Serbia) posed to them during and after the democratic transition in their respective states (Gagnon 1995; Gordy 2007, 283; Woodward 1995, 355).

A number of political parties competing in the first multiparty elections in 1990 in the former Yugoslavia mobilized potential supporters with a discourse that connected their political program with an ethnicity. More specifically, in the town of Knin in the northern Dalmatian region, the Serbian Democratic Party (Srpska demokratska stranka; SDS), which represented ethnic Serbs in Croatia under the leadership of Jovan Rašković, in February 1990 called not only for the decentralization of Croatia but also for territorial reorganization that would provide ethnic Serbs in the Croatian territory with cultural and political autonomy under the organization of Serbian Autonomous Region of Krajina (Srpska autonomna oblast Krajina; SAO Krajina) (I. Goldstein 2008, 659; Rupić 2007). The SDS only won five parliamentary seats in these elections, and in only three municipalities, Donji Lapac (Ličko-senjska županija), Gračac (Zadarska županija), and Knin (Šibensko-kninska županija) (Barić 2005, 61). Another major political party in Croatia, which linked ethnicity and a political goal of independence from the former Yugoslavia in its discourse and program, was the Croatian Democratic Union (Hrvatska demokratska zajednica; HDZ), under the leadership of Franjo Tuđman. The HDZ won the most seats, and more than 40 percent of the total votes, in the first free parliamentary multiparty elections in Croatia, on April 22 and May 6, 1990 (Barić 2005, 53).[15] This relative popularity of the HDZ in Croatia may be understood in the context of both the "perceived weakness of the Croatian Communists in the 1980s and . . . the expansionist character of Serbian nationalism" (Jović 2007, 263). It is important to stress, however, that there was no homogeneity in political preferences among the population in Croatia at the time of the first multiparty elections. For example, based on the study of public opinion in 1990 by the Faculty of Political Science, of the sample of 2,608 respondents from across Croatia, the majority of respondents who identified as ethnic Croats, or 64 percent, expressed a preference for a confederate solution for Croatia within Yugoslavia (Jović 2017, 13–14). Among the population of Croatia, regardless of particular political preferences, there was also an element of distrust toward the central Yugoslav government, in which Serbia historically maintained political dominance through administrative centralization efforts, among other political strategies (Banac 1984; Djokić 2003; Irvine 1993; Jović 2007; Lampe 1996). These historical conflicts over the distribution of political power among the states and autonomous provinces of Yugoslavia were manifested even before the 1980s during Josip Broz Tito's presidency, when disagreements over the centralization of political power in the League of Communists of Yugoslavia figured prominently in the series of nonviolent movements calling for democratization of the party and greater national autonomy in Croatia in the late 1960s and early 1970s (Batović 2017; Irvine 1993, 2007; Jakovina 2012; Klasić 2012). Most importantly, the framing of political goals in terms of ethnicity in the 1990s was not welcomed unanimously by all ethnic group members in Croatia. The results from the first multiparty elections show that there was no homogeneity in political orientation among ethnic Serbs, ethnic Croats, or other ethnic groups in Croatia. It is also important to stress that these elections were not accompanied by violence, and the first casualties of political violence would not occur until late fall of the same year.

The first organized political action that attracted the attention of the national media took place on August 17, 1990 in the region of northern Dalmatia. The movement in this area, which became known as the Log Revolution (Balvan revolucija), entailed the setting up of barricades made of tree logs on the main roads connecting the north of the country with the seacoast. The local leaders of the SDS were encouraged by the promise of support from not only the Serbian government but also the Yugoslav National Army (Jugoslavenska narodna armija; JNA), which was at that time already being transformed from the army of the Yugoslavs into the army of the regime of Slobodan Milošević (Barić 2005, 32; Bieber 2007; Gagnon 2004, 142; I. Goldstein 2008; Magaš and Žanić 1999; Žunec 2007, 184–211). This was the period when the Serbian government and the JNA began covertly arming Croatian Serb leaders (Žunec 2007, 266–267). While this political act created serious disruptions both to the local residents and to the traffic passing through this area during the high tourist season, there was still no violence in the first months of the Log Revolution. The first casualty occurred in November 1990, when the police officer Goran Alavanja was killed on the road between Obrovac and Benkovac (Zadarska županija) by masked attackers (I. Goldstein 2008, 667). While it was not known who the attackers were, the identity of the victim, an ethnic Serb in Croatian police uniform, was an opportunity for the local Serb leadership in Benkovac to frame this incident in ethnic terms (667).

The issue of naming ethnic minorities in the new constitution of the Republic of Croatia became part of the symbolic repertoire of the public discourse before the eruption of violence. The ethnic Serb leaders' distrust of the newly elected government of Croatia increased following the proclamation of the new constitution of Croatia on December 22, 1990, in which the group status of ethnic Serbs was downgraded; whereas before they had been defined as a "constitutive nation" and their status was equal to that of Croats, the new constitution reduced their status to that of "other nations and minorities" (Barić 2005; I. Goldstein 2008). For various representatives of ethnic Serbs, particularly from the geographic areas where Serbs formed a substantial proportion of the total population, this was unacceptable, since based on the historical contribution of Serbs to Croatia, they believed that they should have a group status equal to that of Croats in the Constitution (Barić 2005, 39, 88). Consequently, the leaders of Serbs in Croatia rejected attempts to engage in a dialogue with the central government (88). Even though this constitutional amendment did not have any significant legal consequences for the status of ethnic Serbs in Croatia, it contained a symbolic message, which became, at a time when ethnicity and political goals were being linked in the political discourse, one of the major issues of contention between the leaders representing their respective groups (Barić 2005, 87–90; I. Goldstein 2008, 668; Žunec 2007, 268). The symbolism of this constitutional amendment was heightened by the evidence of actual discrimination against Serbs, including violations of their citizenship rights, their loss of jobs, and requirements that they take loyalty oaths at work (Gagnon 2004, 147; Woodward 1995, 390). These policies were at the time justified by political leaders as a form of "returning Croatia to Croats" (Gagnon 2004, 148). The politicization of the constitutional change was carried out both by the SDS and by the HDZ: "Just as the SDS hardliners pointed to Serbs' subaltern status in Croatia to justify their political control, so too the HDZ's tightening grip on society was justified by pointing to the Serbs . . . who threatened to once again subordinate it to Belgrade" (148). As political tensions heightened in the first part of 1991, additional counties with an ethnic Serb majority decided to join the SAO Krajina with the aim of obtaining ethno-political territorial autonomy within the state of Croatia (Barić 2005, 95–99; I. Goldstein 2008, 668).

The symbolic repertoire of political discourse of the major parties that linked political goals and ethnicity also included references to violence along political and ethnic lines that occurred during World War II, as well as the discursive, and deliberate, association of entire ethnic groups, such as the Serbs and the Croats, with the predominant ethnicity of various armies that perpetrated targeted mass violence during or after World War II. In 1941, when the Axis powers and their allies occupied and divided Yugoslavia, there were three armies that fought in the territory of former Yugoslavia. Ustaša, the army of the Independent State of Croatia (Nezavisna Država Hrvatska; NDH), was allied with the Axis powers and consisted predominantly of ethnic Croats (Lampe 1996, 206–217; Perica 2002, 21–22). Četniks, the army of the Serbian monarch consisting of ethnic Serbs collaborated for most of the war with Germans and Italians (Lampe 1996, 206–217; Perica 2002, 21–22). While members of different ethnicities joined the Partisans, a communist-oriented armed organization that fought against both the Ustaša and the Četniks, Serbs in Croatia joined in relatively large numbers in the first year of the war in response to the targeted mass violence against the Serb, Jewish, and Roma populations by the Ustaša (Lampe 1996, 206–217; Perica 2002, 21–22). The nationalist political parties seeking representation during the period of democratic opening in the late 1980s were aware of the emotional impact of references to these armies in the context of characterizing or labeling people in their communities who did not share their ethnicity. Also, national symbols were reintroduced in Croatia—for example, the medieval checkered coat of arms, *šahovnica*, which was actually different from but resembled closely the coat of arms that Serbs in Croatia associated with the NDH regime, was one of the symbols used by ethnic Serb political leaders to mobilize this population politically along ethnic lines (Gagnon 2004, 147). Emotions were further heightened as the victims of World War II violence perpetrated by one of these armies across the territory of former Yugoslavia were publicly reburied and commemorated (Verdery 1999, 99–100). In addition to the selective use of historical references in political leaders' discourse, church leaders' involvement in the public discussions regarding the interpretation of the events of mass violence during or after World War II, and their open support of the parties that linked ethnicity and political goals in their programs, played a prominent role in political mobilization among people across Croatia throughout this period (Perica 2002, 146–152). There were also instances of selective, and, in some cases, even outright revisionist, use of historical references to World War II in the historiography in the late 1980s and the early 1990s in Serbia and Croatia (146–152). Some of the issues included increasing, without basis in the available historical evidence, the total number of victims who were killed in concentration camps across Croatia during World War II—and most notably in Jasenovac, the concentration camp where Serbs, Jews, Roma, and the political opponents of the Ustaša regime, including Croats, were killed—or decreasing it in other political contexts (S. Goldstein and Goldstein 2011; Kasapović 2018; Lampe 1996, 207; Perica 2002, 147–152; Žerjavić 1992). Another example is the problematic representation of the number of victims, frequently not based on historiographical evidence, of the mass crimes committed in Bleiburg and *Križni put* by the Partisans in the aftermath of World War II against the armies of the NDH fleeing Croatia through Austria (S. Goldstein and Goldstein 2011). The annual commemorations in Bleiburg continue to be accompanied by controversies, though the commemorative discourse has changed over the years as an instrument of political mobilization (Pavlaković, Brentin, and Pauković 2018). The extent to which these top-down mobilization efforts using World War II references were successful, depended, as I argue in the following chapters, most directly on particular local conditions, or processes that facilitated the linking of political and ethnic identities in some multiethnic communities.

Several months before the war started, there were already two highly publicized instances of violence that entailed an attempted violent takeover of local police stations by the local SAO Krajina leadership. Both were prevented by the Croatian special police forces, and there was no escalation of violence at that time. In the first incident, which occurred in early March 1991 in the police station of Pakrac (Slavonsko-požeška županija), there were no casualties, but it was critical as the first attempt to draw new borders and divide the population into newly defined political identities (Dragojević 2016). In the second incident, known as the Plitvice Bloody Easter (Plitvički krvavi Usrks), which took place in Plitvice (Ličko-senjska županija) later in the same month, the local SAO Krajina paramilitary forces clashed with Croatian special police units over the disputed territory, and two people, one on each side, were killed (I. Goldstein 2008, 672). Both incidents figure prominently in the accounts of how ethnicity became a relevant dividing factor on the level of local communities, as well as a shortcut for deducing the political orientation of neighbors, coworkers, and friends among the respondents from this region.

The independence of Croatia was announced officially by the Croatian Sabor, a unicameral legislature, with the proclamation of the Constitutional Decision on the Sovereignty and Independence of Croatia (Ustavna odluka o suverenosti i samostalnosti Hrvatske) and the Declaration of the Independent and Sovereign Republic of Croatia (Deklaracija o proglašenju samostalne i suverene Republike Hrvatske) on June 25, 1991. The main body of the government of the Socialist Federal Republic of Yugoslavia, the National Executive Council, located in Belgrade, annulled both the Croatian and the Slovenian governments' respective declarations of independence on June 26, 1991, and placed the JNA at the borders of Slovenia in order to prevent their secession. Scholars identify a shift in the JNA's strategy after the failure to prevent the secession of Slovenia in 1991, when it increasingly became the army of "the Milošević regime and its military goals in Croatia, Bosnia, and later in Kosovo" (Bieber 2007, 324). However, the JNA's ability to intervene in order to preserve Yugoslavia in 1991 was also hampered by serious recruitment issues, as many soldiers deserted or emigrated so they would not have to serve in the army (Bieber 2007, 324; Gagnon 2004, 2). As early as March 1991, even before the attempted June intervention of the JNA in Slovenia, the role of the JNA changed, reflecting a greater concern for the protection of Serbs in Croatia and, by extension, the protection of the interest of the Serbian state after the army realized that it was impossible to stage a conventional coup and intervene, in an attempt to preserve Yugoslavia, in each of the governments of the republics seeking greater autonomy and eventual independence (Bieber 2007, 320).[16]

Large-scale violence in Croatia began with the attacks of the JNA forces on Glina (central Croatia, Sisačko-moslavačka županija) on June 27, 1991, when the defeated Croatian forces withdrew to the north of the city (I. Goldstein 2008, 698). The JNA withdrew from Slovenia on July 5, 1991, but the forces were later sent to the territories of Croatia where ethnic Serbs were demographically represented in greater numbers. From this point, the war quickly spread to several other parts of the country, or, more specifically, to other parts of central Croatia, Eastern and Western Slavonia, and northern Dalmatia (Barić 2005, 122). In December 1991, after the war was already under way, the SAO Krajina would be named the Serbian Republic of Krajina (Krajina or Republika srpska Krajina; RSK). It covered about a third of present-day Croatia's territory and lasted, in isolation and without international recognition, from 1991 until the territory was reclaimed by the Croatian Army (Hrvatska vojska) in August 1995 as a result of the military operation named Operation Storm (Oluja) after all other diplomatic options were exhausted (Žunec 2007, 745–765).

The armed conflict involved multiple armies and paramilitary formations on both sides that had claims to the same territory. One side included those ethnic Serbs who opposed the independence of Croatia and demanded the autonomy of the Krajina region. The armed forces acting on their behalf included the JNA units and local participants in the SAO Krajina army. After the JNA claimed and seized most of its assets and most of the equipment of the local Territorial Defense (Teritorijalna odbrana; TO) in Croatia in the fall of 1990, the Serb forces in Croatia had a significant military advantage at the very start of the war (Woodward 1995, 137). Moreover, on the Serb side, the forces also included groups of volunteers from Serbia and Croatia who formed numerous paramilitary units, such as the White Eagles, the Serbian Volunteer Guard, Dušan Silni, the Serbian Guard, the Serbian Četnik Movement, and the Martićevci (Kndiže) (Cohen 1993, 254). The other side of the conflict consisted of the supporters of the independent Croatian state, including mostly ethnic Croats but also a number of ethnic Serbs. Given that most of the TO equipment was taken by the JNA, during this time, efforts to arm Croatian forces from abroad began in the fall of 1990

(Hockenos 2003; Woodward 1995, 137). Croatian volunteer forces, which were recruited from among the members of the HDZ, started forming as early as the summer of 1990 (I. Goldstein 2008, 693). In the spring of 1991, four such brigades, which became known as the Croatian National Guard (Zbor narodne garde), formed across Croatia in the cities of Zagreb, Osijek, and Split (693). A number of other paramilitary groups were created, such as the Zebras, the Black Legion, and a formation from the Croatian National Guard, the Wolves of Vukovar (Cohen 1993, 254). Another armed formation of volunteers was the Croatian Defense Forces (Hrvatske odbrambene snage), the military wing of the right-wing Croatian Party of Rights; some of its members were subsumed under the regular state armed forces, the Croatian Army (Hrvatska vojska), in November 1991 (Cohen 1993, 254; I. Goldstein 2008, 693). Many of the paramilitary units were involved in massacres and attacks on civilian populations across the Croatian territory, thus contributing to the sense of insecurity and fear among all local communities in the regions where they were active, regardless of the people's ethnicities (Gagnon 2004, 149–151; I. Goldstein 2008, 699; Woodward 1995, 142, 146, 170). Understanding this general political context in Croatia before and during the war is critical, yet it still leaves unanswered the main question of how it was possible for people who shared in peace the same neighborhoods, villages, towns, and cities in some, but not all, multiethnic geographic areas of Croatia to become such deadly enemies in a relatively short period of time. I address this question in the chapters that follow.

Data and Methods

This book is based on ethnographic research in Croatia conducted from 2013 through 2014, including 131 in-depth interviews, and archival sources collected across regions that experienced varied levels of violence during the war in the 1990s. In addition, in order to explore possible extensions of these findings to different contexts of targeted violence against civilians, I compared the local-level conditions and patterns of violence in Croatia with those in cases of targeted violence against civilians in other locations. While I relied predominantly on secondary sources for the cross-national comparative analyses, I also conducted thirty-six in-depth interviews with a representative sample of respondents in central Uganda in 2015 and eighteen in-depth interviews in western Guatemala in 2016. The studies that were included for cross-national comparison illustrate a variety of socioeconomic contexts and historical conditions in which civilians, who constituted citizens in their respective states, were targeted based on their social identity, whether an ethnic, class, or ideological one.

One of the puzzles that inspired this research came from my initial study of the case of Croatia, where the subnational variation in patterns of mass violence could not be explained solely by examining the military strategies of the warring sides and their factions. For example, why did civilian massacres happen in some communities that were strategically irrelevant to the combatants, such as in the village of Joševica, near Glina, in December 1991? Also, why were some multiethnic communities more peaceful than others? While several studies of Croatia point to such variations, more research in this direction is still needed (Barić 2005; I. Goldstein 2008; Katunarić 2010; Magaš and Žanić 1999). Also, in the Croatian context, it is questionable whether the timing of massacres can be explained purely by military strategies. In one instance of violence in the Lika region of Croatia, the massacre of mostly Croat civilians in Široka Kula on October 13, 1991, was followed by the massacre of mostly Serb civilians in Gospić three days later. Some motives of military commanders trying to conquer a particular territory are clearly rational, but so is an emotional response of revenge, for example (Balcells 2010; D. Horowitz 1985; Petersen 2002). These examples show that violence against civilians may not be always a result of a military strategy.

Mass crimes in which people were targeted on the basis of their ethnicity were committed in the towns of Vukovar, Dalj, Gospić, Baćin, Joševica, and Lovas, among other places across the geographic regions of Slavonia, central Croatia, and northern Dalmatia. While a number of governmental institutions and nongovernmental organizations in Croatia collected the numbers of civilian victims, the total official number of civilian victims for the entire country of Croatia by municipality, including the identifying information of victims, was not available at the time this research was conducted. Based on the existing evidence, however, it can be concluded that a significant number of victims were civilians, that most civilian victims were ethnic Croats, followed by ethnic Serbs, and that there were civilian victims of other ethnicities as well.[17] There are a number of concerns regarding the available estimates and data, which were acknowledged by Croatian scholars and should be taken into account. First, the question of a clearly identified methodology was brought up as one of the issues that needed to be addressed.[18] Second, in the context of the war in Croatia, it was also important to distinguish civilians from soldiers among the numbers of victims, as noted by the sociologist Ozren Žunec (Roginek 2011, 53).[19] Third, apart from these issues related to counting the victims of war, there is also the issue of the possible politicization of numbers by various actors in the manner in which they may be presented in the media, for example. Based on the available information, however, it is evident that in addition to combatants, the number of civilian casualties was substantial, that civilians were targeted, and that there was variation in violence across the country.

For the purpose of the subnational comparative analysis and the selection of places for comparison, I needed to have an estimate of high or low levels of violence during the war across the regions in Croatia. In order to avoid some of the problems raised by scholars, and overcome the problem of not having comparable information for the entire country, I used the existing publications that included verifiable data, such as names and other identifying information of victims, produced by international organizations for the entire territory of Croatia. One such report, the most recent edition of *The Book of the Missing Persons on the Territory of the Republic of Croatia*, published by the International Committee of the Red Cross (ICRC) and the Croatian Red Cross, includes the number of missing persons (ICRC, Croatian Red Cross, and Ministarstvo branitelja Uprava za zatočene i nestale 2012). This publication lists the first and last names of individuals who disappeared in the period between 1991 and 1995, along with the following information for each individual: place and county of disappearance, date of disappearance, gender, date and place of birth, father's name, and the identification numbers of the ICRC and the Croatian Red Cross. While this report lists only the individuals who were still missing as of the date of publication, it provides a proxy for the variation in the overall level of violence across the country. The total number of missing persons in 2012 was 2,322, and it included individuals of all ethnicities, both civilians and soldiers. In addition to individuals born in Croatia, individuals who were born in Serbia, Kosovo, or Bosnia and Herzegovina were also included in this list. However, since it was not possible to verify when these individuals moved to Croatia, or whether they were citizens of Croatia at the time of their disappearance, I only included individuals who were *reported to have disappeared in the territory of Croatia, by place of disappearance, between 1991 and 1995*, regardless of their place of birth or citizenship. More specifically, I included the lists entitled "Tracing Requests by Place of Disappearance" and "Requests for Tracing Human Remains by Place Where Human Remains Were Last Seen." After excluding individuals who disappeared in the territory of Bosnia and Herzegovina and Serbia, as well as those whose place of disappearance was unknown, the total number of individuals included in this study as a proxy for the estimated variation in the level of violence was 2,269 (table 1; see also figure 1). Therefore, the 2012 ICRC report was used as a first step to identify the regions with high and low levels of violence in the early 1990s in Croatia. As part of the subnational comparison, I interviewed individuals from different counties (*županija*) that were ethnically heterogeneous at the start of the war and had varying levels of violence in World War II and in the 1990s (table 1).

Specifically, I looked at five counties in the region of Slavonia: Požeško-slavonska, Brodsko-posavska, Bjelovarsko-bilogorska, Virovitičko-podravska, and Vukovarsko-srijemska županija. On the whole, the region of Slavonia experienced high levels

TABLE 1 Subnational variation of violence in World War II and the 1990s and case selection

	WORLD WAR II (DEATHS)			ICRC 2012 (MISSING PERSONS 1991–1995)			
Total	147,454	% of total		2,269	% of total		Included in the study
Slavonia	41,406	28	H	1,050	46	H	Požeško-slavonska, Brodsko-posavska, Bjelovarsko-bilogorska, Virovitičko-podravska, and Vukovarsko-srijemska
Northwestern Croatia	22,885	16	H	20	1	L	Koprivničko-križevačka
Central Croatia	40,865	28	H	733	32	H	Sisačko-moslavačka and Karlovačka
Lika	19,079	13	M	146	6	M	Ličko-senjska
Gorski Kotar	8,042	5	M	14	1	L	Primorsko-goranska
Dalmatia	15,177	10	M	306	13	M	Šibensko-kninska

Notes: High (H) = over 15%; medium (M) = 5%–15%; low (L) = less than 5%. The World War II data on civilian deaths by region come from Graovac and Cvetković 2005, 61, table 3. The 1990s data include only the number of missing persons in 2012 in the territory of Croatia (ICRC, Croatian Red Cross, and Ministarstvo branitelja Uprava za zatočene i nestale 2012).

of violence both in World War II and in the 1990s. Vukovarsko-srijemska in Eastern Slavonia and Sisačko-moslavačka in central Croatia are the two counties in Croatia with highest numbers of disappearances in the 1990s, based on the 2012 ICRC report.[20] The region of central Croatia experienced high levels of violence in both periods. Ličko-senjska and Šibensko-kninska experienced medium levels of violence both in World War II and in the 1990s. Two counties included in this study with medium to high levels of violence in World War II but a low level of violence in the 1990s are Koprivničko-križevačka and Primorsko-goranska (table 1).

Due in part to the lack of comparable data on civilian victims across the entire territory of Croatia, as noted earlier, and in part due to the methodological and conceptual problems associated with classifying cases of violence against civilians, my research was primarily based on the subnational comparison and analysis of qualitative evidence, including archival documents, periodicals, publications, and in-depth interviews, instead of a quantitative analysis. I carried out part of the archival research in the Croatian Memorial Documentary Center for the Homeland War (Hrvatski Memorijalno-dokumentacijski centar Domovinskog rata). Specifically, I looked at local governance documents in the selected regions of Lika, Banija, Western Slavonia, and Gorski Kotar. I also looked at World War II documents from selected regions in the Croatian National Archive in Zagreb. I complemented this material with documents and publications from the National Archives locations across Croatia, including Rijeka, Split, Gospić, Slavonski Brod, Petrinja, and Požega. Documenta, the Zagreb-based nongovernmental organization collecting data on civilian victims of the war in the 1990s in Croatia, provided materials related to particular cases of violence against civilians, including eighty-two interviews that it conducted with victims and witnesses who reported personal testimonies. Documenta provided me with these interviews for the purpose of this research project to complement my own interviews. In addition, I obtained fourteen interviews, which included both the Croatian Army soldiers and residents in cities affected by violence, from the Institute of Ethnology and Folklore in Zagreb. In the Institute of Ethnology and Folklore, as well as in the National and University Library, I surveyed a large body of literature on the interwar period, as well as the period of the Homeland War in Croatia, in order to complement the interviews and the archival data.

With the help of local research assistants, in-depth interviews were conducted and recorded in 2014 with residents in the following regions across Croatia: Podravina, Western Slavonia, Eastern Slavonia, central Croatia, Gorski Kotar, Lika, and northern Dalmatia.[21] Respondents were selected through local contacts that my assistants established in the geographic regions selected for comparison. In this context, in which interpersonal trust and postconflict reconciliation have still not fully been achieved, it was important to ensure that interviews were anonymous and that the individuals trusted the researcher.[22] Almost all the interviews were recorded; in some interviews, I was present, and I conducted several interviews alone. I selected and trained research assistants in the procedures outlined in the protocol approved by the Institutional Review Board at my institution to ensure the anonymity of respondents. I transcribed and translated all interviews, and any possibly identifying information was excluded from the transcripts.

In Uganda, interviews were conducted in May and June 2015 around the capital city of Kampala and in central Uganda, or the Luweero region. I selected this region because in the early 1980s it was the area where the Ugandan National Liberation Army (UNLA), led by Milton Obote, targeted civilians who were suspected to have aided the rebel army, the National Resistance Army (NRA), under the leadership of the current president of Uganda, Yoweri Museveni. With the help of local research assistants and contacts, I was able to interview thirty-six individuals who were over forty years of age and representative in terms of gender, educational background, and personal experiences during the period of war.[23]

In Guatemala, most interviews were conducted in the western highlands region, where the level of violence against civilians increased significantly in the early 1980s compared to earlier periods in the thirty-six-year-long civil war. Specifically, I interviewed in the regions of Quiché, Sololá, and Totonicapán, as well as in Guatemala City. The field research in Guatemala, carried out in May and June 2016, included eighteen in-depth interviews with residents of these areas, former insurgents, and former members of the military.[24] As in Croatia and Uganda, I relied on local contacts to help me identify respondents, as well as to introduce me to them. Unlike in Croatia, and just like in Uganda, I was present during all interviews and posed comparable, though slightly modified, questions.

The Organization of the Book

The book is organized in the following manner. Chapter 1 identifies conditions and contexts that are conducive to wartime collective crimes. In this study, I do not assume that individuals are targeted on the basis of identities that existed before the rise of political conflict that escalated into violence. Rather, I argue that new identities, referred to as political ethnicities, form in those communities where state-level processes of ethnicization, or the fusion of ethnic or cultural and political identity, coincide with local processes of ethnicization. State-level processes of ethnicization begin most commonly in the discourse of political leaders, in media representations, and, most decisively, with the use of violence as a political strategy. Local-level processes of ethnicization, in turn, are triggered by the complementary processes of the exclusion of moderates and the production of borders. The common thread connecting collective crimes in time of war, in other words, is the context within which they occur. It is a context in which the perpetrators believe that their actions are not going to be penalized, that they are acceptable under the given circumstances, and that they represent a form of self-defense. It is also a context in which those who wish to prevent such crimes are made to feel that they are outsiders—traitors, even—and may also become targets of violence. Thus, in my conceptualization, the moderates are not people who are neutral bystanders to violence but rather those who actively challenge the new order and the ethnicization process in their communities. This is the context that I conceptualize as amoral communities. Instead of punishing the perpetrators of criminal acts, the leaders in power place more emphasis on resolving a political crisis, winning a war, or eliminating those defined as enemies. In amoral communities, not only is the violence against civilians tolerated by the authorities, it may also be covered up, presented as the result of random accidents, or justified as a necessary sacrifice for a greater political goal.

Chapter 2 focuses on one of the characteristics of amoral communities, the ethnicization of everyday life, which was evident across different regions in Croatia, such as in the examples from central Croatia and Eastern Slavonia, in the workplaces, where people started to group along ethnic lines; in public spaces, where symbolic messages signaled ethnic polarization; in schools, where students made comments to other classmates that they had heard at home; or in the way that certain political messages were framed and interpreted by the local media, local government representatives, and informal groups of citizens on the neighborhood level. While the process of ethnicization initially occurs on the state level in the discourse of political leaders, it may or may not lead to polarization along ethnic lines in some communities.

In chapter 3, I consider the first of the two mechanisms that trigger the local-level conditions necessary for the formation of amoral communities, the exclusion of moderates. This chapter shows how such exclusion is achieved through threats, selective targeted violence, social ostracism, and other forms of in-group policing. For example, moderates may be excluded through efforts to recruit supporters and participants by offering only two options—you are with us or against us—because it eliminates a third possibility, that of remaining part of the same community as a neutral member. Even if, in rare cases, individuals manage to remain neutral in this phase, they will likely be seen as disloyal, or, worse, as opportunists trying to benefit their personal situation by exploiting both sides, or even as spies. The individuals who do not align with one or the other side, or who do not share the political views that are imposed on their own communities by the more extreme members, the local leaders, or different armies, may become targets of violence in these communities.

Chapter 4 shows how the second mechanism that triggers the formation of amoral communities, the production of borders, begins initially as the setting up of barricades, checkpoints, or roadblocks with an aim to control the population. Insurgent-dominated communities are blocked off by the wartime dividing lines for extended periods of time with no access to food, medicine, basic supplies, or any state-provided services. As a result of the production of borders, civilians in these areas may become easier targets of violence. Also, given that people have limited opportunities to leave when surrounded by armies, recruiting civilians for the insurgency is also easier.

Chapter 5 examines critically the hypothesis that the violence against civilians in some communities was in some way associated with the history of violence against civilians in that region or community. Respondents were asked whether they had been told of violence that took place earlier in their local community and whether they thought that there was a connection between historical and modern cycles of violence. I found that personal, intergenerational, and local memories varied to a great extent and may or may not have been political in origin or interpretation. This variation was evident across individuals in the same region, and even in the same communities. For this reason, it is not sufficient to analyze solely the role of memories of previous waves of violence in people's perceptions and motivations.

In chapter 6, I show how the wartime violence against civilians in some communities was a political rather than a military strategy because the violence occurred after the perpetrators took control of the territory, and people who were perceived as adversaries based on their political ethnicity were targeted. These individuals were defined as a threat. Their elimination, or forced displacement from the defined territory, was seen as a justified goal in the context of war, or during the "state of exception," even when the perpetrators acted in an area under their control and against noncombatants who did not pose any realistic military threat to them. Targeted violence, in turn, further contributed to ethnicization and divisions based on newly defined identities in the communities where such violence occurred in the first year of the war.

1
THE MAKING OF AMORAL COMMUNITIES

What context is conducive to collective wartime crimes? How does such a context form? In this book, I show how the context in which the perpetrators believe that their actions are not going to be penalized and that their actions are acceptable is created on the local level in some communities.[1] It is a context in which moderates, or those who wish to prevent such crimes, are excluded for putting their desire to protect all civilians, regardless of their identity or political orientation, ahead of the security-related needs that are presented by their leaders as more pressing concerns in time of war.[2] This is the context that I conceptualize as *amoral communities*. Instead of punishing the perpetrators of criminal acts so that civilians and prisoners of war are protected under all circumstances, the leaders in power place more emphasis on resolving a political crisis, winning a war, or eliminating those defined as enemies (Anderson 1983; Esposito 2011; Foucault [1978] 1990; Haleem 2012). In amoral communities, violence against civilians not only is tolerated by the authorities but also may be covered up or presented as a necessary sacrifice or the result of random accidents, given the need to respond urgently to a security crisis or a war. Furthermore, in such communities, it is not necessary for the government to send its own armies because the local population is disposed to take part in the violence.

Collective Crimes in Time of War

Rather than assuming that individuals are targeted on the basis of identities that existed before the rise of political conflict that escalated into violence, I define *collective crimes* as wartime targeting of individuals and their immediate social and cultural environment on the basis of newly created identities that merge a particular political identity with a particular ethnicity, referred to in this study as a *political ethnicity*. I show how political ethnicities were created in some communities through several complementary processes of *ethnicization*, such as the *exclusion of moderates* and the *production of borders*, as well as by the *use of violence as a political strategy*.[3]

The *term collective crimes* is closely related to the concept of genocide, defined by Raphael Lemkin as "acts of barbarity" and "acts of vandalism" and included in the Convention on the Prevention and Punishment of the Crime of Genocide, adopted by Resolution 260 A (III) of the UN General Assembly in 1948 (Lemkin 1933). The intersection of political and sociological elements of the concept was recognized by Lemkin.[4] Scholars of mass ethnic violence showed that it is possible to "eliminate ethnic groups if their culture disappears, even if there is no physical removal of persons" (Mann 2005, 11). Hence, in the concept of collective crimes, it is crucial to include the act of destruction of cultural property that is symbolically connected with a particular political or ethnic group, such as cemeteries, churches, books, and the like.

I build on Lemkin's notion that political groups should be included in the conceptualization. This idea is not new; other scholars have also included the targeting of political groups in conjunction with the term *genocide*. For example, Barbara Harff defines both genocides and politicides as "the promotion, execution, and/or implied consent of sustained policies by governing elites or their agents—or, in the case of civil war, either of the contending authorities—that are intended to destroy, in whole or part, a communal, political, or politicized ethnic group," and in politicides, "groups are defined primarily in terms of their political opposition to the regime and dominant groups" (2003, 58). I depart from Lemkin and Harff, however, by placing political groups at the center of the analysis and showing how religious, ethnic, or racial identities become relevant only after the political adversaries in a given conflict have already been identified.[5] Rather than employing the term *intentional*, as used by scholars of genocide, I include acts categorized as *targeted* violence. In the use of either term, the act of violence is categorized as intentional or targeted after it has occurred. In order to prove that the action was intentional, however, it is necessary to consider documents and other evidence that proves that a particular action was planned.[6] For many of the acts of violence against civilians, unfortunately, such evidence does not exist, while the evidence proving that civilians were targeted may be deduced from a combination of factors, such as the nature of the act (killing, forced displacement, torture, rape, destruction of religious sites, etc.), the circumstances under which the act took place (the deliberate bombing of a residential community or other civilian location, such as a bomb shelter or hospital; massacres of civilians in particular villages, etc.), and the characteristics of the victims. Thus, I prefer to use the term *targeted violence* in my analysis.

In the literature on violence against civilians, the definitions that come the closest to the definition used in my study are provided by Kristine Eck and Lisa Hultman (2007, 235) and Laia Balcells (2017, 21–24). Eck and Hultman distinguish "one-sided violence" from other forms of violence, as it "encompasses only those fatalities that are caused by the intentional and direct use of violence" as a result of "the use of armed force by the government of a state or by a formally organized group against civilians which results in at least 25 deaths per year" (2007, 235). Balcells distinguishes direct violence and indirect violence, and defines the former as the form of violence "carried out with light weaponry . . . in a 'face-to-face' type of interaction" (2017, 21). Furthermore, Balcells argues that direct violence "involves individual identification of victims, but it can also involve executions *en masse*" and it is "shaped" by "the interaction between the armed groups and local civilians" during the war (21). In a similar way, in Eck and Hultman's definition of one-sided violence, "intentional killings" includes "any action that is taken to deliberately kill civilians" and excludes deaths that occur, for example, when noncombatants are caught in crossfire, while "direct deaths" includes deaths caused by "bombing or shooting" and excludes "deaths caused indirectly by an ongoing conflict, mainly due to disease or other health problems" (2007, 235). In my work, the elements of the identification and targeting of certain civilians over others in a given community are the most relevant in these scholars' definitions. However, the concept of collective crimes, as employed in my study, is broader,[7] as it also includes the forced displacement of civilians, arrest, torture, rape, and the destruction of cultural property.

This brings us to another key characteristic of the definition of *collective crimes* that is employed in this study: crimes occurring over the course of war, as well as crimes occurring immediately before or after the war, are included (Shaw 2007, 155).[8] Even though I consider collective crimes to be tied to a war, defined as a violent political conflict, like Shaw, as well as Eck and Hultman, I also acknowledge that particular acts of violence are one-sided. One of the difficulties when analyzing collective crimes in some wartime contexts may be in distinguishing between combatants and noncombatants. In wars, such as the war in Croatia, where former members of the same community participated on opposite sides, it may be difficult to determine with certainty whether a person was a civilian or a combatant or, in some cases, even whether a person was a perpetrator, a collaborator, or a victim. By placing the analysis of collective crimes in the wartime period, it becomes possible to gain a better understanding of the situations in which the same individual may transition from one to another of these categories. As Virginia Garrard-Burnett (2010, 168) shows in her study of violence in Guatemala, it is assumed that violence, and political violence in particular, constructs warring sides' identities. Specifically, as Garrard-Burnett argues, violence "constructs people who might once have been friends, neighbors, even kin, into intractable internal enemies" (168). This is one of the principal reasons for my decision to examine collective crimes in the wartime context.

Amoral Communities

In addressing the question of the conditions under which collective crimes in war occur, it is necessary to consider state-level processes taking place before, as well as during, the time that collective crimes occur. I build on theoretical insights put forward most compellingly by scholars of nationalism,[9] ethnic violence,[10] and political, or sovereign, power[11] to develop the concept of *amoral communities*. It was inspired by a number of scholarly contributions to the field of nationalism, but most directly by Benedict Anderson's concept of "imagined communities," defined as "nations" whose members share a certain "image of their communion," and as communities that are sovereign, or free to govern, within their territorially limited space (Anderson 1983, 6–7). The amoral communities are the "imagined communities" under the condition of war, in which the use of unlimited violence with the aim of eliminating external and internal enemies is justified by the necessity to protect the image of a nation-state as a representation and extension of a human life (Anderson 1983; Esposito 2011; Foucault [1978] 1990; Haleem 2012). In this image, a nation, like a human body, is defined by a certain physical space, but a nation's life is seen as worthy of sacrifice in part because it is potentially eternal, unlike a human life.

The use of violence in such communities is seen amorally, as a medical or surgical necessity, rather than as a crime, because the "enemy" or the "other" is seen as the source of the threat to the survival of the community (Esposito 2011). In that way it is akin to, but also different from, Hannah Arendt's concept of the "banality of evil" (Arendt [1963] 1996). Conceptually, it is similar in that individuals under the conditions of an amoral community are not free to act based on "ethical reflexivity," or individual moral values (Amoureux 2015, 30; Haleem 2012, 35). It is different because the concept of amoral communities directs the analysis away from the individual-level characteristics of people, or potential perpetrators of violence, toward greater understanding of the local context, or the conditions that make it possible for a community of diverse people, in terms of personal, political, or ethical values, to transform itself into a community where former neighbors would turn against one another (Forti 2015; Haleem 2012).[12] The alternative to the amoral community is simply a community where this type of mass violence remains inconceivable by local residents, rather than an ideal type of community, such as a "moral community," defined by Seyla Benhabib as "a community of interdependence" where it is possible "to settle those issues of common concern to all via dialogical procedures in which all are participants" (2002, 36). While such a community would be a highly desirable one, another study would be needed to establish which conditions may be conducive to its creation.

Within a single state, amoral communities may coexist with communities that categorize the use of violence against civilians as collective crimes and continue to value human life even under the conditions of war. For this reason, I look at the subnational level of analysis and consider the national-level conditions only as a set of political factors that are necessary, but not sufficient, in explaining why collective crimes occur in some areas and not in others within the same state and during the same war.

In states in which state formation is accompanied by the processes of the "ethnicization of statehood," the state-level context is favorable to the exclusion of ethnic minorities (Cederman, Gleditsch, and Buhaug 2013; Straus 2015; Wimmer 2001). Indeed, when ethnic groups are excluded from political power in a given state, either through limits in access to state power or through recent loss of state power, internal conflict is more likely to occur (Cederman, Gleditsch, and Buhaug 2013). In such states, the ethnic or racial minorities may be seen as the threatening "other." The exclusion may take different forms, ranging from subtle forms of discrimination to the most extreme forms, such as genocide, ethnic cleansing, or mass violence against the ethnic minorities (Cederman, Gleditsch, and Buhaug 2013; Mamdani 2001; Mann 2005; Straus 2015; Wimmer 2001, 2013). What makes the violence in this context particularly pervasive is that the processes of state formation, self-determination, and democratization have shifted the political power from the elites to the regular citizens (Foucault [1978] 1990; Mamdani 2001). It is the citizens of those modern states who decide who belongs, or who is one of "us," and who is an outsider, or who is seen as a threat to "our" lives. Michel Foucault argues that genocide was made possible in modern states precisely "because power is situated and exercised at the level of life, the species, the race, and the large-scale phenomena of population" ([1978] 1990, 137). The survival of a nation-state, in turn, just as the survival of a nation-as-a-body, is equated to the survival of the state's population, or the population that claims the legitimacy of their own political power within the territorial boundaries of the state (137). This represents a change from the time when wars used to be "waged in the name of the sovereign," or the monarch, to the period when wars "are waged on behalf of the existence of everyone" (137). The goal in this situation becomes not only a political victory over those who are defined as enemies in the war but also their elimination (Esposito 2010, 2011; Foucault 2003, 256; Girard 1972, 266).[13] Giorgio Agamben (1995) builds on Foucault's thesis, presented here, to argue that phenomena like genocide are not just "exceptional" cases but rather that such acts of violence are possible in any state where the "state of exception" becomes the norm through the legal framework on which the particular state is constituted. Even after the wartime violence entailing genocide or ethnic cleansing ends, the protection of the nation-state does not end because existential threats continue to be perceived by the nation's guardians (Hajdarpašić 2015).

An act of preemptive violence against individuals who represent a threat to a community in a crisis, or during the "state of exception," would constitute a defensive act. In amoral communities, such an act of violence is not only tolerated but also justified, even if it "completely disregards the humanity of the other," as argued by Irm Haleem, who convincingly criticizes the logic of justice in the "Just War Doctrine" that categorizes an act of political violence as "'moral' as long as it is argued to be a product of 'necessity' and 'supreme emergency'" (2012, 128). The community that perceives the threat, thus, may justify turning against its members by claiming a need to protect itself preemptively. Given these inconsistencies in the arguments justifying the use of political violence, particularly in cases in which it may be more difficult to distinguish the perpetrators of violence or the militants from civilians in particular communities, I use the term *amoral*, meaning an absence of any morality or justice, in the cases in which violence against some human beings, however their status may be defined, is not considered as a criminal act.

At least two questions remain, however, that scholars have not directly addressed: (1) How is the "state of exception," or the situation of crisis in which crimes would be tolerated, constituted in some places and not in others within the same nation and during the same war? and (2) How does a certain group of individuals or identity within a given body politic become a threat?

These questions are particularly important in the context of a theory that applies to democratic political systems in which, as mentioned earlier, the sovereignty represents the power of the people, or of the state's citizens. Related to the second question, if the leaders seeking to constitute *amoral communities*, or communities in which crimes against certain members of the community who are perceived as a threat would not be considered as crimes, claim to be representing the citizens, or their constituents, what would be a democratic way to prevent this from occurring? In *Rogues: Two Essays on Reason*, Jacques Derrida poses a related question: "Must a democracy leave free and in a position to exercise power those who risk mounting an assault on democratic freedoms and putting an end to democratic freedom in the name of democracy and of the majority that they might actually be able to rally round to their cause?" (2005, 34). In other words, given a democratic political system, how can the state of exception that makes collective crimes in wars possible be avoided, while at the same time ensuring that democratic values are upheld for all people in the state's territory? Derrida builds on Carl Schmitt's conceptualization of the "sovereign" to address the question of how a state of exception becomes institutionalized in a democratic polity.

In such a state, it is the sovereign who determines when the state of exception is appropriate (Derrida 2010, 7–8). How does the sovereign claim this power, and how are individuals who represent the "beast," or the target of unsanctioned violence, identified? Also, who is permitted to die as a result of war, and whose death is recognized or commemorated? Rene Girard (1972, 271), for example, suggests that the victims constitute the "others" among "us," where the differences between "us" and "them" may be so subtle that they may be imperceptible to people who are indeed outside the given community. Schmitt writes that the decision of who the enemy is constitutes a "political decision" that precedes the actual war, or the state of exception ([1927] 2007, 27–34). Even though Schmitt emphasizes that defining the "enemy" is a political act, it is possible to infer from Schmitt's text that there is an ethnic or racial aspect, in a primordial sense, in his concept when he writes that in order for an individual to be labeled as an enemy, "it is sufficient for his nature that he is, in a specially intense way, existentially something different and alien" (27).

In this study, I would like to delineate more clearly that what is "existentially something different and alien" has been made so not as a result of any preexisting racial or ethnic differences but rather as a result of the sovereign's categorization of the members of a society into two groups: those who are perceived to present a political challenge to the dominant power structure and those who are not perceived in such way. In order to facilitate the identification and possible elimination of those who are seen as a threat to the dominant order, ethnic or racial traits of the majority of political opponents are transformed into the *markers* of any potential political opponent of the dominant regime. In this process, the opponents' political position is deliberately *ethnicized* or *racialized* (Bergholz 2016; Fujii 2009; Gagnon 2004; Mamdani 2001; Žarkov 2007). While the impetus for the ethnicization process tends to come from the top (Straus 2015), the power of identifying and eliminating those labeled as "enemies" is not purely in the hands of the state institutions and officials; it may be carried out by individuals' own communities, consisting of former neighbors, friends, and even family members (Bergholz 2016). As scholars have already acknowledged, violence may not always be carried out by the state; rather, it is "exercised in three distinct ways: top-down by elites, bottom-up by popular pressures, and coercively sideways by paramilitaries" (Mann 2005, 8). This is why it is critical to move the study of wartime collective crimes to the local level of analysis, with an aim to understand not only the conditions that contribute to the formation of amoral communities but also the conditions that make the prevention of collective crimes possible in other communities, even in time of war.

Local Conditions for the Formation of Amoral Communities

Given a state in which the dominant contending political factions are framed in terms of ethnicity, what accounts for wartime collective crimes in some communities and what accounts for their absence in others? In other words, what are the local factors, actions, or conditions that contribute to the formation of spaces within which attacks on certain members of the community and their respective cultural symbols are seen as a justifiable form of defense? On the other hand, what are the conditions that prevent such forms of political violence in some communities, referred to by scholars as "peace enclaves" (Katunarić 2010; Varshney 2002)?

Scholars who conduct a subnational comparative, or micro-level, analysis conclude that violence against civilians could be explained as part of the rational strategies of various participants in war, with the goal being to gain military control over a particular geographic area (Kalyvas 1999, 2005, 2006), the civilian population (R. Wood 2010), or the adversary (Hultman 2007; Metelits 2010). Opportunities such as access to local or international material or military resources and support may also motivate wartime violence against civilians in some cases (Bulutgil 2010; Weinstein 2007). While these studies are valuable in explaining the violence against civilians when it is a result of a strategic goal or a rational opportunity, most of the studies of political violence, with exception of the work of Balcells (2017) that reintroduces political strategies into the analysis of violence against civilians, still do not account for targeted violence in cases in which the episodes of collective crimes against civilians occurred even when there was no clear military or strategic advantage to perpetrators because the territory had already been occupied.

In my study, I focus on analyzing the processes that connect the national-level (i.e., macro-level) and local-level conditions (i.e., both micro-level and meso-level) that may be associated with violence against civilians (Balcells and Justino 2014; Cederman, Gleditsch, and Buhaug 2013). A gradual process of ethnicization, beginning on the national level, creates new social identities, *political ethnicities*—political identities that aim to reduce a multiplicity of personal views and political preferences to political views that become defined primarily in terms of race or ethnicity, among other possible markers of groups (Straus 2015).[14] These national-level processes may or may not lead to polarization along ethnic lines in some communities locally, however, as previously discussed. I refer to communities in which ethnicization is successfully carried out as *amoral communities*. In such communities, the process of ethnicization is triggered by the exclusion of moderates from the political and social space through violence, threats, or social ostracism and by the production of borders along which the population that once shared the same community is divided.[15] The process of the exclusion of moderates has already been identified by scholars of political polarization and political violence (Bergholz 2016; Bermeo 2003; Gagnon 2004; Hajdarpašić 2015; Heberle [1940] 1970; Straus 2012, 2015). In his classic study of the rise of Nazism in German, Rudolf Heberle shows "how in an atmosphere of intimidation, hopeless resignation, and self-deceiving compromise" and with the use of "a great number of ingenious devices of 'social control,' aimed primarily at the attainment of conformity in overt behavior," gradually "it became increasingly difficult to abstain from more or less active support of the regime" ([1940] 1970, 126). Similarly, in her analysis of cases of democratic breakdown in Europe and Latin America, Nancy Bermeo shows how polarization, conceived as a multidimensional process, resulted when "elites overlooked the moderate forces in the voting public" (2003, 229). When the process of the exclusion of moderates is accompanied by the process of the production of borders, initially through barricades or checkpoints and later through wartime dividing lines and state borders, it results in the physical manifestation of the division of communities. This is when the abstract notions of "us" and "them" become a reality. One of the consequences of these processes is the formation of new identities—political ethnicities.

If ethnicization occurs on the local level, it may be observed in the everyday lives of individuals: in the workplaces, where people start to group along ethnic lines; in public spaces, where symbolic messages, which may be more or less subtle, signal the ethnic polarization; in schools, where students make comments to other classmates that they hear at home; or in the way that certain political messages are framed and interpreted by the local media, local government representatives, and informal groups of citizens on the neighborhood level. Ethnicization processes, in turn, may create conditions for violence along the newly defined sociopolitical boundaries. One reason for this is that ethnicization processes reduce the plurality of political preferences,[16] thereby creating an artificially polarized society. Most people's opinions and views do not fall neatly into categories that correspond to their ethnic identities. If the ethnicization process is successful on the societal level, in any conversation, people can use ethnicity (or race, religion, and language, among other relevant cultural markers), rather than the substance of the conversation, as a shortcut to identify individuals with shared political views. In such an environment, individuals assume that if they know each other's identities, they know everything about each other's political opinions. Another reason that ethnicization processes may create conditions for violence in a society is that these processes facilitate identification of "others" who may be the potential targets of violence. This is related to Mahmood Mamdani's concept of the process of racialization (2001, 13). Easy identification of "others," in turn, facilitates attacks in the context of intense political competition, campaigning, revenge, or simply preemptive behavior against individuals who, on the surface, appear as political opponents or enemies, even though the targeted individuals' real political views are not known. Violent incidents may take place at any time in a context of war—before, during, or after a war. If they happen before the war in a community where ethnicization has already taken place, however, these incidents further hinder the communication and trust in such a community, and may even serve to further mobilize societies politically and polarize their members, thus contributing to the formation of a community, an amoral community, in which collective crimes against some members of the community may be tolerated or justified.

In amoral communities, the violence against the side categorized as a threat is more easily justified and accepted not only by the army and the police but also by ordinary citizens who, unlike the political leaders and their armies, see violence against those on the other side of the dividing line as a form of self-defense and part of their own survival strategy under the state of emergency or the "state of exception."[17] Regardless of how the actual perpetrators understand the violence against civilians in amoral communities, I show that this type of violence represents primarily a political strategy rather than a military strategy. This is so, first, because it occurs after military control over the territory is attained and when the civilians once categorized as a threat no longer represent a realistic and objective threat. Second, most cases of mass violence occur in the beginning of war, or during the time when political control is just in the process of being established. When *political* control is more certain, violence subsides until the next challenge to political control. Third, only those who are seen as enemies politically or ethnically are targets of violence. Finally, even the cultural symbols of the perceived political or ethnic enemies may become the targets in the social and physical spaces where the new political regime is attempting to establish its power. Therefore, collective crimes are not irrational acts but rather part of a political strategy. They are made conceivable and possible in those communities in which the exclusion of moderates and the production of borders gradually lead to the ethnicization of everyday life that divides ordinary people with diverse personal and political opinions into merely two groups—the "citizens" on this side of the border and the "enemies" of the state on the other side of the border.

2
EVIDENCE OF AMORAL COMMUNITIES

What distinguishes *amoral communities* from other types of wartime settings in which violence, looting, and the destruction of property are commonplace? The principal characteristic is that the connection between ethnicity and a political identity extends into everyday facets of life. In communities where the *ethnicization of everyday life* is present, instead of perceiving each other in terms of personal traits or community roles, people first consider ethnicities, or, more specifically, *political ethnicities*. This becomes evident, for instance, in the workplace, where people start to group along ethnic lines; in public places, where symbolic messages reflect the new polarization; and even in schools or on playgrounds, where children repeat comments they heard from adults in their lives. In amoral communities, when civilians become targets of violence on the basis of their political ethnicities, these acts of violence may be presented as necessary for the restoration of order or as a consequence of wartime conditions.

The formation of political ethnicities, or the linking of ethnicity and political goals, usually starts from the top: in the discourse of political leaders, in the media, or in the new policies and decrees of the government. Over the course of this process, statehood is redefined in terms of the political inclusion of certain political ethnicities and the exclusion of others. If violence results, political leaders who have already engaged in the ethnicization process justify the targeting of civilians associated with an excluded political ethnicity by portraying them as an existential threat under the condition of war, or the "state of exception," both to the state and to the population the state was going to include (Agamben 2005, 2). The role of the national leaders is, therefore, a necessary condition for the formation of amoral communities, yet it is not a sufficient condition because local-level processes, which are examined in the following two chapters, also matter. In some communities, divisions along the new political ethnicities may sever interpersonal relationships that existed before the onset of violence. In those communities, violence against former neighbors or friends becomes permissible under the conditions of war and in the context of the resulting lack of security. Even before the start of the violence, the evidence of amoral communities in such places may be found in the ethnicization of everyday life, or the divisions of the population along new identities across multiple levels of society. In other communities, where ethnicization processes do not spill over into the everyday life of residents, however, despite some tensions, the prewar social ties of most of the residents remain unchanged both throughout the war and afterward.

Discourse of Threats and Top-Down Ethnicization

In the context of Croatia, the wartime violence and the nationalist political discourse of dominant political leaders touched many people more or less directly in the first part of the 1990s. Many respondents, even in the regions of Croatia where mass violence did not take place, noted that the discourse in the national media contributed to their sense of fear at the start of the war. For example, the following respondent from northwestern Croatia mentioned how the news contributed to the general panic that people felt when the first local attacks started:

> RESPONDENT (R): The war in Yugoslavia started on the news. I was very upset, and it frightened me . . .
> INTERVIEWER (I): Could you tell me more?
> R: We spent a lot of time hiding in basements when the first sirens started. We were afraid, but as time passed and nothing dangerous was happening, we thought that the war cannot happen here, and that there won't be grenades and such things here. We relaxed a bit. And then, one day, grenades were launched on the nearby military headquarters. Then we all realized that this was happening to us. One journalist literally spread the panic through the local media. He was saying that the fifth column[1] is here and that they are targeting people on the roads with snipers.
> I: How did you react to this? Did you believe him?
> R: While we were in the shelter, we believed him.[2]

The anticipation of the war that the media built up contributed, in this respondent's view, to the general sense of panic once the first attacks started. This is one of the arguments of the book *The Body of War: Media, Ethnicity, and Gender in the Break-Up of Yugoslavia* by Dubravka Žarkov (2007), which documents the role that the media had in constructing ethnicity.[3] In some instances, the state-controlled media made references to the World War II armies the Ustaša and the Četniks as a "form of frightening people."[4] The media also exposed people to politicized symbols and ceremonies that represented a "constitutive element in preparing for the war" (Kale 2016, 125). One respondent stopped reading the newspapers during the early 1990s because she thought that the "media war" contributed to the polarization of the population on the basis of ethnic differences in her town.[5]

In the view of the respondent from northwestern Croatia, political leaders presented the events at the beginning of the war as an emergency or a crisis in order to motivate ordinary people to take part in the war.[6] The residents of central Croatia date the beginning of threatening discourse to the period of the first elections in 1990. In their perspective, the electoral discourse of the nationalist parties that called for linking the political goal of statehood with ethnicity, most notably in the discourse of the HDZ relative to other nonethnic parties, such as the Social Democratic Party, was particularly powerful in the period when people were still trying to make sense of the new political order during the democratization phase.[7]

The electoral rhetoric and nationalist symbols used in the campaigns of political parties emphasized the link between statehood and ethnicity, such as in the discourse of the HDZ and the SDS. In the following discussion, respondents from northern Dalmatia describe the use of such symbols in the campaign discourse of the HDZ in their area:

> RESPONDENT 1 (R1): If anyone wants to talk about this last war and describe it, then it is important to start with the very beginning . . . what [Franjo] Tuđman was saying before he won the election. He went all around Croatia except here where we were. He organized the gatherings with Ustaša symbols, Ustaša songs, and threats to Serbs. I remember I watched this on television. It was public knowledge. Until Tuđman won, people in these areas where Serbs lived didn't do anything. But once he won, then they sent from Zagreb the police to change the police in Knin. Then people in Knin rebelled. Then it started in other parts of Croatia, and then the war started.
> I: When you mention "other parts," what do you mean?
> R1: In other parts where Serbs were in the majority, such as Gračac, Udbina, Benkovac, and Banija. Those were all places where Serbs were

in the majority, and in those police units, there were mainly Serbs because they were local majorities. Then they all rebelled against Tuđman and the police from Zagreb in their towns.

I: What did this rebellion look like at first?

RESPONDENT 2 (R2): That is when the barricades started.⁸

These two residents perceived the political campaign of the former president of Croatia and the leader of the HDZ, Tuđman, not only as excluding ethnic Serbs but in fact as a threat to them. The political and armed mobilization of the local population in their region started shortly after the HDZ won the first multiparty elections in Croatia in May 1990. On the Serb side, politicians exaggerated the threat that the new political system in Croatia represented, in the view of another resident from the region. For those who did not believe that discourse or those who did not want to take an active part in the new sociopolitical system, life during that time was "a struggle."⁹ The media from Serbia that was circulated among the population in the regions with a high proportion of ethnic Serbs further contributed to the construction of threat:

> R: I didn't have any ambition to participate in the local political life. Among those newspapers that were coming from Belgrade, one could have made one very nice catalog. In *Večernje Novosti*,¹⁰ even before the first gun was fired, there was an article about how Croatian police officers were killing Croatian children for money from the HDZ government.
>
> I: And that article about some agreement [among political leaders], what was the purpose? And wouldn't that contribute to the loss of the desire to fight if there was already an agreement?
>
> R: This was targeted to the population in Krajina.
>
> I: Only Serbs?
>
> R: Yes, to show them how there is some conspiracy against them to motivate them to rebel against it.
>
> I: People believed that?
>
> R: Yes, they believed that. The article was [about] how Tuđman and [Alija] Izetbegović¹¹ agreed to move out the Serb population from Croatia, to divide Bosnia, and to expand Croatia all the way to Zemun [near Belgrade], and so on, in order to stir the population here.
>
> I: Not [Slobodan] Milošević?
>
> R: No, Izetbegović. There were meetings between Milošević and Tuđman indeed, but that article was about the meeting between Tuđman and Izetbegović.¹²

The discourse of threat was, thus, present in the media on both sides. Just as previous respondents who lived in the predominantly ethnic Serb regions were exposed to the discourse that the victory of the HDZ under Tuđman was a threat to Serbs in Croatia, ethnic Croats received messages that the victory of the nationalist party in Serbia, the Serbian Socialist Party (Srpska socijalistička stranka) under Milošević, was a threat to them and to Croatia.[13] In both perspectives, even though they are diametrically opposed, the new political regimes and the new definitions of statehood, primarily in ethnic terms, were being linked with respondents' existential concerns in their respective Yugoslav successor states.

In addition to individual differences, there were also important regional differences across Croatia in how people understood the political discourse in the 1990s. In Gorski Kotar, the region that had a strong antifascist movement historically, any openly nationalist discourse that excluded people on the basis of their ethnicity was connected to fascism:

> The fact is that politicians . . . or the Greater Serbian nationalism [*velikosrpski nacionalizam*] started the matter. That is how the ideology, which was a pro-fascist ideology, with a goal to have all Serbs in one state, [was] based on their slogan [*Svi Srbi u jednoj državi* (All Serbs in one state)], and so on. Then these nationalist slogans started and that simply led to the rise of emotions among the people. . . . But there was no one to stop them and that is why it manifested itself in the tragedies that happened. The defenders [*branitelji*], or the participants of the Homeland War, just like Partisans in World War II who were fighting for freedom, fought against this fascism. And we can openly label that as the Serbian fascism.[14]

These respondents interpreted political discourse that linked ethnicity and the political goal of statehood, or in this case Serbian nationalism, in the context of their own local World War II experience of the antifascist struggle. The significance of this view was that in detaching ethnicity from the political goal of state formation, this perspective did not actually fit in the dominant national narrative during the 1990s. Similar perspectives that considered ethnicity separately from the dominant political options were shared by a number of respondents. For instance, a veteran of the Croatian Army decided to take part in the war "not because of some animosity or revenge, but because of the movement that took place in Europe with the destruction of the Berlin Wall and the desire to attain greater political freedom for independent states when bigger states, such as the USSR and Yugoslavia, were falling apart."[15] He was critical of violence, and of the abuse of power that he witnessed both during the war and afterward, and would have preferred a peaceful political solution for all sides in Croatia to a war. Political leaders' ethnicization discourse thus had a different effect in areas such as Gorski Kotar in part because local histories differed.

When remembering this period of the early 1990s over the course of the interviews, many respondents interpreted the attempts to link ethnicity and a political goal in critical ways. However, at that time, as one respondent recalls, it was not easy to view such messages, which were widespread in popular culture and the media, critically:

> I was a child, but I remember some images. That song, "My Country" [Moja Domovina], which some people consider very funny today, raised some patriotic sentiments [in the 1990s]. And, sometimes, you even cried. On television, during that time, you couldn't watch funny shows, like today. What was being shown was a program calling people to go to war. . . . They were playing some of these songs. So, you sat by the television. You were not allowed to leave home because you didn't know when the air raids would start. . . . We didn't know in our building, and I remember immediately the song of [Đorđe] Balašević,[16] "Skyscraper" [Soliter], we didn't know who was a Serb and who was a Croat. Later, we realized what was happening when people were disappearing overnight. Then we asked, "Where are these neighbors?" Until yesterday, we were playing on the playground. Then you heard that they fled across [to Serbia]. We lost a friend. These were strange situations. You would ask why these people left. And it was difficult for parents to explain this to a ten- or an eleven-year-old.[17]

Listening to patriotic music was normal during the period of war when it was difficult to understand why some new things were happening around them. For another respondent, these songs connected all of them during this time of "fear" and uncertainty.[18] Battle songs and patriotic music, combining the sounds of weaponry and oriental melodies invoking the "invented tradition" of the geographic frontier region, were commonplace on airwaves during this period (Hobsbawm and Ranger [1983] 1992; Kale 2016, 130).[19] The context in which patriotic songs were frequently played on the radio was one in which one perspective was emphasized while excluding other views, experiences, and sentiments from consideration in order to ideologically unify the group.[20] It was a situation that created a sense of urgency to act on behalf of those whose suffering was broadcast, or, in other words, not people in general but rather Croats in the Croatian media and Serbs in the Serbian media. This was manifested in some communities across Croatia in ways that affected ordinary people in their neighborhoods, workplaces, and schools, where social divisions along ethnic lines became more pronounced during this time.

Everyday Ethnicization in Public Places

The ethnicization of everyday life was reflected in changes in interpersonal relations with coworkers whose ethnicities had not been considered relevant before the war. These divisions in some cases started even before the first violent clashes, while in other cases they corresponded to the outbreak of violence. In the following experience of one respondent from central Croatia, for example, workplace divisions coincided with the first local violent incidents in 1991:

> I: In what way did it [social division along ethnic lines] manifest itself or did you notice it?
>
> R: For the big part, ethnic Serbs, under excuse . . . First, there was an unpaid vacation leave at work. You could take that if you were working in agriculture. This was used generally by the rural-based Serb population. They worked at home. In essence, what was worked on was the preparation of the rebellion and the uprising. This was the beginning of the Log Revolution and then the war.
>
> I: How did you find out about that? Through friends?
>
> R: That was known. There were very few of us at work, around thirty. There were Muslims, Serbs, and Croats. So you could notice. We and Muslims were working, while Serbs were missing work more and more. Those more extreme, those who were more nationalistic, were the first ones who were leaving. Then we noticed it.
>
> I: Tell me, did people pay attention in the factory before 1991 to ethnicities?
>
> R: No, only based on the first and the last names.
>
> I: How did the situation further develop when you noticed that Serbs were grouping themselves and withdrawing to villages?
>
> R: At work, I didn't notice too much. Maybe during the breaks, there were some comments. During the night shifts, when there was more time, [people were asking] why they were leaving and what they wanted. We still didn't have an idea of what they wanted. Nobody even imagined that this separation of the parts of Croatia [was planned].[21]

In this case, stark interethnic divisions were evident only after some of the respondent's coworkers started missing work both shortly before the Log Revolution and after the violent incident in the police station in Plitvice on March 31, 1991. The respondent assumed that people who were missing from work were of Serb ethnicity and that they took unpaid leave in anticipation of the armed conflict so that they could join the insurgency and the effort to create the RSK.[22] In his view, those who went to the other side of the barricades and the dividing line automatically represented the "other," or the extreme, while those who remained on his side and joined the Croatian Army were "normal."[23] For another resident from central Croatia, separations into distinct groups coincided with the start of the violence. People who were once friends suddenly became "Serbs" and "Croats" following the escalation of violence and the start of the war in this respondent's region.[24] Political leaders' discourse of ethnicization was thus reinforced locally after the barricades were set up and the violence started.

Individual perceptions can vary widely, however. One respondent from central Croatia who also reported workplace divisions along ethnic lines perceived ethnic divisions several years before the war when she was warned by a family member against marrying a Serb. In her opinion, Serbs in her community started emphasizing their ethnic identity before the war started. This was evident at work when people separated into groups on the basis of ethnicity and when graffiti, such as a symbol with "SSSS" (meaning *Samo sloga spašava Srbina* [Only unity saves the Serbs]), which was used by the nationalist-oriented Serbs during the war, appeared occasionally on the walls of her workplace. While this respondent did not care about ethnicity before the war and did not even pay attention to her family's advice about whom to marry, her account shows that she became more conscious of ethnicity as a result of the subsequent divisions at work.[25]

In addition to adults in the workplace, children and young people also experienced divisions along ethnic lines, in school and among friends. According to the following account of one respondent, he became more aware of his own ethnicity as he became a bit older and overheard conversations with references to different ethnic groups in his own home:

> I: When you were in school before the war, were there Serbs and Croats in your class?
> R: I was in a completely mixed class.
> I: Did you know who was a Croat and who was a Serb?
> R: I knew that after the fourth grade. In the first and the second, I didn't know.
> I: You didn't know because it was not important at that time in that society or because you were not interested in that?
> R: Both things. It was not important. This was not talked about in front of children. Normally, as you get older, you are going from the first to the eighth grade, you listen to what people are talking about . . .
> I: When did you hear in your family that you are a Croat? Was it from a young age?

R: Look, from a young age, I knew I was a Croat. Now, I cannot tell you when and how I learned that exactly. I knew I was a Croat. Probably not when I was three or four years old, but I knew it when I was seven or eight.

I: So, at your home, was it mentioned?

R: Yes, but there was no ideological indoctrination. It was talked about in the economic context, which was a fact. This was a multiethnic area, and Serbs had the best jobs as presidents, or in the police, in commerce. Generally, Serbs had the top positions. That was a fact, and this was talked about. I cannot say it was not talked about. Not to me directly, but I was a curious child who overheard it.[26]

This respondent recalled how knowledge from the conversations of adults around him played a role in his understanding of his own ethnic group as the one that had been disadvantaged under the previous political regime. Even for respondents who were not exposed to similar topics of conversation in their families, schools and streets were places where they came into contact with people who learned about their ethnic background at home:

I: Do you remember whether in this period before the war, given that you were in high school, someone identified as a Serb or a Croat?

R: No, personally, I didn't know what I was because this was not a topic of conversation in our house. It was not mentioned until the war. The only thing that was weird that I remember was that my girlfriends who were sitting next to me in the classroom used to draw some weird symbols on the desks. That was right before the beginning of the war. Until then, it was never important what I was or who I was. I remember from that period right before the war some changes in their behavior and their behavior toward me. There were very few Croats actually compared to . . . There were more Serbs in our class, even though, as I said, I didn't know that before. I was not brought up like that. But I noticed some distance. They formed a group . . . I don't know. I have one experience that to me now is funny. I was going home, and I was already a big girl. At that time, girls of fifteen were grown up already. There was a car that passed and they yelled at me that I was Šokica. I know now that Šokica is a term used in Slavonia for a Croat. I went home and cried. I was thinking whether I was stinking or there was something on me. My parents never taught me this. Even when I arrived home that time, my mother didn't explain to me what that meant. She just said, "Let go of those stupidities." And the drawing of Cyrillic "SSSS" on a school desk, which was drawn by women in class. It was not something I noticed among men, but among women who behaved strangely. They distanced themselves and there were no more common topics. I was always worried that I was somehow guilty for that because I didn't know the reason for all that.²⁷

In this account, the respondent did not learn about ethnic differences at home, and as a result, she did not recognize the ethnic symbols that her classmates drew on the school desks. She became aware of her ethnicity in school when she was gradually excluded as a Croat minority by her classmates and on the streets of her city, where she was categorized ethnically for the first time. During the early 1990s, even some children in elementary schools were witnesses of divisions along ethnic lines when symbols of the former Yugoslavia, such as the statues that honored individuals who fought against fascism in World War II, were removed or destroyed in their schools. In that context, ethnic differences among students translated into fights along ethnic lines between younger and older students, frequently placing their teachers in the role of observers or bystanders.²⁸ Gradually, ethnicity started to matter among friends in ways that created a certain distance and distrust that previously had not existed between them.

In addition to schools, streets and public spaces across cities in Croatia were also an arena of everyday local-level ethnicization among residents:

> I: When were the stars and the Yugoslav flags removed from public places?
> R: That went down immediately.
> I: When exactly?
> R: In 1990.
> I: Were Croatian symbols placed right away?
> R: Yes, the Croatian symbols were placed. There was still a road over there when Tuđman photos were carried.... Our people [Croats] were carrying those photos. I put a big photo of Tuđman on my back, and someone from the passing car swore at me. I responded, "I know who you are." That meant that he was a Serb who saw I was carrying Tuđman on my back. I still have a photo of Tuđman rolled up on top of the closet. It was difficult here, toward Kutina, and toward Dvor when tanks were pushing their own people. They ran over their own people with tanks.... There is a Četnik village ... over there. People from there couldn't not be Četniks because they had to be Četniks. There were some people from there who were much younger than me. I didn't know they were Četniks, but they knew who they were and who I was. We were naïve; we the Croats are naïve people.²⁹

Political views were expressed not just by voting for or politically supporting particular leaders but by identifying with political leaders ethnically. This process excluded the possibility that a Croat would criticize a political leader who claimed to represent ethnic Croat interests or that a Serb would support a leader claiming to represent ethnic Croat interests. By automatically labeling a person who criticizes a particular political leader as a Serb or a village with a Serb ethnic majority as a Četnik village, an assumption was made that all members of the same ethnic group shared the same political views, such as the view of the hardliners among the Serb minority who advocated for political autonomy or separation from Croatia for areas where ethnic Serbs constituted a significant proportion of the population.

Thus, through political leaders' discourse of the state of exception, as well as through the cultural and political messages conveyed in the media, in some communities across Croatia, the process of the ethnicization of everyday life was set in motion even before the start of the war. While in the following two chapters I analyze the local-level processes that contributed to the ethnicization of everyday life in some communities, in the next section, I show some similarities between the top-down ethnicization processes in Croatia and in other countries with entirely different historical and political conditions that experienced wartime targeted violence against civilians that is comparable to the violence that took place during particular periods of the war and in certain parts of Croatia.

Ethnicization in Comparative Perspective

Similar processes of top-down ethnicization were present in other countries where targeted violence against civilians occurred. In a comparative study of genocide in Africa, Scott Straus argues that state leaders' ideology of including or excluding particular ethnically defined groups in the state, or their "founding narratives," constituted an important precondition for genocide, which he defines as "the group-selective violence that requires coordination and the sustained application of violence against an identified population" (2015, 10–11). In countries with a history of colonialism, it could be argued that the modern efforts to link ethnicity and political ideology were more or less directly inspired by the social division that colonial authorities initiated or exploited.

In Uganda, under British control, the ethnic Baganda (i.e., the population of the central kingdom of Buganda) were given greater autonomy than other groups as a form of "indirect rule" (Buckley-Zistel 2008, 59).[30] Even though ethnic groups like the Baganda were not homogenous culturally or politically, some of the intergroup differences were politicized by political leaders, such as the leader of the

Uganda People's Congress (UPC), Milton Obote, who struggled for power following independence from the British (Nsibambi 2014, 42). In 1966 Obote carried out a coup, which resulted in the change of the constitution, the elimination of the autonomy of the region of central Uganda, and the exile of the *kabaka* (king) of the Baganda. This act, considered by some of my respondents as a deliberate effort to weaken the political influence of the Baganda in the state, led to the animosity of the Baganda toward Obote and the UPC.[31] Obote's coup in 1966 and the removal of the king of Buganda from power, among other policies of Obote, thus contributed to the gradual political and ethnic homogenization of the population in central Uganda.

As Obote, and his policies, became perceived by people from central Uganda as anti-Baganda, it was not a surprise, from the critical perspective of one of my respondents, that the leader of the opposition movement (National Resistance Movement) and the insurgent forces (NRA), Yoweri Museveni, chose central Uganda, or, more specifically, the Luweero region, as the area for recruitment and the base of the insurgency when Obote claimed victory in the disputed 1980 elections. This was the area where the opposition to Obote was already present among the majority of the local population. The rigging of elections by Obote served as an opportunity for Museveni to build social support for the insurgency in the region where Obote was already highly unpopular. Museveni built his social support during this time by connecting the political goal of rebellion against the oppressive government with the political goals of the Baganda, the ethnic majority in the region where the rebellion was based.[32]

In the analysis of another respondent, ethnicization became a strategy of mobilizing political support in the aftermath of the disputed elections.[33] However, one of the former insurgents wrote in his memoirs that rather than being a conflict in which ethnicity or even a particular ideology played an important role in motivating resistance, it was primarily an anti-Obote, anti-UPC, and anti-UNLA movement, and the "chief campaign manager and mobilizer for the anti-UPC regime was the UPC itself" because of Obote's policies, such as the removal of the king of Buganda from power and the reduction of the political autonomy for central Uganda (Kutesa [2006] 2008, 53).[34] While this former insurgent acknowledged that the perception of threat and the need for survival were principal motivating factors in joining the insurgency, he also contradicted himself when he described how members of the guerrilla forces received "political training" in the goals of the resistance movement from the leaders, known as cadres (122–123). Thus, the awareness that the sense of threat contributed to the condition of the state of exception under which violence may be seen as a justifiable form of "survival" or self-defense was probably created after the insurgents were already recruited. Additionally, as a result of the guerrilla strategy to "nurture a close bond with the population," civilians in the Luweero region became identified with the insurgency (Kainerugaba 2010, 91). Gradually, not only the insurgents but also the civilians in the Luweero region, who were mostly the Baganda, perceived the UNLA soldiers as a threat to their survival and were prepared to defend themselves (Kutesa [2006] 2008, 114). In turn, the process of linking a political goal and regional or ethnic identities began as part of the strategy of bringing civilians into the armed struggle.[35] Ultimately, civilians in central Uganda found themselves between the two sides.[36] To summarize, the case of Uganda in the 1980s shows how the dominant political leaders brought civilians into the conflict through the process of linking ethnic or regional identities with their political programs in the aftermath of the disputed 1980 elections.

Ethnicization was also evident in Guatemala, where violence against individuals of Mayan ethnicities in the western highland region of the country became part of the systematic counterinsurgency strategy relatively late in the protracted civil war, which lasted from 1960 to 1996, or under the governments of Lucas García from 1978 to 1982 and Efraín Ríos Montt from 1982 to 1983. The government under General García in 1978 began a new counterinsurgency strategy that was "planned carefully" and included a "mass repression in the countryside, assassinations and selective disappearances accompanied by a direct attack on the urban guerrillas" (Santa Cruz [2004] 2006, 48).[37] Under the government of García, and subsequently that of Montt, the geographic regions inhabited predominantly by the Mayan population, such as Ixcán, Alta and Baja Verapaz, the Ixil region, and El Quiché, were considered the insurgency territory, or the "red" zones (Recuperación de la Memoria Histórica [Recovery of Historical Memory Project; REMHI] 1999, 7). Thus, in areas marked by the military as "red," under the state of exception of the counterinsurgency strategy, both the insurgents and the civilians were considered legitimate targets of military violence.[38] With the goal of defeating the insurgents, "particularly between 1980 and 1983, the army annihilated entire communities considered to be the guerrillas' social support base" (133). Any evidence of Guerrilla Army of the Poor (Ejército Guerrillero de los Pobres; EGP) activity marked all residents of the town of Chupol in El Quiché as potential enemies (McAllister 2013, 99).[39] From the perspective of the government, cultural identity, ethnicity, and place of origin thus became shortcuts to identify potential enemies. In some cases, even cultural symbols, such as language or a traditional dress, associated with one of the geographic areas of the insurgency "led to threats and abuse" (Rothenberg 2012, 68). The violence in this period thus contributed to ethnicization processes.

Before the mass violence in the western highlands of Guatemala and the targeting of groups based on their ethnicities, the National Police (Policía Nacional) developed an elaborate system of "control and surveillance" with an aim to "prevent and combat crime" (Archivo Histórico de la Policía Nacional 2013, 267).[40] The National Police received information on "alleged subversive activities" not only from the members of the military or the police but also from individuals who considered themselves simply as "patriotic Guatemalans" (306).[41] Therefore, the intelligence system aimed at identifying political enemies extended from the top of the government all the way into the communities that had at some point been full of guerrilla members or collaborators.

The war did not make sense, from the perspective of some respondents, since it created conditions for people of the same communities to turn against one another. As a result, in some areas of the country, such as the region where the Ixil people lived, known in military terminology as the Ixil Triangle, residents were killed indiscriminately and on a large scale during the military operations against the insurgents.[42] In the view of another respondent, "we were fighting the war that was not ours," and in the end, the population mobilized by the guerrillas or living in the areas where the guerrillas were based did not benefit: "Now, these areas are weak and the government can obtain permits from big mining companies even against the will of the local population. If the population protests, they send the military and the police to protect not the people but the companies."[43] From the perspective of the leaders of the indigenous communities, part of the struggle was about land ownership (Menchú and Burgos-Debray [1983] 1994, 125). It was a conflict, in other words, over the control of land as the critical resource for survival. According to another respondent, the conflict was, and continues to be, essentially about power and the entrenched racial hierarchy. It stems from the colonial period, when the descendants of white colonizers, referred to as *ladinos*, established both political and economic power over the territory of present-day Guatemala. In his view, the conflict was thus over the empowerment and the inclusion of the population that has been exploited, marginalized, and oppressed since the period of colonization.[44] The insurgency then contributed to the ethnicization by turning the Mayan communities into the "other" or the "enemy" of the state from the perspective of the Guatemalan military (Short 2004, 52).[45]

In the case of Guatemala, as in the cases of Uganda and Croatia, ethnicization processes preceded the instances of targeted violence against civilians. In all three cases, ethnicity and political goals were linked in the state and insurgent leaders' conceptions of statehood. The processes of ethnicization started from the top with the discourse referencing the need to defend "the life of the community," or the nation-as-a-body—defined by a singular dominant ethnicity and a singular political orientation—against the threat of the "other," who is, from the perspective of "us," outside the norms and laws that apply to the state (Derrida 2010, 70; Esposito 2011, 5; Foucault [1978] 1990, 137). Violence against the "other" was, in turn, justified in light of such "supreme emergency" (Haleem 2012, 128). Violence outside the established norms, including indiscriminate mass violence, was free of judgment in the context of amoral communities because it was perceived by the perpetrators as self-defense or as a defense of the nation or the state against an imminent threat. Even though ethnicization processes were initiated from the top, usually by the political leaders representing the state or the insurgents, there were regional differences in the ways that divisions of the population manifested themselves in everyday life.

Wartime Communities in Croatia without Mass Violence

In the case of Croatia, in the multiethnic regions of Podravina and Gorski Kotar, most of the population, including ethnic Serbs, continued to live in the same towns or neighborhoods throughout the war. These regions of Croatia did not experience targeted violence against civilians on the scale of the violence in other regions, such as Eastern and Western Slavonia, central Croatia, Lika, and northern Dalmatia. In the areas with lower levels of ethnicization, it was not unusual for ethnic Serbs to join the Croatian Army, as one of the commanders of the Croatian Army recounted in the following example from his experience on the front line:

> I had wonderful people who were ethnic Serbs, and sometimes, I trusted them more than some of the people of my own ethnicity. . . . We had many people who were ethnic Serbs from our region. There is a very big difference among our people here. . . . During one operation . . . one young man from here probably saw something in me, and from fear, he was always behind my back. When it was all over, he personally told me, "I thought that you would kill me in this operation and it would be presented as if I died in battle." Why? Because he was a Serb, and he thought of that, and not everyone thought like that, but he was thinking that, and he was afraid. . . . I don't know of any [other examples like that]. I didn't experience that. That is what I wanted to say, about this difference between Gorski Kotar and Lika. We accepted all those people who were with us in the battle. Simply, I don't know why some people were against them [Serbs who fought on the Croat side in the war], and they [Serbs] helped them [Croats]. . . . Let's say, there in Dalmatia, a Serb who was in the battle was later expelled from his apartment. . . . Here in our region, there were no such things for sure. . . . They [Serbs] were wonderful people. They were eager to go. They lived here and it was a beautiful life here and why not. They didn't agree with that [RSK],

their occupation, and what they wanted, to connect [the territory of RSK] to Karlobag [city on the Adriatic coast]. They didn't agree with that. They are still here, and they live here and work, or they are retired.[46]

This example shows that, during the war, ethnicity became an important divisive characteristic, but that in the regions that were not part of the Krajina (RSK) territory, such as the region of Gorski Kotar, people had more freedom than in northern Dalmatia, for example, to express and act according to their personal political views, regardless of their ethnicity. In other regions that were affected by wartime violence, ethnic Serbs, even those who joined the Croatian Army, were afraid for their own safety or uncertain of fair treatment after the war.

Generally, in peaceful regions, it was rare for people to divide on the basis of ethnicity. Also, in those areas, most residents remained living in their homes throughout the war, regardless of ethnicity. Cases such as one in which a former neighbor was convinced by his coethnic Serbs that he should leave were extremely rare in one community in Gorski Kotar. In this case, the pressure to leave came from the neighbor's Serb coethnics rather than from Croat neighbors. In this community, based on the respondents' accounts, people still valued other human qualities, such as hard work and collegiality, over a person's ethnic identity.[47]

Another respondent from a nearby city said that there was something culturally different about this region: "In this region, people are not categorized by ethnicity. For example, I am an ethnic Croat, and I know that, but that identity has never been something that I use to judge people."[48] Unlike in other regions, where the population was divided along ethnic lines and displaced by violence, in most villages in the county of Primorsko-goranska, ethnic Serbs and ethnic Croats continued to live relatively peacefully throughout the war:

> R: People get along. Look, everyone has the same problems. Everyone has the same concerns. Every person has blood under their skin and the same things hurt them, as they say. This is how it is here, as far as that is concerned. Even though I am a Serb, I work here, and I travel from a nearby village where only Serbs live. . . . When the planes were passing, we were all hiding in shelters and we were all together.
> I: I am sure it was a bit difficult during the war, though.
> R: Of course, to use simple language, there are problem-makers on both sides. That is the case everywhere, . . . however, most people here are reasonable. As I said, we all have the same problems and we are all struggling to make it the best we can.
> I: People didn't leave from here?

R: No, maybe, you know how many left? Maybe four or five families. Those were the more extreme ones and that was better for all. I am being honest. Maybe they would have created trouble in our town.

I: But from here people didn't have to leave, like maybe in some other parts where people were afraid?

R: No, nobody forced them. Now, whether they were afraid of something they might have done that we didn't know, that is something I cannot say. They simply left.

I: But here there were no threats, like in other places?

R: No, no. Nobody did that. We slept peacefully each in our bed here, the entire war.[49]

The respondent clarified that in her region, they did not experience mass displacement, general fear, threats or targeted violence on the basis of one's ethnicity, or mass violence. She emphasized that people in her area were equals, sharing the same worries and problems, regardless of ethnicity. Only a few, in her view those who might have been "more extreme," left the area without being forced to do so. The respondent emphasized that they were not forced and that this was probably their own preference, given that the majority of the people in her village shared similar and moderate political views that did not align with either of the two dominant ethnicized political positions.

These cases show that in some multiethnic regions of Croatia, there was minimal ethnicization of everyday life, both before and during the war. These areas were not affected by the mass violence and the forced mass displacement of the population. What explains these regional differences? In other words, what local conditions at the start of the war, or even before the start of the war, distinguish these communities from amoral communities? These questions are addressed in the following chapter.

3

THE EXCLUSION OF MODERATES

> RESPONDENT 2 (R2): Those who were for that idea [the creation of the SAO Krajina], they left.
> RESPONDENT 1 (R1): They left.
> R2: Six or seven people left right away as soon as they saw that they cannot do anything.
> INTERVIEWER (I): So, there were good relations among most people here?
> R2: Yes, Gorski Kotar is known for that. There were [a few] individuals, but they didn't succeed in anything.[1]

Gorski Kotar is a multiethnic region with similar preconditions for mass violence as other parts of Croatia that had a high proportion of ethnic Serbs and where local Serbs were initially armed by the JNA (Glad 2017, 179). However, in contrast to other regions, here, the moderates—the individuals who resisted the process of ethnicization—were not excluded by the local communities. Local activists, such as Franjo Starčević from the village of Mrkopalj, played an important role in preventing political violence on the scale that other regions in Croatia experienced. He traveled across the barricades in the summer of 1991 to neighboring villages, promoted nonviolence, and successfully facilitated negotiations between the leaders of conflicting sides (29, 181, 415). It was unusually risky and difficult to preserve peace when the leaders were calling for people to distrust and fear the other side, take up arms, and demonstrate loyalty to a given group. While the activity of individuals like Starčević was important, it was not sufficient—what was needed was also the commitment to peace by local governments and local armed forces (212). For example, when Josip Reihl-Kir, the police chief of Osijek, attempted to remove the first barricades and facilitate negotiations between the conflicting sides in Eastern Slavonia, he was killed in the summer of 1991 (I. Goldstein 2008, 674). Other early peaceful initiatives, such as the Anti-war Campaign, founded by a group of young activists in Zagreb in the summer of 1991, were also ultimately unable to prevent the mass violence that ensued in many areas of Croatia in the latter part of 1991, even though they initially formed a network of organizations across Croatia and even across the other territories of former Yugoslavia (Bilić 2012; Dević 1997; Komnenović 2014). It appears that the ability to create favorable local conditions for the activity of peace activists and moderates, instead of excluding them through the use of threats and violence, marked a turning point that set some communities on a trajectory toward conflict de-escalation. In the Primorje-Gorski Kotar region, the local residents and their leaders even refused to follow certain top-level political and military orders assessed to be harmful for their own communities. Here, the majority of local Serbs were not in favor of joining the SAO Krajina.[2] In the broader region, the local Croat armed forces defied the Croatian government's orders to attack four local JNA headquarters after they assessed that the decision to do so was a political one, rather than a purely strategic military one, given that the JNA's military capabilities exceeded those of the local Croat forces.[3] These examples from Croatia raise the following questions: How are some communities able to resist the pressures from the top and prevent the formation of amoral communities, characterized by the ethnicization of everyday life? And how do amoral communities form in other places?

In the political science literature on civil wars that explains local-level variation in violence against civilians, the existing explanations tend to attribute wartime violence against civilians to military strategies aimed at gaining control over territory, the civilian population, or the adversary (Hultman 2007; Kalyvas 1999, 2005, 2006; Metelits 2010; R. Wood 2010). This set of theories, however, would not explain adequately the instances of violence against individuals on the basis of their political and ethnic identities that took place, for example, when the targeted population did not represent an objective military threat. In the scholarship addressing this question, the importance of perceived political loyalties, and emotions in responding to fears and threats, has already been recognized (Balcells 2017; Petersen 2002). In addition, political violence and nationalism scholars have already highlighted the significant role that the exclusion of moderates plays in the increasing polarization of societies preceding mass violence (Bergholz 2016; Bermeo 2003; Gagnon 2004; Hajdarpašić 2015; Heberle [1940] 1970; Straus 2012, 2015). For example, in communities in which mass violence takes place, the moderates may be silenced by threats, destruction of property, or violence against them (Bergholz 2016, 31). In this book, I build on this existing research as I analyze how the exclusion of moderates is facilitated or triggered through the following complementary mechanisms or tactics: *social ostracism*, *in-group policing*, and *targeted violence and threats*. Gradually, in the places where these processes played out, conditions favorable for the formation of amoral communities were created.

Social Ostracism and Pressure to Choose Sides

When the national-level discourse categorized different political options in terms of ethnic belonging in the early 1990s, it was hard to remain neutral in many communities across Croatia, even in those places that did not eventually transform themselves into amoral communities. Individuals with a more ambiguous ethnic identification or political views that were not easily connected to a particular ethnicity were viewed by hardliners with suspicion. The difficulty of predicting the direction of their loyalty added an uncertainty that local actors engaged in ethnicization tried to eliminate. As a result, many individuals who wanted to remain neutral and those who had ambiguous ethno-political loyalties experienced social ostracism and, in some cases, even threats. Given this context, it is not surprising that this was an exceptionally difficult period for multiethnic families.

Social distancing along ethnic lines as a form of exclusion occurred gradually as people became more careful about associating with former friends and neighbors in public spaces. In the account of one of the respondents, a woman who identified herself as a Catholic married to an Orthodox person, the initial pressure to take sides began when many of her friends changed suddenly and, in her words, "started to turn their back" on her and her husband, even though the couple was not involved in politics and lived in the area that did not experience extensive violence in the 1990s.[4] Subtle forms of social ostracism during that time were present in both the regions with high levels of violence and those with low levels of violence. For instance, a respondent from Eastern Slavonia, the region with high levels of violence, talked about pressure from other Croat neighbors not to talk on the street with their Serb neighbors.[5] The in-group censoring of people became pervasive at the level of society beyond the political circles. Those who did not want to be excluded by their communities simply communicated in public places solely with people who were perceived to be of their own ethnicity during this time, even if they did not have a strong personal preference for doing so.

A couple of residents in Eastern Slavonia described early signs of the reordering into ethnically defined groups in their workplace before the war started: "You didn't know back then if someone was an extremist or not. But in 1990 . . . on our Christmas, how we called it back then, we would bring food, and on their Christmas, they would bring food. Then, the [1990] Orthodox Christmas came, and I remember this one colleague of mine . . . they have their traditional *česnica* [honey and walnut cake]. I asked her, 'So, where is *česnica*?' They were eating separately. This was my colleague, and I asked what the reason for divisions was. . . . We stopped going into a deeper conversation. We realized that something was not right, but we didn't know that this was it."[6] While it used to be common in this multiethnic region to share the traditional holiday food for both the Catholic and the Orthodox Christmases, months before the war started, divisions along ethnic lines were already noticeable as people started socializing with others who presumably shared their ethnicity. Another respondent from the same region also confirmed divisions along ethnic lines in the workplace, which he noticed as early as 1987, even though his own social circle remained "compact until the very end."[7] Yet another respondent from this region noticed divisions along ethnic or religious lines as far back as 1985 when he attended a wedding for the first time:

> In 1985, I went to a wedding for the first time in my life. This was a Catholic wedding. As it was a tradition, it didn't bother me. But when I stood up while they played the Croatian anthem, I was not indifferent. Until that time, since I moved here as a child, I never learned it in school. My wife and I both stood up. Then I went to another wedding of a relative, and the same thing happened. That was already an indication of something. In that wedding, my uncle ordered two songs that were Vojvodina songs, but they stopped playing them right away and moved to Slavonian songs. . . . The nationalism was the strongest during the Christmas time. At midnight mass, there was already separation. One group attends one set of services and the other group the other. The police had to watch Serbs in their church since Serbs had a tradition to shoot at Christmas, and this was interpreted in the Croat media as political violence.[8]

While some divisions between those who were Catholic and those who were Orthodox may be traced back to the 1980s, in this respondent's town, they were mostly visible during celebrations that involved different cultural traditions. It is possible that over the course of this personal reflection and analysis of how and when the first divisions started, the respondent gave significance to his recollections of divisions because of the violent events that ensued much later. In the weddings, regional songs could have denoted subtle ethnic differences among wedding guests, even though both regions, Vojvodina and Slavonia, share very similar cultures and are highly multicultural, with residents of many different ethnicities, including Hungarians, Slovaks, Roma, Ruthenians, Romanians, Germans, and others. During Christmas, divisions were more clearly visible because the Catholic Christmas Mass was attended by Catholics at a different time, two weeks before the Orthodox residents attended their Christmas church services. In the respondent's account, it was not until the political situation became more tense in the 1990s that the police had to get involved in overseeing these gatherings. It was around the same time that even the traditional use of weapons in these celebrations among Serbs became framed as political or threatening. This is in stark contrast to the way in which local residents and the police handled wedding celebrations before and during the war in Gorski Kotar. In that area, a respondent from a Serb village remembered how locals who were organizing a wedding would inform the local Croat police and residents of the surrounding villages in advance so they would not get alarmed if they heard gunshots coming from the neighboring village.[9]

Once the war started, individuals who wished to remain neutral were pressured to leave, as described by one respondent: "I tried to talk to both sides. Then Serbs told me that I was favoring [Franjo] Tuđman, and asked what I was doing with Croats. Later, they provoked me by calling me on the phone, both sides. They called me and then they would breathe in the receiver. Basically, it was pressure to choose one or the other side. It was difficult to survive as a neutral person. Then I had an opportunity to go abroad, and we left."[10] By forcing those who are seen as a potential challenge to the dominant political goals to leave or choose sides, or to exhibit loyalty to a single ethno-political group, a certain illusion of security in times of war is maintained. An added element of uncertainty was that it was not known where the attack on those who wished to remain neutral would come from—the neighbors, the infiltrated paramilitary organizations, their own political leaders, the local authorities, or others. In the words of one respondent, the pressure that she and her family felt to choose sides came from the local officials and armies representing her own ethnicity, while neighbors and friends, regardless of their ethnicities, helped them:

> I went and requested to transfer us over the dividing line between the so-called RSK and the remainder of Croatia. . . . That period was really horrible. There were these mobilizations and raids. Well, I understood that the war was over stupid things. And then I thought why they would need [my relative] . . . Military police literally gathered all the men from the streets. He was picked up at the market when he was buying cheese. I just heard that they all were taken to the front lines. . . . there were

many other men who didn't want to go [to war]. Some people were wearing wigs, others masks, and others changed appearance to look like women by wearing housedresses. These were golden times for madmen who were nothing [before the war]. They put on uniforms and took weapons into their hands, and all of a sudden they had power.[11]

This respondent analyzed how difficult it was to remain neutral and not take part in the war by also taking into account the dimension of the gender divide. Even though the respondent did not depart significantly from the traditional gender roles—men's concern for war and women's concern for family life—she recognized that many men tried to avoid mobilization by disguising themselves as women. Through this act, a number of men symbolically (and practically) rejected militarism and, by extension, their own society's gender roles. Also, unlike the previous accounts, this one shows how the efforts to remain neutral actually unified the like-minded, and more moderate, people in this community across ethnic lines in their efforts to protect one another from individuals who were more extreme and who came to power in local institutions.

While the previous respondent recalled an instance of wartime interethnic cooperation despite the conditions that characterized amoral communities, the interviewee in the following statement discusses how his father, who wanted to maintain neutrality and remain in the territory controlled by the Serb forces, experienced pressure from people on both sides of the dividing line, including pressure from ordinary residents and armed forces:

> R: My father is a Croat and my mother a Serb. . . . When all of this started . . . he was supposed to leave. Now, the question that came up was what would happen with me. My mother would stay and he would have to leave? That was the hardest decision—what to do with a child? To whom should I belong? At the end, he stayed here the whole time and he had problems.
>
> I: So what happened? Was he harassed by Serbs and your mother by Croats?
>
> R: No, no. He was harassed. They broke into his apartment. . . . They beat him up, and they threatened him with a gun.
>
> I: Was it soldiers or ordinary people?
>
> R: Some were soldiers and some were ordinary people. . . . Many people criticize him for having stayed.
>
> I: Who criticizes him, Croats, Serbs?
>
> R: Croats criticize him for having stayed. Serbs criticize him for being a Croat. This was a common experience. Among most of my friends, coincidentally, there are so-called intermarriages. I don't like that

word, but use it because it is easier to understand. The common thing is that we lost either way. Someone always criticizes the other side. . . . Whoever is there, and there were all kinds of madmen, and usually it was madmen who had some power and to whom nobody could say anything.

I: Do you have some examples?

R: For instance, a friend whose mother is a Croat and father a Serb was beaten up several times . . . by his own friends. That is one of many examples. Of course, the opposite happened after Oluja [Operation Storm]. People didn't like that his father was a Serb. Somebody is always calculating this. This is one of the examples. But not everything was that bad. There were many normal people here who helped us and who were our friends. So, in the war here, it cannot be said that it was all that black.[12]

As in the other examples, members of society who saw themselves as local enforcers of ethnicization did not tolerate ambiguity in personal identification (i.e., Yugoslav or any other nonethnic or nonreligious identity) because the role of ethnicity was to serve as a shortcut for inferring individuals' political preferences and potential loyalty to the political regimes (i.e., nationalist) that were dominant at the time. Those who automatically connected ethnicity and shared political goals considered the presence of individuals such as this respondent inconvenient in their communities during this period of wartime uncertainty because their ethnically mixed backgrounds made their loyalty unpredictable. A similar situation was described by other respondents from this region who have different ethnicities represented in their family: "It was horrible because you couldn't choose sides. I didn't get involved because I couldn't. I have both sides in my home. You know. I cannot go either against Croats or Serbs because I am connected to both ethnicities."[13] Even before the war started, in some communities, it was intolerable for those pushing for ethnicization if people wanted to remain neutral. Once the war started, however, when people, regardless of their ethnic heritage, decided on a particular side of the dividing line for whatever personal reason that may or may not have to do with politics, they were expected to prove their loyalty to the given group repeatedly. But if they chose neutrality openly, regardless of their ethnic background, in some communities where ethnicization processes were carried out, they experienced great pressure through social ostracism, threats, or, as will be shown next, even violence that caused them to leave their respective communities.

Threats and Targeted Violence

Even before the war started, in some multiethnic communities of Croatia, there were instances of disappearance, threats, and property destruction that contributed to the ethnicization of everyday life, thereby weakening the power of those individuals who advocated moderate political options or of those who may not have had a strong preference to identify ethnically and politically. Scholars of political violence have already shown how violence, rather than deep-seated preexisting cleavages related to ethnic or cultural difference or ideology, can have a polarizing effect on communities (Bergholz 2016; Fujii 2009; Gagnon 2004, 8–9; Kalyvas 2006; Žarkov 2007). This book complements existing literature in its argument that violence is one of the triggers of ethnicization. Where I add to the existing scholarship is in my claim that small-scale, targeted violence was one of the factors that contributed to the formation of amoral communities.[14]

Before the first prewar disappearances or murders, news of which was communicated mainly through word of mouth, there were several prominent prewar instances of violence on a larger scale that were widely reported by the media. Several respondents mentioned how the events surrounding the ambushing and killing of twelve Croatian policemen by the Serb paramilitary forces in Borovo Selo on May 2, 1991, changed the way they perceived the influence of political changes on the level of personal security in their region.[15] Even before the violence in Borovo Selo, volunteer units from Serbia with Četnik symbols, under the leadership of Vojislav Šešelj, the president of the nationalist-oriented opposition party, the Serbian Radical Party, started arriving in Eastern Slavonia in April 1991 (I. Goldstein 2008, 674). In this context, the Belgrade-based media was already reporting about the "patriotism of volunteers defending the threatened Serbian people" (674). In response to the tensions in the region, several individuals who were part of the Croatian government fired three grenades in Borovo Selo at the end of April 1991. This led to a quick escalation of violence. First, the special police units from Serbia captured two Croatian policemen. Then the Croatian police rescue unit was caught in an ambush in Borovo Selo, and the result was the murder of twelve policemen and the wounding of more than twenty others. The Croatian president, Tuđman, announced that this was "the start of the open war against Croatia," while Šešelj confirmed that paramilitary formations of volunteers under his leadership participated in this operation in Borovo Selo (675). This event and the way it was framed in the media by various political leaders, unlike any other political tensions beforehand, led to a general sense of fear among the residents of Eastern Slavonia. In the following interview, a local resident recalls the atmosphere: "I remember very well the time after May 2nd. We went to a May 1st celebration, as usual. The next day, there was some chaos. Everyone stopped their work, and people started walking around. We received the news that Borovo Selo was attacked and that some people died there. I remember that people in our village organized themselves with hunting guns out of fear that some policemen would attack us here, and that they would kill us for some reason."[16] This account shows how violence occurred unexpectedly, provoked fear, and compelled some local residents to take up arms even though they did not fully understand what was happening. Early May 1991 was also a critical time in the account of another respondent from the same region, when the relations among former neighbors and colleagues at work started to deteriorate rapidly.[17]

In contrast to the respondents who interpreted the first instances of violence as a sign of trouble and were prepared to organize themselves accordingly, in the following interview, the respondent describes her belief that the situation would stabilize in her region even after the violence started on a large scale:

> The war had already started . . . and as a result of what happened in Borovo Selo, all of us knew that something was happening, but until the very end we couldn't believe what ended up happening. That is how we thought, that someone got into a conflict somewhere and that someone will pacify the conflicting sides. We didn't, or at least I didn't, know that there would be some interethnic conflict because here, we didn't experience that before. We heard from people that some Serbs were stopped by some soldiers and were beaten. Then there was a bomb in the house of a local Croat. But we believed that this was something else that is not connected to ethnicity because we continued to have coffee with our neighbors as usual.[18]

Given that her community never experienced conflicts along ethnic lines before, divisions into warring ethnicities were unthinkable from the perspective of this respondent, even after violence became increasingly more common.

In the region of Eastern Slavonia, the first barricades that were set up after the violence in Borovo Selo were removed due to the mediating activity of the moderate person in power, Josip Reihl-Kir, the Osijek-based police chief, though they would be set up again in the summer of 1991. Reihl-Kir was killed later, in the summer of 1991, by the local Croat extremists, for whom his moderate stance represented a threat (I. Goldstein 2008, 674).[19] The summer of 1991 was mentioned in a number of interviews as the critical period when divisions along ethnic lines became more relevant *as a result* of violence. For instance, one respondent mentioned that in July 1991, he was stopped at a checkpoint when going to his weekend house and asked to provide a permit of passage that only a local police chief could issue.[20] Shortly after that experience, he witnessed his relative being arrested one night in his neighborhood, and later he found out that he was badly beaten and then used as a human shield in order to pass through one of the checkpoints. He survived, but another family member, who was also arrested in the fall of 1991, was murdered. In this period and in this area, based on the account of another respondent who suffered a loss in the summer of 1991, "nobody was able to protect oneself," regardless of one's ethnicity.[21] In this atmosphere in which it was not clear who would be attacked next and why, people shared what they heard from others as they tried to decide whether to leave or to stay behind, potentially risking their lives. One respondent, for example, mentioned how after he heard about a local person who was killed, he discussed with his colleague the possibility of leaving the area.[22] He decided to leave in the end, and he later heard about several people who were killed after they decided to stay despite the threats they received. Several other respondents from this region lost family members in the summer of 1991.[23]

One respondent described the situation in her region around this time in the following way:

> R: It was not possible to go to Serb villages because of the barricades. Serbs placed barricades so it was impossible to enter the villages, and also Croatian police placed barricades in front of the villages so it was not possible to go out of those villages. So there were double barricades.... That was right before the war started. I cannot generalize about the villages around here.... Our town was full of uniformed people. That army was called the ZNG [Zbor narodne garde; Croatian National Guard] and they had camouflage uniforms. They usually carried Kalashnikovs. What was the most interesting was that they weren't carrying them on the shoulders but in their hands. That was strange for me because I knew that soldiers always carried guns hanging on the shoulders. Then there were cars without license plates.... There were searches in the houses where they knew people had hunting guns, which were registered in the police. If the members of the family were not at home, they entered by force and took the weapons away. Every day in the afternoon or in the evening, there was a convoy of cars ... with flags, and they were singing songs.
>
> I: What kind of songs?
>
> R: I don't remember the songs. I was not brought up in such way to identify people based on ethnicity.... We never made any difference between Serbs and Croats. And when these flags started appearing every afternoon and evening, around 6 or 7 p.m., in May, June, and July, it was not logical. I was confused. Then in June and July, in the

> evenings, bombs started exploding in Serb businesses. . . . We never went to sleep before 1 or 2 a.m., because we knew there would be some explosion at night. These were plain provocations. Sometime in early summer, we heard that one person was killed.[24]

These statements illustrate several changes that contributed to the gradual ethnicization. First, there were double barricades—Serb barricades at the entries of predominantly Serb villages, and Croat ones farther ahead of the Serb barricades, preventing the free passage of people in and out of villages. Second, uniformed people and new armies started to appear. Third, cars without license plates driven by uniformed individuals, random house searches, and a general atmosphere of unrest increased the sense of fear and insecurity. Finally, targeted acts of violence further contributed to the ethnicization—the connection of ethnicity and the political agenda of the local strongmen on both sides of the divide.

The targeting of residents on the basis of ethnicity, which included threats and the destruction of property, also occurred in northwestern Croatia, even though the communities there did not experience a division of the population with barricades in this period, or mass violence against civilians, on the level that other regions did at a later time:

> On Easter of 1991, they marked our doors and the façade with a sign containing "SSSS." So that was marked as Serbian. My husband never . . . I am Catholic and he is Orthodox. He was even joking about that by saying, "If they didn't mark that for me, I wouldn't even know I was a Serb." We didn't pay any attention to that at all. We considered it all as some joke still, nothing serious. Later, however, a bomb was thrown in our weekend house. Until then, we used to sleep there. . . . Then, here in town, another bomb was thrown in front of the house. Nothing happened, but we got scared. . . . And, after that, they saw that we didn't leave. They tried to force us to leave with bombs. They didn't succeed in that. Where would we go? My husband was never in Serbia before . . . so he didn't feel like a Serb at all. He was not involved in politics. He worked [here] all his life. . . . My son was in the Croatian Army defending Croatia. That was horrible for me.[25]

The pressure on this multiethnic couple to leave increased gradually as they tried to continue living in their community throughout the war. Simply by being who they are, people who did not consider ethnicity ahead of human qualities when forming a family, their loyalty to the new political project of ethnicization would likely be questioned by the hardliners on either side of the divide. What distinguished this case from the cases of threats and violence that occurred in amoral communities, as in the previous example, was that apart from the threats and the destruction of property, there were no disappearances or deaths in their family, in their social circle, or in their wider community. There were also no barricades dividing the population physically, as in Eastern Slavonia, for example. In other words, there was no escalation of attacks, and despite the fear that they experienced initially, the respondent and her family felt sufficiently safe to remain at home throughout the war.

Just like the violent incident in Borovo Selo was the defining point for some of the residents of Eastern Slavonia, the Plitvice incident, which took place a couple of months earlier, in March 1991, and was reported in the media as "Bloody Easter," was a turning point in the conflict for some of the residents of the region of Lika. One respondent from this region did not pay attention to the ethnicities of her coworkers until ethnic Serbs stopped coming to work, in her recollection, shortly after the violent clash in Plitvice. That was the turning point, in her view, and it was when the local divisions and the mobilization of civilians started. Even though she initially joined the civilian protection, she was disillusioned early on after realizing that civilians, regardless of their ethnicity, were not receiving an adequate level of protection from the local representatives claiming to be protecting them. For those who held power locally, on both sides, civilians were quickly transformed into the "ethnic other," or the enemy.[26]

Partly in response to the first instances of violence, and partly in response to ingroup policing, which will be discussed in the next section, in many instances in the regions with greater levels of violence, such as Lika and central Croatia, people were more cautious than the previous respondent in making decisions that caused them to stand out in any way. For one respondent, the changes in his immediate surroundings were so sudden that he did not have time to think.[27] Any decisions were difficult to make because this respondent, like others around him, was not only concerned about his own life but also about his family.[28] In one perspective, the atmosphere of distrust and segregation of former friends and neighbors into groups started before the war in central Croatia, but it was only after the attack of the JNA that the population became divided along ethnic lines, a division that remained for a period of four years while the war lasted, with only a few exceptions.[29] This was comparable to the situation described by the respondent in Eastern Slavonia at the time of the JNA's attack on his own community: "To the last day, I had friends of all ethnicities, and when grenades and shooting started . . . while the first grenades were falling, and I was here in the downtown with my friends, and nobody mentioned anything [about ethnicity]. There were no disagreements as far as that is concerned. But then, when shooting started, it started, 'These [people] are shooting, or those [people] are shooting.' And, everyone went on one's own side."[30] Thus, the top-down political discourse that linked ethnicity and political goals did not contribute directly to ethnicization on the local level since there were areas of Croatia where such conditions were not created throughout the war. It was the actual instances of violence, including the bombings, the murders, and the disappearances that were never investigated—which were accompanied by physical divisions of the population—that contributed to the local ethnicization and to the silencing of individuals who could have presented a moderate political stance. Other respondents expressed similar sentiments showing how violence silences those who may wish to demonstrate opposition to events that may have been against their own personal beliefs:

> R1: You had to be with your own people. Everything else, in these small communities, was . . . You could not choose.
> R2: It is different in big cities. People are more mixed in cities.
> R1: Here, you have to be with your own, and if you don't want to be, then you have to flee.
> R2: It was ugly back then. But you could lose your head overnight, and you don't know from whom, from yours or from the others. How many people were still not found until this day?
> R1: It is easy to emphasize individuality now when there is no more [war].
> R2: There were people here who publicly said, "No," and they didn't go to sleep peacefully for a long time.[31]

Unlike the rare individuals who refused to participate in the civilian defense after encountering injustice and situations with which they did not agree, these respondents did not describe such empowerment. Even though they mentioned that they helped Croats who were arrested, over the course of the discussion, they emphasized mass psychology, collectivity, and being led by others. One of the most striking themes in this conversation is the varying levels of freedom that people felt they had to talk or challenge the dominant political views during the period of violence and afterward ("It is easy to emphasize individuality now . . .").[32] At the end of their conversation, however, these respondents came to the conclusion that the war was not inevitable, and that if it were possible to disagree openly, or if educated people stepped up as more reasonable and moderate leaders ("to calm us down"), perhaps the mass violence could have been avoided. One of the respondents even acknowledged that there was always a choice and that those who were educated should have done something.[33] These contradictions show how the decisions of people in times of high levels of insecurity, and, in part, in response to the exclusion of moderates and a survival impulse, were inconsistent with their own beliefs. Only later, many years after the war, did they realize that they, as well others, could have acted differently and could have perhaps done something from their end to prevent the extent of violence and the losses that occurred in their own communities.

Targeted violence against moderates or individuals who wished to maintain neutrality was used in settings beyond Croatia where wartime amoral communities were created. In Uganda, for example, during the period of insurgency, it was risky for those who refused to take sides because these individuals were suspicious to both sides and could be killed or punished under the accusation of being spies. One respondent who managed to remain neutral and gain trust in his own community was still in danger when he crossed new roadblocks set up by the government soldiers, traveled through unfamiliar rebel-controlled territories, or came into contact with people who did not know him.[34] In addition to visible markers, such as scars (a possible sign of having participated in violence as a member of some armed forces), what made some people targets of government violence, for example, was if they were members of Yoweri Museveni's political party, or if they were wealthy and prominent members of their communities.[35] Such use of violence created a general sense of fear that anyone could be a target of violence, whether by military, insurgents, thugs of war, or a stray bullet.[36] Disappearances contributed to the general sense of fear and distrust; as one respondent said, "Your very brother could betray you. . . . We were told not to trust even your very shadow."[37] Being made aware, through violence or threats, that it was very easy to be killed by standing out in any way or appearing suspicious to rebels or the government, people became less willing to oppose the increasingly more oppressive conditions that limited their ability to express personal views or act in ways that did not conform to one of the dominant political or ideological options. Political leaders, as well as military and guerrilla commanders, used violence not only to silence the moderates, the opponents of one of the dominant political options, or the opponents of war more generally but also to divide people, including civilians, into two camps.[38] Both sides in the conflict needed civilians because they relied on their electoral or logistical support.[39] One way in which the dominant warring adversaries divided the civilian population was through the performance of violence in order to create the wartime conditions in which a general sense of fear, insecurity, and distrust justified collective crimes before they even occurred.

In similar ways as in Croatia and Uganda, the extensive evidence in published scholarship and reports documenting violence in other cases shows how violence effectively constrained people's behavior. In the case of El Salvador, Jocelyn Viterna (2013, 82) categorized three paths through which women joined the guerrilla forces—politicized, reluctant, and recruited. In her study, she found that men generally had fewer options and, due to the wartime conditions in their communities, they had to decide between the military or the guerrilla forces in order to survive, since younger men would not be accepted at refugee camps and they would probably be killed if found at home by the military, under the presumption that they were collaborators or supporters of the guerrilla forces (109).

One way in which the possible nonviolent options of moderates in predominantly indigenous and economically underdeveloped communities in the highlands of Guatemala were restricted was through the closing off of nonviolent political routes for political action and change. For example, "community structures responsible for conflict resolution or development were eliminated by the criminalization of any type of leadership not under military control," and those "who tried to step into a significant organizing or community role" were "harassed and denounced" (REMHI 1999, 42). Many local leaders who did not show "obedience and submission to military authority" were replaced or murdered (42). These circumstances, which severely limited nonviolent political action, "led many people in certain areas to join the war effort, either voluntarily or by force of circumstance" (8). According to one former participant in the guerrilla movement, people in his community did not feel that they had civilian leaders who would advocate or "stand up for them" (8). In other words, they saw armed rebellion as their only option if they wished to fight for greater representation in the state and better conditions in their communities. A similar sentiment was expressed by a person who was able to stay neutral throughout the war precisely because he was not a member of the community in which the guerrillas started to organize and that was targeted by the army:

> I: And was it possible to stay neutral? Was it possible to stay outside of it all?
> R: No, not in those communities because these are small communities that are easy to control. What happened was that most members of the community at that time were Catholics. So, there was a group in the Catholic Church called Acción Católica [Catholic Action]. They managed the collective consciousness and the social work through the church [by addressing concerns, such as] land, social justice, and all those aspects. Nobody could stay [out]. As we realized today, in a community ... there are many agents, there are many leaders who make decisions, and all the people support a leader. In that situation, it is not easy to say, I will stay out of that. Then, the community ... if I say, "I am not participating," the community would come to me and say, "You are not with us. You are with them." So, that was not possible ... it was [an act of] rejection [of one's community]. So, let's imagine I was a person who rejected my community where my grandparents lived, my parents, where I lived all my life, and to reject all

that, that is hard. And I don't have another option but to be on the side of my community. So, for that very reason, many communities didn't have a choice to decide, "We are neutral." It was not possible. On top of that, the army and the government never considered those possibilities. They simply assumed that if someone from the community was [a member of the guerrilla], then everyone was.... There was no option.[40]

As evident in this statement, religious organizations, like Catholic Action in this particular community, which were helping to provide access to education and health care and other services, played an important role in creating awareness of the social inequalities and injustices that indigenous populations experienced relative to other, more privileged, and generally *ladino* populations in the country. Yet the ideological orientation of religious activists, or even the ideas to which people were exposed, did not fully explain why it was impossible to remain neutral. Individuals' choices were also constrained by external pressures, both from their own communities and from the military. From the community's point of view, an individual's declaration of neutrality would automatically mean rejection of one's identity and the most intimate social circle. From the military's perspective, the possibility of a neutral individual in a community where guerrilla organizations were active did not exist; it was assumed that all the people in such communities were supporters of the insurgency, as confirmed by another respondent from the Ixil region, where scorched-earth campaigns were carried out by the military.[41] Her account showed not only that it was difficult to remain neutral due to pressures from one's own community but also that it was not possible to continue with one's work because of the limitations imposed by the military. The military may have justified these controls by the extraordinary circumstances of war and guerrilla activity in the area. Nevertheless, the restrictions, such as the prohibition against selling products to guerrillas even if insurgents were armed and threatening the shopkeepers, pushed the residents who attempted to remain neutral toward a situation in which it was impossible to survive.[42] Also, the military recruited indigenous populations in the areas affected by war either by force or through incentives (Menchú and Burgos-Debray [1983] 1994, 174–175; REMHI 1999, 126).[43] For example, the military would pass in trucks and pick up young people, seventeen- or eighteen-year-olds, from streets, city squares, and markets.[44] One of the respondents was recruited on his hometown square by force in the early 1980s, and he was sent "to the mountains to fight, or to kill."[45] These circumstances limited the options that residents, particularly those in small communities, had at the time. The use of violence, threats, and social ostracism made neutrality difficult, and in many cases impossible, in those communities that were gradually transformed into amoral communities. Another way in which moderates were excluded in those communities was through in-group policing, which I turn to in the next section.

In-Group Policing and the Exclusion of Moderates

I define *in-group policing* as an effort of members of a particular social group to prevent defection or strengthen social boundaries in order to create distance between themselves and those who are seen either as a threat or as members of inferior groups. One way of preventing the future defection of individuals from groups into which their local communities initially place them is by excluding or punishing those who choose to follow their personal beliefs rather than the political views associated with their presumed ethnicity, thereby challenging the newly dominant categorizations. As scholars of genocide have argued, in-group policing, or "a process that could include the removal or marginalization of those who actively oppose a policy of violence," is necessary in order to attain the support of the population that political leaders seek as they carry out political projects entailing targeted violence against a particular social group (Straus 2015, 82).[46] In a historical micro-level study of targeted violence against civilians in Kulen Vakuf, a Bosnian community in World War II, Max Bergholz also documented "threats or acts" of "intra-ethnic violence" perpetrated in order to create a more unified group and exclude coethnics who may have a more ambiguous stance toward a particular political goal, the use of violence, or their own sense of identity (2016, 154–155).

In the context of Croatia in the 1990s, in Lika, just as in other communities where ethnicization was more prevalent in everyday life, it was challenging for people who wished to stay in their communities and did not fully agree with the policy of violence advocated by the leaders of their own groups:

> R2: Here, it was a different scenario. You are here at night, and you are gone in the morning. You are dead.
> I: When was that, recently?
> R2: No, that was in the 1990s. You have to keep quiet or there would be a problem.
> I: And that was from the same side?
> R2: From the same side. There were people who were talking to some extremists and there would be problems. A person had to maneuver [relationships] well in order to avoid making mistakes on either side.

> We are among those who managed to maneuver the situation well so that we would eventually not have problems with either side. We could have had problems, however. Generally, we didn't have problems, only with some individuals on both sides.
>
> I: How did you deal with this? You watched what you said? Were you neutral?
>
> R2: Yes, neutral.
>
> I: People were killed like that?
>
> R1: People disappeared.
>
> R2: As I mentioned, in the morning you are gone. He disappeared and nobody talks about it anymore. Nobody dares. There is danger. Silence. He is gone.
>
> R1: Let me tell you. People were always whispering here. Whispering. The walls could hear everything. Now, you can say anything.[47]

This example shows that in certain communities, people were afraid of different armies as much as of hardliners in their own ethnic groups. According to the interviewees' account, that was the situation during the war, when people used to speak in a whispering voice to one another out of fear. Without going into details, the interviewees stated that some people from their community disappeared when they "talked to extremists," probably in a critical way or in order to express a wish to remain more moderate and neutral. Even though the murders and disappearances of dissenters were not publicized widely in the media, people heard about them. The word-of-mouth accounts of these extreme forms of in-group policing spread even beyond the region where they occurred, as the following excerpt from an interview in Gorski Kotar illustrates: "They [Serbs] killed their own, too. They killed a man . . . only because he didn't want to join the [RSK] military. . . . They did this. For Serbs in these areas these times were very uncertain."[48] Thus it was highly risky to resist recruitment or refuse to comply during this period and in certain communities during wartime.

Distrust, suspicion, and fear characterized the acts of in-group policing. As a result, people were put to a variety of "loyalty tests" by members of their communities. For example, in the very beginning of the war, in August 1991, some representatives of a community in central Croatia proposed a rule that those who were absent from work for five days should be automatically fired since they were potentially on the "enemy" side of the dividing line.[49] Another, less drastic proposal was that those individuals who did not support the SAO Krajina, or pro-Serb political autonomy within the territory of Croatia, from the very beginning needed to be checked well before being given any position in the new governance structures.⁵⁰ The fear of the "other" thus mirrored the fear of "traitors from within," and reactions to the "internal other" became progressively more violent as the war went on. This would explain why coethnics found on the territory of the opposing ethnic side were punished harshly in some cases, as in the case of the Serb prisoners of war after the Serb occupation of Vukovar who were beaten more than ethnic Croat prisoners because they were considered "traitors of their own nation."⁵¹

As already seen in the previous sections, those whose identities were ambiguous from the perspective of their community, such as children whose parents were of different ethnicities, represented especially vulnerable targets. In this context, multiethnic families were in some cases targets of in-group policing simply because of their assumed dissent to the leaders' more extreme policies.⁵² In some cases, individuals with mixed heritage were expected to show even greater loyalty to the group by being more vocal supporters of the dominant policies or participating in violence, as observed by a respondent from Eastern Slavonia who noted that the harshest enforcers of in-group cohesion on the Serb side were those who had Croat relatives, because they had to prove their loyalty to Serbs.⁵³ This observation was echoed by a respondent from Western Slavonia: "I also had another friend . . . she used to visit here . . . and we had coffee. But, right before the war . . . she told me, 'You are a real Četnik now, and all you need is a beard and a *kokarda*.'⁵⁴ I swore at her. That same friend was fine until then. This wouldn't hurt me so much if she had been a pure Croat, but she was of mixed origin [*križanka*]. She needed to prove herself."⁵⁵ By making comments signaling her loyalty to a particular group publicly, the person in this respondent's example alienated more moderate people like the respondent but protected herself from possible attacks from the extreme, and potentially violent, members of her community who would consider her family background as evidence of ambiguous loyalty. This sense of a need to prove oneself as loyal to one group or to play a more active role in creating and enforcing group unity also fits with earlier analyses showing how the process of ethnicization began under the condition of a high level of uncertainty.

The rumors that neighbors or armed units sent from elsewhere would attack further contributed to the sense of fear that was already present at the time in amoral communities (Petersen 2002).⁵⁶ Yet fear for one's security was sustained not only by rumors but also by actual incidents of violence against those who resisted joining in with their respective ethnic groups in engaging in armed struggle. For example, the municipal president of Vrginmost, Dmitar Obradović, who was identified as a moderate following the attack on the Glina police station by local leadership, was seen as an obstacle that needed to be controlled.⁵⁷ He was killed in 1992, allegedly by the more radical members of the Serb forces.⁵⁸ Another act of in-group policing was the already noted murder of Josip Reihl-Kir, the Osijek police chief who initiated negotiations between the two sides in Eastern Slavonia. Similarly, Milan Levar, a Croat who testified to the International Criminal Tribunal for the Former Yugoslavia (ICTY) about the killing of Serb civilians in Gospić, was murdered in his hometown in 2000. Thus, in-group policing entailed constant vigilance and distrust among individuals on the same side of the wartime dividing line, and in some cases, the punishment of those considered "traitors" extended well into peacetime.

This in-group vigilance was not unique to the context of amoral community formation in Croatia. For example, in one instance during the NRA insurgency in Uganda, Shaban Kashanku, one of the combatants, was shot by a firing squad consisting of his fellow insurgents because Commander Sam Magara of the NRA doubted his loyalty. Kashanku's assignment throughout the war was to serve as a messenger between the insurgents and the Kampala-based supporters because he was an expert in urban warfare. Due to his long absence from the battle and adoption of the dress and behavior of the city population, he was perceived as "being a 'soft fist' and a malingerer" and "accused of being an enemy agent" when he returned to the front line. Even though "not everyone supported" Kashanku's execution, the witnesses did not dare object to the extreme decisions and orders of the military commander and prevent his execution. Kashanku's execution thus served as a mechanism of double exclusion—the elimination of Kashanku as a symbol of ambiguous loyalty and the silencing of those who disagreed with the views of the hardliners (Kutesa [2006] 2008, 118).

The exclusion of certain members of a community and the pressure to join one of the dominant sides of the war do not work out neatly precisely because, when wartime violence begins, there are usually more than two dominant sides, reflecting the plurality of political options that is found under ordinary conditions in most communities. These observations complement the insights of other scholars of civil wars and ethnicity who show that macro-level cleavages and divisions along ethnic or ideological lines do not map out automatically on the local level, or on the ground (Driscoll 2015; Gagnon 2004; Kalyvas 2006). In the Ugandan context, the fighters and recruits were more likely to know the person on whose side they were fighting than the program for which they were fighting.[59] There were, however, efforts by top-level commanders to educate the recruits, as evident from the memoir of one of the former commanders of the NRA, who argued that "everyone knew what we were fighting for and why and how we were going to win the war" (Kutesa [2006] 2008, 120).[60] It is possible that the training and education of recruits once they became members of a particular faction played an important role in their motivation and performance. Nevertheless, this example suggests that an initial division into warring factions was more likely to occur through processes other than the preexisting commitment of potential recruits to a particular political program of a warring group or a movement.

Similar observations regarding recruitment and in-group policing processes were made by witnesses of violence and former insurgents in the Nakaseke District in Uganda:

> I: There were three factions. How come you remained with this faction?
> R: We were determined because as soon as we were recruited in the guerrilla movement, whatever faction, as soon as you would defect, you would be killed. So as soon as you got in there, there is no way you could get out.
> I: How did the factions get recruited in the beginning?
> R: That very gentleman was the one recruiting.
> I: Tell us, please.
> R: At the beginning of the war, there were three factions. There was the Western Nile front. Then, Museveni . . . at the beginning of the war, there was an agreement that Moses . . . would fight from the north, Kayiira east, and Museveni [in the] center and west. But during the time of the fighting, one person would come from [one region to another], from Kayiira, [he] would come from the east into the central [region]. That would cause conflict. People should have concentrated in their areas as demarcated. But whenever a person moved from one area to another, the conflict erupted. Some of the conflicts erupted in these very factions conflicting [with each other]. Our target was to overthrow the government, but this crossing over from one area of jurisdiction to another area, that was a problem. Then Museveni's strength was that he concentrated on this area and won effectively.[61]

According to these respondents, once individuals were recruited, often based on the ways in which geographic territory was divided among the leaders of various guerrilla movements, it was difficult to switch to another faction. In order to avoid drawing attention to themselves, or to avoid risking their lives if their group leaders used violence as a form of in-group policing, people did not switch from one to another guerrilla faction once they were recruited. The competition and conflict between various guerrilla factions was a "problem," in the words of one of the former insurgents who participated in the recruitment efforts for Museveni's army, the NRA, because it undermined the insurgents' pursuit of their common political goal, which was the overthrow of the government. One way to maintain order and avoid conflict between various guerrilla factions was to demarcate the areas under the control of each group. These became de facto in-group, or within-insurgency, wartime dividing lines that limited the movement and choices of people in communities where the guerrillas recruited from among the local population. Thus it was difficult, or impossible, to maintain any neutrality in certain communities in Luweero, Nakaseke, and other districts that various insurgent factions used as their geographic and logistical bases during the war.

According to one of the former insurgents, it was possible to change factions if individuals seeking to make the switch previously approached their leaders and asked for their permission.[62] Trust was lacking in wartime, when violence, or a threat of violence, was a way to reinforce obedience and, through the exclusion of anyone without a strong commitment to the given faction, introduce a veneer of predictability in the behavior of group members.[63] The exclusion of individuals through violence functioned both within the group, as in-group policing, and outside the group. Within the group, individuals would be punished, or, in more extreme cases, even killed, if they were suspected to be traitors, spies, or defectors.[64] For example, the reading of the names and the subsequent caning of members of the in-group who were identified as defectors, or traitors, by their fellow insurgents functioned as a violent and fear-inducing public performance through which belonging, loyalty, and group homogeneity were forged in a powerful manner.[65] Outside the group, individuals would be punished or killed because they represented to others an enemy, regardless of their personal political views, simply by virtue of having participated on one side of the conflict.[66] Both types of violence contributed to the process of ethnicization, or the fusing of the group's cultural (whether regional, ethnic, religious, or tribal) identity and political goal or orientation. Thus, once recruited, the insurgents could perhaps change factions if they were convincing or lucky, but they could no longer decide "to turn back" and refuse to take part in violence halfway through the war.[67] These cases illustrate how difficult it was to trust anyone in the areas where amoral communities formed.

In the case of Guatemala, neutrality was also made more difficult because of violence and the processes of in-group policing, among both the government army and the guerrilla soldiers. The Maya populations in certain regions of the country were subjected to in-group policing by both sides. For example, David Stoll (1993, 95) shows how Ixils joined the insurgency in such large numbers less because of their ideological orientation and more because they were trying to survive the wartime condition of finding themselves "between two fires," that of the army and that of the guerrillas. While there were individuals who sympathized with the guerrillas because they were influenced by ideas of revolutionary change aimed at promoting greater social justice and equality, there were some people who felt that they had no choice when approached to join the struggle.[68] In the areas of the country that experienced the highest levels of violence in the early 1980s, the population was generally poorer and less educated, and those circumstances further limited people's options and choices, particularly their ability to leave the area and start a new life elsewhere.[69] Even women were obligated to contribute to the guerrilla forces with food, though they were not forced to take part in the fighting.[70] In one account, a respondent described the circumstances when his cousin came to recruit him, his father, and one of his uncles.[71] As the recruiter for the guerrillas was the respondent's own cousin, the respondent felt more empowered to ask questions and even attempt to stay outside the conflict. At that time, there were only seven people in the respondent's village who were not members of the guerrilla forces. This instance shows how, in these small communities, it was difficult to remain neutral, and it confirms findings documenting the role that communities play in recruitment (Petersen 2001; E. Wood 2003). The high level of involvement of civilians in the insurgency in these communities also shows how difficult it was to make a clear distinction between civilians and participants in some cases. Some people who were a bit more affluent managed to leave the area of conflict and remain unaffiliated with either side. However, they had to leave behind everything they owned, and they later had problems reclaiming property because they did not stay to fight and help their neighbors.[72]

Neutrality was also a problem because neither side of the conflict was certain about the loyalty of neutral individuals, and any error made by such individuals could cause them to be accused of being a spy (*orejon*) and become an easy target for the guerrilla forces or the military (REMHI 1999, 9).[73] In a village neighboring that of one of my respondents, the guerrillas killed individuals who talked to others about guerrilla plans, those who drank too much and presumably could not be dependable, and those who failed to follow orders.[74] Individuals who took initiative were also punished, as in the case of a priest: "The guerrillas killed four members of his church for filling in stake-pits that the EGP had dug as a defense measure" (Stoll 1993, 124). Also, within the guerrilla ranks, a person who was only suspected of being a spy would be killed quickly, without investigation or trial (Santa Cruz [2004] 2006, 103). Lists of "enemies," or individuals who were not loyal to one or the other armed group, were produced by some members of communities, sometimes because those individuals were forced to betray their neighbors and were trying to save their own lives, or in other cases because they wanted to take advantage of an opportunity to seek revenge for personal reasons (Montejo 1987, 36). Whatever the reason for producing the list, the goal was to increase group homogeneity by eliminating anyone whose loyalty was questionable in some way.

As mentioned earlier, the exclusion of moderates, or those who display an ambiguous level of loyalty to the in-group, reduces uncertainty in wartime and leads to greater group homogeneity. But this only benefits the warring sides, not the civilians, because the exclusion of moderates also triggers the processes of ethnicization, or the linking of political identities and racial or ethnic identities, and the formation of amoral communities. As a result, entire communities, and not just armies claiming to represent them based on the communities' political orientation, become labeled as "enemies" and are now seen as legitimate targets of violence by opponent armies. This outcome is best illustrated in Guatemala, where the residents in war-affected regions were "forced" to participate in civil patrols following Efraín Ríos Montt's arrival to power and implementation of the Victoria 82 campaign (Schirmer 1998, 64). Part of the Victoria 82 plan was to turn roughly 70 percent of the population away from supporting the insurgency through development projects and to use violence against the remaining 30 percent (23). By the middle of the 1980s, around eight hundred thousand men had been mobilized into the civil patrols (Sieder 2001, 188).[75] During this time, civilians in the war-affected region became "a primary objective" for both sides of the conflict (Santa Cruz [2004] 2006, 111–112).

Under Montt, based on the account of one of my respondents, former members of the guerrilla forces were recruiting residents for civil patrols after amnesty was granted to the guerrillas and the population was informed by the military that it was safe to return home:

> R: I was returning in fear that they would kill us all. That was the end, though. It calmed down. We met with the military and the commander of the guerrillas who started talking with them. The person in charge of the military said that if we all agree, "we are here to serve and support you. At this time, if a family has still not returned, please let them know that they can return without worry." That is how it was. It calmed down. After, he told us, "For now, we are going to organize the community. Do you agree? We are going to take turns."
>
> I: Patrols?
>
> R: Yes, patrols . . . before with the guerrilla, and now with the military. I asked the person in charge of the guerrilla, "And with this new organization we are going to join, are we going to do turns apart?" "No," he said, "this is the end, guerrilla is over. Now we are going to turn ourselves over to the military. And the military ordered us to control the area and they would protect us." He said, "Now we are no longer against the military, but for the moment, we are against the guerrillas."[76]

These statements illustrate both the distrust and the confusion that people felt as a result of the sudden change of circumstances when the former guerrilla members began recruiting the population in their region on behalf of the military. Many patrollers were not even armed adequately because the army "could not be sure of the communities' loyalty" (REMHI 1999, 122). Loyalty was demonstrated most effectively through in-group policing, or violence, against other locals. Communities that had previously been pressured by the army were now putting pressure on other neighboring communities to organize into civil patrols (119). Men in these communities were expected to join civil patrols in order to survive, and the population found itself "between two fires" (REMHI 1999, 23; Schirmer 1998, 81; Stoll 1993, 93–94).[77] The population's fear of both the guerrilla forces and the army was justified, given that after the civil patrols were organized, the guerrillas started killing individuals who acted as military commissioners and supported the army efforts to organize civil patrols in their communities; in the words of a former insurgent, "Selective repression, never indiscriminate, was an essential part of the politics of fighting against the members of the military intelligence apparatus" (Santa Cruz [2004] 2006, 131–132). It was after the civil patrols organized that guerrilla massacres of civilians in the war-affected regions became more commonplace, as in the case of thirteen Cotzaleño civil patrollers and their wives who were killed by the guerrillas in the summer of 1982 on the road (Stoll 1993, 115).

One of the key functions of civil patrols was in-group policing, or reporting on and eliminating anyone who was not loyal to the government and forcing people to demonstrate their loyalty, even by participating in violence against members of their own communities (Garrard-Burnett 2010, 99; Schirmer 1998, 81, 91; Sieder 2001, 188). The following excerpt from a war memoir depicts the reluctance, the fear, and the complicity of civil patrollers in the murder of members of their own community: "A military officer had forced them to join and had threatened to kill them if they refused" (Montejo 1987, 18–19). People identifying members of their communities wore hoods, and "in some cases there were visible signs that they had been cruelly tortured" (REMHI 1999, 123). Even the army's "pamphlet" referred to civil patrols as "the eyes and ears for the Army" (Schirmer 1998, 90). Those who did not want to participate "were threatened with prison and were told that to oppose these measures was to be an enemy of the government" (Montejo 1987, 12–13; REMHI 1999, 8).

In-group policing was also evident in the communities' creation of lists of people who were involved in the guerrilla movement or identification of hiding places of the guerrillas (Schirmer 1998, 52–53). Only in rare cases was a person able to remain on the outside of the conflict. In the case of one of my respondents, it was because he was not a member of the community.[78] Yet his perspective as an "outsider," a person who did not depend on either the community or the military, reveals that a person's ability to resist the rules and orders was directly related to his ability to leave the area of violence safely. While residents of communities in war-affected areas of the country had limited choices, some individuals took risks and challenged the established rules. In a few cases, civil patrollers played a positive role in protecting their communities, finding family members who were victims of violence, advocating for the release of prisoners, or even refusing to join civil patrols in the first place (REMHI 1999, 125). But these were very risky acts that the majority of people did not attempt. Community leaders also adopted an approach of "two faces," feigning support for the army in front of the army and displaying another "face" in front of their supporters from the community (Nelson 2009, 13–14). Even my respondent who was not from the area of conflict recognized that, in retrospect, he risked his own life and was lucky that he was able to enter and leave freely while maintaining neutrality.[79] These accounts showed very clearly how the process of in-group policing was set in motion in tight-knit communities through new sets of rules and the elimination of those who threatened the new status quo when former guerrillas switched sides. Even if individuals participated in civil patrols reluctantly, or only to obey the orders of the military and save their lives, the recruitment of locals in areas affected by the war managed to ethnicize some communities in Guatemala. Both the insurgents' and the government's armed forces reduced individuals' freedom to act in accordance with their own personal views.

In all three cases, Croatia, Uganda, and Guatemala, the exclusion of moderates limited the number of political views, polarized communities, and created an artificial homogeneity of identities that I refer to throughout the book as *political ethnicities*. Individuals were targeted because their perceived ambiguous loyalties represented an obstacle to achieving the maximum degree of group homogeneity, which would reduce the level of uncertainty under wartime conditions. For that reason, it was very difficult, and even impossible in most cases, to remain neutral once the process of the exclusion of moderates started. In this way, the national-level cleavages between the rebels and the government were transposed, and made relevant, locally. Such strategic use of violence throughout the war had a two-pronged effect in local communities where the conditions for mass violence against civilians were created. First, as shown in this chapter, through the exclusion of moderates, or those who in some way posed a political challenge to mobilization and recruitment into one of the two dominant sides in the war, local-level ethnicization processes were set in motion. Second, as will be shown in the next chapter, through the production of borders, or wartime dividing lines, it became possible not only to physically divide and control the civilian population but also to transpose the dominant national-level political cleavages to the local communities, where people were more diverse politically, religiously, or ethnically and where such divisions were not relevant previously.

4
THE PRODUCTION OF BORDERS

When moderates are excluded through social ostracism, threats, violence, or in-group policing, it becomes easier for political leaders to divide people who previously lived peacefully in their communities. When the exclusion of moderates is accompanied by the production of physical borders, or the setting up of barricades, checkpoints, and, eventually, wartime dividing lines, then the conditions for the formation of amoral communities are created. In those communities, physical borders force individuals to choose one of the sides, and the population is both divided and policed accordingly.[1] In the communities in which these processes of creating new political identities, which are ethnically or culturally defined, are set in motion, the military and political leaders gain greater control of the civilian population by limiting their political options, artificially reducing ambiguity in the identification of potential members of the out-group, and preventing in-group defection. Given that in amoral communities individuals' freedom to express or act on the basis of their personal views becomes extremely limited, especially if those views do not fit into the new social ordering, favorable conditions for targeted violence against civilians are created.

In the context of Croatia, even before the war had started, the discourse of leaders such as Slobodan Milošević and Vojislav Šešelj in Serbia, who called for a state in which all ethnic Serbs would be unified, or that of Franjo Tuđman, who called for a state independent from Yugoslavia for all ethnic Croats, represented, in the view of one of my respondents, clear examples of attempts to redraw the borders and create new ethnic states when the political transition from a single-party socialist regime to a multiparty democracy in Yugoslavia began in 1990.[2]

Yet physical borders corresponding to these envisioned states were not drawn in all regions across Croatia with ethnic Serb minorities. For example, the multiethnic regions of northwestern Croatia and Gorski Kotar remained part of the territory of Croatia throughout the war.[3] In Gorski Kotar, more specifically, local disagreements among the ethnic Serb population, in addition to the eventual success of the more moderate factions that preferred to remain administratively in the Republic of Croatia rather than in the RSK, influenced the ultimate decision of local authorities not to engage in the production of borders separating various communities along ethnic lines.[4] Residents in those communities successfully resisted the border placement that would have made them more vulnerable to the local-level ethnicization that multiethnic communities in central Croatia, northern Dalmatia, and Slavonia experienced.[5] In those regions where borders materialized, people who used to live peacefully in the same communities were separated by the new dividing line that defined the wartime territory controlled by ethnically defined armies for four years.

Barricades and Local-Level Ethnicization

Barricades, roadblocks, and checkpoints are usually the first types of borders that may be erected to separate neighborhoods, villages, or entire regions even before the start of a war. If the conflict does not escalate, these temporary barriers may be removed. In the region of Western Slavonia of Croatia, however, barricades ended up dividing former neighbors, friends, and, in some cases, even family members along ethnic lines throughout the war (figure 3). When asked who set up the barricades in his community, a respondent from this region stated that he did not know, but he observed that people were divided almost overnight.[6] Until then, everything functioned well and people did not divide by ethnicity at his workplace. Because of the barricades, he, like others from his village, was unable to continue working, given that he lived in a village and commuted to his job in a city. Several other respondents from this region also described how barricades prevented them from going to work thereafter.[7]

Choosing one side of the border was difficult for the people who lived in multiethnic communities that they considered their home:

> INTERVIEWER (I): Tell me, now, how did that start to change in the period immediately before the start of the war? Did you notice that something was happening?
> RESPONDENT (R): Some barricades were set up. Then we were informed who could pass where and why they couldn't pass. Barricades were

outside of the city. . . . Something was being prepared. You could sense it in the atmosphere. Some people were going to the military headquarters. I don't know why, maybe it was into those reservist units. My husband didn't want to go, so we hid. . . . One night we would sleep in his parents' house, for instance, in order to hide ourselves. We didn't want that [conflict]. We were not members of any political party. It seemed to me . . . you could feel that something was happening, but what? We were not in contact with people who knew what was happening. Then there was some referendum for the independence of Croatia. That was already a sign that people started dividing into Serbs and Croats. Serbs didn't want separation from Yugoslavia, and Croats wanted it. That was tense. . . . At the end, my husband is, if that is important, of Serb ethnicity. That is something specific, for instance. Maybe I am a good example.[8]

After the barricades were set up, people became afraid and started to separate along political and ethnic lines already after the first elections and the referenda, about a year before violence started in this respondent's region. For her family, however, it was difficult to make sense of the situation, not only because she and her husband were of different ethnicities but also because their personal views did not align with either of the two dominant political options. This example shows that rather than automatically choosing a side of the dividing line simply based on their own ethnicity, when forced to choose by the circumstances of the barricades, individuals ultimately considered other practical or personal reasons. She and her husband finally chose the Croat side of the dividing line, while her other relative remained on the Serb side because she was close to her Serb neighbors and wanted to stay in her own home.[9] Another respondent's son, who lived in an urban area, was "caught" on the other side of the dividing line for the remainder of the war only because he was visiting his mother on the same weekend that the barricades were set up.[10] Similar experiences were shared by a respondent in Eastern Slavonia, where communities were divided by the first barricades early on. There, permits to travel around the area were issued by the local police chief "only for lots of money or with connections."[11] Consequently, everyone's ability to travel was limited, regardless of ethnicity, in the wider region in those communities where barricades were set up.

Even if people managed to obtain permits to travel, barricades introduced distrust and suspicion into communities. In the case of one respondent, when the first barricades were set up in the summer of 1991, his relative who used to visit him on the Serb side was killed one day when he returned to his own home on the Croat side.[12] The reality of barricades made the ethnicization discourse of

FIGURES 3A–D. Near the dividing line in Lipik and Pakrac, Western Slavonia

Source: Author's photographs, June 12, 2014.

political leaders more believable to people who previously did not divide along ethnic lines:

> When the war started, our first neighbors were Serbs, and they were, in the beginning, in the shelter of my relatives. There were, and that you probably already saw or heard, some young men who were mobilized. Some wanted to participate, others had to, and others [didn't] because of a family situation if a spouse is of another ethnicity, for example, and so on. Only then when it started, then we could see in our neighbors that they knew something about this from before. Probably they were talking in their houses. We have here some villages that are one hundred percent ethnic Serb. Those Serb villages, later I heard that from my father, were inhabited in a planned way. You couldn't cross this entire area around us without passing through a Serb village. And there were barricades. You couldn't go to any other town in the area without passing through a Serb village and barricades.[13]

Thus, the erecting of barricades was a significant factor that set the course for the distrust, division, ethnicization, and subsequent instances of violence in some multiethnic communities in Croatia. The barricades played an important role not only in the local process of ethnicization but also in creating the wartime "enemy" category before the actual war had even started, as people on the other side were converted through the media, but also stories told in close social circles based on fears during the time of political insecurity, or even rumors that further fed into fears, into an existential threat that was identifiable ethnically. For example, a respondent mentioned that he heard that after he stopped going to work because barricades impeded him from traveling, his coworkers thought that he and other people from the surrounding villages who stopped going to work were gone because they were organizing an insurgency.[14] It was in those communities that the macro-level ethno-political cleavages were successfully mapped locally with the help of the barricades, and it was there that targeted violence against individuals perceived as suspicious, whether due to their ambiguous ethnicity or ambiguous political stance, was facilitated. These cases show how even though the process of ethnicization had already begun in the discourse of political leaders, on the local level, ethnicity started to matter and to serve as a marker dividing the population *after* the first barricades were raised.

In other contexts, beyond the case of Croatia, the first divisions between warring sides, and respective populations, were roadblocks and checkpoints, sometimes reinforced by landmines and other barriers preventing the free movement of people. For example, in Uganda, the use of roadblocks and landmines by both guerrilla forces and government forces limited free movement and travel between the geographic region corresponding to the Luweero Triangle, where the NRA and other guerrilla forces were based, and other parts of Uganda, particularly the capital city of Kampala (Kutesa [2006] 2008, 121). This permitted the insurgents, for example, to govern the territory and population during the wartime uncertainty more effectively.[15]

While the roadblocks added to a false sense of control and predictability under wartime conditions both for the civilians on either side of the divide and for those who were armed, whether insurgents or government forces, the roadblocks actually disadvantaged civilians in a number of ways.[16] More specifically, the roadblocks themselves represented a source of fear and insecurity that characterized the wartime reality of all citizens, regardless of their political, religious, or ethnic identity: "Elderly men and women walked with their heads heavily bowed down. Ours, too. Incidentally, even ours! Because at this roadblock one looked up only at his or her own risk. If a response was required from you, then you gave it to the boss while either looking down or at your shoulder, depending on where the boss was standing. The law! The unbreakable law!" (Wayenga 2009, 152). Fear for one's life and uncertainty regarding whether one would be considered innocent by the armed guards were typical sentiments of people attempting to cross the wartime dividing lines in the central region of Uganda. For example, in one case, several humanitarian aid workers were stopped at the roadblock and asked for money they did not have. They were lucky that the guards accepted some blankets instead of money and let them through.[17] The roadblocks and barricades may have added an element of certainty and control for the armies, but these barriers made civilians even more afraid, as people did not dare to reason with the guards or show any sign of disapproval of even the most oppressive and unjust treatment.

Similarly, in Guatemala during the war, segregating and isolating the population in the parts of the country where the insurgents were based served as a form of control by inhibiting travel, communication, and commercial activity. In the following interview, a respondent who was able to move freely across the barriers because of the nature of his work describes the differences between the war-affected areas and the peaceful areas of Guatemala:

> R: But in the case of Quetzaltenango and the capital city, Guatemala was seen as a peaceful place where nothing [bad] was happening, no major problems.
> I: Everything was seen to be working well?
> R: Yes, there was no conflict that was visible. There were no battles, killings, everything was happening here. I think that the representation of the news contributed to one's understanding that this was a different

world and that one was not affected by that. During the time of my adolescence and youth, I was traveling frequently . . . and slowly I started to notice the difference. Because near here, where we traveled, you started to feel the absence of people. Another thing was that the buses would not stop. They would pass as fast as possible. There is a spot . . . [on the way] where you could see houses, but no movement of people. One time, when I was traveling on that route, somebody stopped the bus, this close [to the bus]. The driver and the assistant noticed him and talked, and I remember the words of the driver saying, "We are going to take a risk and stop." They stopped, but they didn't stop stop. They just slowed down, quickly pulled the man inside, and we continued as fast as possible. . . . At that time, I still didn't fully understand the suffering of brothers from here and in other places. They were completely isolated. . . . There was something interesting. I was in a community that was blocked off for fifteen days by the military. They didn't let anyone enter or leave. And people literally died of hunger. They could not go anywhere outside of their houses . . . this was in '83–'84. I came to that community to work with them, but always with a different understanding than people who were actually living there and living the war. . . . One did not fully know what was happening. When I started working with these communities, my encounters with the military became more intense. They didn't allow other people to enter these communities. . . . They placed roadblocks [*reténes*] . . . like checkpoints. . . . There were several communities I visited, but I visited them on foot. Sometimes I walked more than an hour. And sometimes I had to go up and down the ravines. I would enter in one community and exit from another. I had no choice.[18]

In the Guatemalan western highlands, certain communities that were associated with insurgents became gradually isolated and invisible to the peaceful regions of the country. It was as if parallel worlds existed in the same country—the war-affected communities, without freedom of movement, and the peaceful communities. For those who were free to travel across the country, like this respondent, crossing checkpoints, whether the military-controlled or the guerrilla-controlled ones, was always risky. But for others, it was not even possible to travel. They were completely cut off from the rest of the country for as long as the barriers were in place. Those who traveled through these regions during the war acknowledged that they were lucky to have survived. This was the case of a former soldier who was stopped twice at guerrilla checkpoints, but he managed to conceal his identity successfully.[19] In some cases, people were mistaken for others because they happened to share the name of a person on the lists that were provided to the men at checkpoints by local spies (*orejas*), as these lists did not have any photographs next to the names.[20] These first barriers in form of checkpoints, roadblocks, and barricades, therefore, physically separated the population and facilitated the ethnicization processes that began from the top in these local communities.

Wartime Dividing Lines and the Formation of Amoral Communities

With the increase in the frequency and scale of violent incidents in the areas of Croatia where barricades were set up, these first lines of division were gradually transformed into the front lines of the war, which people could not cross freely for the duration of the war.[21] As seen already, dividing lines did not just control and limit the movement of people and communication. They also distributed the population into warring sides. Even more significantly, the production of borders complemented the processes, such as top-down ethnicization and local-level exclusion of moderates, that created conditions conducive to targeted violence against civilians. Over time, the people, and not merely the warring armies, on the other side of the dividing line became the enemy, who were now identified both politically and ethnically.

Given the significance of the dividing lines for the local processes of ethnicization in Croatia, it is not surprising that when any question of opening connections across the dividing line came up, local hardliners often blocked such efforts. This was evident most directly in the context of the Daruvar Agreement (Daruvarski sporazum) in the Western Slavonian region of Croatia. The agreement, which was signed by several local representatives among ethnic Serb leaders on February 18, 1993, was ultimately rejected by the local hardliners. It called for the repair of local roads and train tracks, the establishment of communication across the dividing line, and the facilitation of the return of expellees to their homes, among other measures aimed at the "normalization of life" in communities across Western Slavonia that had been affected by violence since 1991.[22] In the meeting of the Fifth Regular Session of the local government on March 21, 1993, the political atmosphere in the aftermath of the signing of the Daruvar Agreement was characterized as "heated" by one of the representatives.[23] The decision of some representatives to cross over to the Croat side of the dividing line (referred to as "Ustaša territory" by one of the representatives in the minutes) and sign the agreement with the warring side on February 18, 1993, on the initiative of several members of the local government was characterized as "an act of treason" (*akt veleizdaje*).²⁴ Until that date, according to one of the representatives who criticized this act, the local representatives' "ideas were the same," but after February 18, they "diverged," and this agreement was not "supported by the Government of the RSK or the people of Western Slavonia" but rather was a result of "naiveté from [the representatives'] end."²⁵ Another representative disagreed with him: "Croats are our reality and we are their reality. We cannot call these people [who signed the agreement] traitors."²⁶ After this contentious discussion and the vote, before which two representatives left, the Daruvar Agreement was ultimately rejected by the local representatives.²⁷

The resistance to the signing of the Daruvar Agreement was not the only instance of opposition to opening the lines of communication and transportation across the wartime dividing lines in Croatia. After the 1994 opening of the Zagreb–Belgrade highway that reconnected the two sides of the dividing line for transportation in the region of Western Slavonia, the local government wrote a letter of protest to the central government of the RSK in Knin calling for limitations of movement along the highway.²⁸ In this document, the local representatives from Western Slavonia wrote that as a result of the opening of the highway, their region was "open for the Croatian intelligence and propaganda," in addition to "illicit trade" and "illegal crossings," including the mass departure of "our citizens" to the territory of Croatia and their application for Croatian citizenship and passports.²⁹ This shows that the borders were put in place not only to protect the population from possible attacks but also to control the local population.³⁰ As evident in the cases of the Daruvar Agreement and the Zagreb–Belgrade highway deliberations, the production of borders further empowered the local hardliners who wished to exclude the moderates from their communities.

The war in Croatia ultimately ended with Operation Storm (Oluja) on August 4, 1995. This military operation, which was carried out by the Croatian Army in central Croatia and northern Dalmatia, resulted in the mass displacement of predominantly ethnic Serbs from the territory delineated by the RSK borders. Most people fled over the course of a couple of days across the territory of Bosnia and Herzegovina toward Serbia.³¹ In the rush to leave, most people took with them only what they could carry in their vehicles:

> R: The fighting had already started and the civilians still didn't know that. Then it was only at the moment when the Croatian Army was already near . . . , in the cannon range, at one moment, the general mobilization, not mobilization, but evacuation, was declared. General evacuation was declared, and simply, the army of the RSK went to all houses and apartments, from apartment to apartment, and ordered everyone within half an hour to gather all of their belongings

and to start in the direction of Bosnia first, and then toward Serbia. It was ordered like this, "They are coming, they will kill all of you, you have to leave." People were . . . those images that are well known of people on tractors fleeing. They were in tractors, cars, and in whatever they could find, on foot, or in whatever form. They took with them all that they could fit in there, only some documents, some money, some gold if they had any, and everything else was left behind. Their whole lives stayed behind, their furniture, their pictures, everything that they amassed throughout their lives.

I: And maybe nothing would have happened to civilians?

R: Look, some civilians, the elderly especially, didn't want to leave. They went to the UN base. And nothing happened to them. Some old people who stayed at home were killed. And they were not killed by the Croatian Army, but by those trailing paramilitary formations, different ones. The volunteers who were operating there, in principle, the criminals. People who were in the Croatian Army and who participated in those operations said that they went through the region and everything was fine. They would be there for two weeks, and on the way back, the same areas they passed that were not touched and where the houses were standing or not robbed, [they] were now burned, robbed, and so on. . . . The good thing was that my family was on both sides; when that operation was over and it was possible to go to that territory with special permits, you couldn't go right away . . . then one of my relatives secured permits. . . . So they came with trucks and took their furniture, things from their apartments that were already being prepared for other people to move in. They brought them here and stored them. They waited for people to return. Then ten years later, when people returned to their apartments and houses, they brought them back their furniture and personal belongings. That meant a lot to them to get their photos, books, furniture, and things from their apartment.[32]

In areas where borders separated communities, anything was possible during the war. In some cases, civilians were harmed; in others, they survived. In some cases, property was looted or destroyed, and in others, it was saved. Given the uncertainty and the general wartime "psychosis," in the respondent's words, in the areas under the RSK, most civilians left when the Croatian Army advanced during Oluja. People were aware that civilians were in danger of being targeted precisely because the dividing line served both to protect them and to convert them into an "enemy" who was defined ethnically. As a result of "choosing" to live in the

RSK territory, they, and not only their armies, represented (or were represented by political leaders as) a political threat—a threat to the statehood of Croatia and, by extension, a threat to the people on the other side of the dividing line.

The ethnicization process further ensured that once people chose a particular side of the divide at the onset of the war, they could no longer change it. Even if they physically crossed to the other side, their own borders would travel with them. This was the case for an ethnic Croat who was seen as a traitor by his fellow coethnics because he spent the war on the Serb side of the dividing line.[33] In describing how he was punished by his coethnics for having stayed on the Serb side during the war, the respondent expressed particular distress that he was the only one who was beaten by a woman. In the context of a patriarchal society, this for him represented a form of public humiliation. He felt that this act of violence thus made him appear doubly weak—first, for having betrayed his nation, and second, for being so beaten by a woman.

Given that one of the roles of the wartime dividing lines was to reinforce the process of ethnicization locally, it was also difficult for individuals who chose the side of the border where they constituted an ethnic minority. This was the experience of one respondent who was originally from the territory under control of the RSK during the war but was trying to register as a refugee on the Croat side of the dividing line:

> The woman taking my information asked for the first and last name, and ethnicity. I said I didn't have an ethnicity anymore. There were no more Yugoslavs by then. Then she said, "You are an Orthodox Croat." I said, "No, I am not." I am an atheist, I don't go to church, and I was not even baptized. I don't have an idea about religion. She continued to insist until I took my card and said, "You cannot help me, that is my right." Then I went to find another worker. My friend who was with me then was in an even worse situation. She was an Orthodox whose parents stayed in the RSK. When she heard how this woman talked to me, and when it was her turn to answer the question about her ethnicity, she said, "An Orthodox Croat." That is how they registered her then. The story goes then, her father and mother both Serbs, I asked her, "How were you not ashamed to say you were a Croat? You don't feel uncomfortable about how it was imposed?" That was my first experience with being a refugee . . . Ah that. Listen, the fact is that very few Serbs stayed . . . [in the territory of Croatia that was not the RSK] as refugees. They either stayed in Krajina [RSK], or after a short time, they left Croatia altogether. There were very few like my friend and me. In that first period, people distributed themselves wherever they thought they should go. Simulta-

neously with all of this, you had a feeling that you would go home very fast and not that this was a war that would last for quite some time.³⁴

It is evident, in this example, how the wartime dividing lines reflected the state policies of ethnicization and reinforced the ethnic divides among civilian population. People who attempted to challenge these imposed borders by using commonsense, or by self-identifying with a category outside of the imposed categories, encountered resistance from some state officials. In other words, there was little to no room for personal choice under the circumstances described by this respondent.

Just as in the case of Croatia, the borders separating the Luweero Triangle from the remainder of Uganda also produced new political identities. As in Croatia, some people who had a choice moved from this rural area to the city of Kampala, in part, because life was difficult without basic security and the basic necessities while the road connecting this region to Kampala was blocked.³⁵ In some cases, people who did not want to join either side could "hide" more easily there than in the war zone.³⁶ Also, as in Croatia, a number of families were separated by the wartime dividing lines for many years, and some could not even recognize their own family after they reunited.³⁷ Those who remained in the Luweero area under the insurgent political leadership participated in the creation of a territorially delimited "subnation" that was politically aligned with the opposition to the Obote regime and ethnically identified with the majority group in this region, the Baganda. The population in the Luweero region helped the insurgents by providing food and logistical support, and they were "governed" internally by the system of resistance councils. For this reason, the population that remained behind the wartime dividing lines in the Luweero region was assumed to be antigovernment and pro-insurgency. This became such a prevalent categorization that one of the commanders of the NRA was caught by surprise by a person from this region who was on a reconnaissance mission on behalf of the government forces (Kutesa [2006] 2008, 159). This example illustrates how territorial and ethnic identities, following the physical separation of territory during the conflict, serve as shortcuts in identifying those who belong, or who may be trusted by the army and the government, and those who are excluded, or those whose torture and murder were considered acts of self-defense in the context of amoral communities.

Similarly, in Guatemala, one of the counterinsurgency strategies that the military implemented was to isolate a community associated with the guerrillas for a period of time or to gather people from different regions into a single community "to be more easily controlled" (Falla 1994, 117). Civilians in those communities had no access to food, medicine, basic supplies, or state-provided services during the war. Lack of access to basic necessities for survival was one of the main reasons that some communities were ready to turn against the guerrillas and participate in the government-organized civil patrols when the possibility of amnesty was introduced by Efraín Ríos Montt (Stoll 1993, 125). When civil patrols were put in place by the government as part of the counterinsurgency strategy, "the commissioner or the patrol commander had to authorize the departure and issue a pass that had to be presented by the military authorities upon the arrival at the destination" (REMHI 1999, 124). In rare cases, people were able to leave communities to avoid being targeted or recruited by either the military or the guerrillas.[38]

Many people from these communities, however, could not even leave because they were surrounded either by the army or by the guerrillas.[39] As a result of the wartime dividing lines, people whose freedom of movement was limited not only faced difficulties in earning their livelihoods but also became targets of violence by the army or by the insurgents.[40] According to one respondent's account, when he and his family had to flee their village to save themselves from an army attack, as his wife and his children were hiding in the ravines, they were completely encircled by the military.[41] Another respondent described how they were surrounded by both the army soldiers and the guerrillas, and "many people died," while others left or hid in the nearby forest.[42] In some communities, such as Cuarto Pueblo, which was politically and ideologically diverse before the attack, residents who supported the right-oriented Movement of the National Liberation (Movimiento de Liberación Nacional) did not feel they were in danger when the army arrived, and they did not leave (Falla 1994, 68).[43] The army carried out the massacre indiscriminately, assuming that the entire community supported the insurgency. People in areas isolated by the wartime dividing lines were also targets of recruitment by both sides: "[It was] pure pressure because in the zone of conflict, communities . . . the military would arrive in the conflict areas and the communities are pressured. They recruited people for the military. Just like the guerillas also recruited people. They pressured them [people]. So, if they [people] didn't join one side, they would join another side."[44] In Guatemala, by limiting the movement of people or their freedom to choose neutrality, the barriers, checkpoints, and, eventually, wartime dividing lines contributed to the formation of amoral communities, where civilians became the targets both of violence and of recruitment for the armed forces on both sides.

The production of borders represents, therefore, a strategic form of control and recruitment of populations. From the point of view of the armed forces on either side, the borders introduce a sense of certainty and predictability because they make it easier to control the civilian population and to target individuals, or entire communities, presumed to be supporting the enemy forces. Yet the civilians suffer from this strategy because they become easy targets both within their communities, as part of the in-group policing process, and of the out-group army.

In this and the previous chapter, I showed how local-level conditions conducive to the formation of amoral communities were created in some regions through the complementary processes of the production of borders and the exclusion of moderates. My analysis, thus far, has not included an examination of the role that local memories of historical waves of violence may have played in the formation of amoral communities in some regions. I turn to this question in the next chapter.

5

MEMORIES AND VIOLENCE

> INTERVIEWER (I): When you look at the Homeland War now in retrospect, do you think it was connected with events from World War II?
> RESPONDENT (R): I don't think so. In my opinion this was like when two brothers are fighting over how they would divide what they have—"You got more, and now I'll get you, and you'll get me"—and that is what I think happened here. If the borders were known, why would Serbia attack or send tanks from Serbia to Croatia, to destroy the entire city and all the people? The grenades were falling and anyone could be killed, a Serb or a Croat.[1]

According to this respondent, memories of events or violence from World War II have little to do with what occurred in the most recent war. His opinion, however, was not shared by all interviewees. Some strongly agreed that the violence of the recent war was connected with memories and events of World War II, some strongly disagreed, and still others had a more ambiguous stance toward this question. Similar disagreements may be found in the existing scholarship. Some scholars argue that residents in regions with a history of violence during World War II were more likely to mobilize for violence in the 1990s because the narratives of historical violence contributed to their heightened perception of threat (Posen 1993; Schiemann 2007). Yet the patterns of violence indicate that there may not be a direct relationship between the history of violence in World War II and the level of violence in the 1990s in Croatia, given that some multiethnic areas that experienced significant violence in World War II, such as northwestern Croatia or the region of Istria, were areas with lower levels of violence in the 1990s.[2] These patterns invite a more nuanced and systematic analysis in line with other studies examining how people make sense of past waves of violence and how they are interpreted in the present (Brown 2003; Jambrešić Kirin 2000; Jansen 2002; Katunarić 2010).

In the field of memory studies, which contains many studies from geographic contexts beyond the region of the former Yugoslavia, scholars have argued that collective memories play an important role in collective identity formation, and sometimes may even account for certain patterns of collective political behavior.[3] Scholars have also recognized collective memory as an instrument of political mobilization.[4] Yet the question of under what conditions top-level mobilization efforts evoking historical memories of violence are actually successful on the local level still remains to be examined.

My research thus builds on this extensive interdisciplinary scholarship, but differs in its aim to distinguish more rigorously between the processes of collective memory formation and the processes of collective identity formation, or ethnicization, on the level of local communities.[5] I started by posing the question of how local narratives of historical waves of violence may have informed respondents' interpretations and understanding of the most recent political violence in their region. In short, my approach was to study memories in the individual and the social spaces, or, more specifically, the places in which varied levels and types of collective violence are encountered.[6] Based on the evidence from my interviews in Croatia, Uganda, and Guatemala, in this chapter, I argue that it is not possible to predict or generalize about how memories of historical violence shape political behavior solely by examining the content of the memories or individual interpretations because they vary both within regions and across individuals to a great extent. And yet memories of past waves of violence figure prominently in the interviews, confirming that they may matter a great deal, particularly because they help people "make sense" of current events (Portelli 1991). But in order to understand why these local or individual memories are "activated," particularly when political leaders mention them over the course of their efforts to mobilize the population politically through the processes of ethnicization, in some regions and not in others, it is critical to take into account the local conditions and processes, such as the exclusion of moderates and the production of borders, that may cause memories of past waves of violence to become powerful instruments of political mobilization.

I begin my study of the role of memories in local-level ethnicization processes by exploring the ways in which family or local narratives emerge and reemerge over the course of people's lives. While some of these narratives may be employed by political leaders in their discourse aimed at mobilizing supporters or participants in mass violence, my respondents' stories emerged from their families' genuine personal memories and experiences. Even though these memories may be political, respondents referred to events mainly as they were connected to personally relevant experiences, or teachings, that were conveyed to them by others in their family or community with previous war experiences. The second section of this chapter considers community-level, or local, memories in the context of local-level ethnicization processes. In this analysis, I also look at silences, absences, or what I refer to as *silenced memories*. These memories, like any other memories of violence, may be politicized easily because they are connected to personal or intergenerational experiences that are considered inconvenient truths since they may reveal the negative, or even criminal, aspects of the incumbent political regime's activities. Finally, the third section considers my respondents as teachers by presenting their own thoughts regarding whether they find any connections between their communities' memories of historical violence and the wartime targeted violence against civilians in those communities across Croatia, Uganda, and Guatemala.

Intergenerational Narratives of World War II Violence across Croatia

Families are recognized as important social spaces for the intergenerational transmission of memories of wars and related traumas (Halbwachs 1992; Hirsch 2008). In the context of Croatia, the work of Slavko Goldstein titled *1941: The Year That Keeps Returning* (2007) represents an important example of both a family story that centers on the World War II experience of his father, who lost his life in the concentration camp Jadovno, and the history of violence in Croatia under the Ustaša regime in World War II. As an intergenerational narrative, this book presents a carefully researched account of tragic events and a lesson for future generations of possible signs of danger that should be prevented or avoided. In that sense, it plays a similar role as the family stories mentioned by my respondents in that it transmits a message of courage and hope, or simply valuable life lessons for younger generations, rather than reinforcing the ethnicization that was present in the media and the discourse of political elites at the onset of the violence in the 1990s. In contrast, a number of books were published in the early 1990s that made references to World War II violence, but many were written in the context of political mobilization and ethnicization discourse, or, in Goldstein's words, when it was "too late for cautious research and impartial discussion" (2007, 457).

What kind of a role do families play in this transmission of memory? What types of narratives of past wars are told? When are they told? Are there any regional disparities in the types of stories told or the practice of telling stories within families? What are some dominant elements, values, or teachings accompanying the stories? How do these stories, when told, help older and younger generations make sense of current political events? These are some of the questions that I considered in my analysis of the interviews that were conducted across regions with varied levels of violence in the 1940s and 1990s in Croatia.

Several respondents reflected on the different values that stories told within families may convey to younger generations. In one case, a respondent thought that intergenerational narratives of violence from previous wars not only are irrelevant but may even be harmful in making sense of the events in the 1990s.[7] By referring to stories as "old wives' tales," the respondent differentiated between "written history" and "oral history" and implied that the latter history is based on potentially unreliable word-of-mouth accounts or rumors. Without getting into a scholarly debate on the credibility, limitations, and advantages of oral sources for historical research (Passerini [2007] 2014; Portelli 1991; Radstone and Schwarz 2010; Thompson [1978] 2000), which is not the principal goal of this study, it is important to note that this respondent discredits the practice of telling stories of local and family history as a useful process not only for the transmission of history but also for the development of a personal worldview consisting of a certain set of values and beliefs. The most salient element in this respondent's analysis is the emphasis on the potentially harmful consequences that these stories could have for the development of young persons' values, such as tolerance, and for interpersonal relations in the broader community, particularly if used to form ideas about potential friends and enemies, ethnically defined. From this perspective, the family narratives of World War II are more likely than other sources to be based on selective and possibly even erroneous information that could divide a community along ethnic lines. This concern that stories of past cycles of violence were used in the 1990s to divide people, not by politicians but by people in those communities, was also voiced by another respondent: "As soon as you put ethnicity in front [of historical episodes of violence], the old people are reminded of World War II. One older war veteran said, 'It will be the same thing again.' I asked him what would happen again. He said, 'Serbs won't be able to say anything again because they will end up in Jadovno.'[8] And, from ... [the respondent's community] during World War II, some three hundred and more people were taken to Jadovno and thrown into a hole. And now when you think about this, listen, this was talked about at home to younger generations."[9] The manner in which these stories are told is critical, based on this respondent's personal experience. Ideally, they should be told without an intention to divide people on the basis of ethnicity or religion but rather to recount what actually occurred. That is how stories about what happened in this respondent's family in

World War II were conveyed, with the intention of teaching younger generations to be more tolerant. But, as with any stories told in families, they will differ from family to family, and they will also have a different effect on each individual.

Memories of past traumas or violence may or may not contain any political elements or values. Stories about the experiences of older family members may be shared as encouragement for younger generations, demonstrating that even in the most difficult situations, there is hope for survival. The storytelling may be prompted by certain current events that remind older generations of their own experiences, or stories they had heard from their elders. For example, the air raids and the consequent need to hide in the basement in the 1990s reminded one respondent of her grandmother's account of her experiences during World War II, which seemed significantly worse than their situation and helped give her courage.[10] In other cases, for the individuals who had firsthand experience with violence in World War II, the start of the violence in the 1990s may have actually triggered memories of the traumas from World War II and had psychologically detrimental effects on them and their families.[11] Therefore, in times of crisis, memories shared in families may inspire courage to overcome difficulties, fear, sadness, anger, or a mix of different emotions.

The types of memories that are passed on from generation to generation may also vary within the same families. As one respondent noted, her own side of the family was not directly affected by the violence of World War II, but her husband's side of the family was:

> I was born in World War II, so I cannot say that I experienced anything. Even my father and members of my most immediate family were not in any army. My father was older . . . so he didn't participate in war. So, in my family, I didn't hear anything. But on my husband's side of the family, there were stories. As a child, he survived . . . the children's concentration camp. . . . His mother was in Jasenovac, and there his mother, his sister, and two . . . [relatives] were killed. . . . An aunt of my husband was so brave, a peasant woman, older woman, very brave, managed to pull her children from the camp and took them home, and then returned to get the mother of my husband. But when she returned, his mother and her daughter were already dead. That is courage.[12]

It may be difficult to make generalizations based on experiences and memories of traumatic events from World War II even within a single family. In this case, some members of the family were survivors of violence, some were witnesses, some were participants, and others were not directly affected by the same war. Moreover, each individual survivor deals differently with his or her experiences.

The stories usually carry a message for younger generations, and in the case of this story, it illustrates courage, as well as the tragedy of one family.

Just as memories vary within (and across) families, they also differ from region to region, and from community to community. It is important to remember that even though intergenerational stories may play a role in individuals' sense of collective identity, the exposure to other sources of historical narratives, including some state-sponsored educational initiatives or commemorations, may also matter. One respondent, for example, said that most of her knowledge about World War II came from school, except for the family story about her grandfather who refused to wear the official army uniform and secretly helped the Partisans by transporting their weapons throughout the war.[13] In the account of another respondent, she remembered that after her father joined the Partisans, her mother was beaten so brutally by Ustaša in the basement where they were hiding with other members of the family that she died three days later.[14] A respondent whose parents had moved to the region of northwestern Croatia from other parts of Croatia did not hear stories from his family, but he heard them from the local museum staff, who had heard them from the survivors of the local concentration camp, Danica, and other witnesses of the crimes and mass violence that took place there.[15] This respondent also noted that such "horrible stories" were mentioned very rarely. Another respondent heard stories from his friend's grandmother about Danica.[16] This is the site he also visited with his school occasionally. From these stories, he learned that while local Serbs and Jews made up the majority of prisoners in Danica, many Croats who were against the NDH were also imprisoned there. There were cases of a few local Croats who helped testify in favor of local Serbs in order to save them.[17] Another respondent mentioned good interpersonal relations in her community before World War II.[18] These examples illustrate how local stories of solidarity across ethnic and religious lines, especially before World War II, were also available to respondents.

The region of northwestern Croatia is notable for violence not only during World War II but also following the war when the Partisans committed violence against the members of the NDH armies, and in some cases their families, who were attempting to escape through Slovenia and Austria (*Križni put*). A family memory of one respondent from this region refers to this post–World War II episode of violence:

> I have one story that I don't remember very clearly. When I was little, I heard this story from the older family members. It was a story about how people were standing in front of their houses and watching how Partisans were taking away their husbands to shoot them. They weren't even

> allowed to approach them or say goodbye, but they could only watch how the convoy was leaving for the place where they executed them. . . . That story probably refers to 1945; that would be the most logical time of that. And people from our region were the ones who were killed. Maybe even from my distant family. I don't know exactly who because I was too young when I heard the story and I don't remember it. I was too young. But then on the other hand, we know many examples of crimes from that other side, from the NDH and the Ustaša government. For example, the concentration camp Danica, where too many people were killed. It turns out that in World War II, both sides were committing crimes. The same happened in the Homeland War, but again, this is something that is not talked about very eagerly.[19]

The lasting image of people who suffered the loss of family members reminded this respondent how some parts of history may be confined to the family circle exclusively during certain times when they may be considered to be politically inconvenient to the governing regime. In these cases, the stories remain political even if shared only in the private sphere, but they are not used for a political purpose. Another respondent from this region also mentioned how some of his older family members talked about being arrested or having to hide for several years and even emigrate after World War II because they were in the Croatian Home Guard (Domobrani) armed forces.[20] Some memories of violence thus may be discussed only in private circles as people seek to make sense of both past and present events under changing political circumstances.

The change of political atmosphere in Croatia in the 1990s was described in the following way by one of my respondents from northwestern Croatia:

> The situation in my town, given how we were brought up at that time, we didn't, for instance . . . My grandmother never talked about these things, or my grandfather who had experiences from both World War I and World War II. . . . He was in both armies, in the army of the old Yugoslavia, and in Domobrani. It was not talked about in my family until the 1990s. Then, in some way, we were mildly directed toward one side. Older generations started talking about things that they might have suppressed all this time vis-à-vis the environment in which they lived. Only after, we started realizing, or hearing, some other stories about how all the things we used to think or experience were not that great. There were also many things that were hidden. Simply, in some way, we didn't . . . how would I say, we didn't notice some things. For instance, we didn't notice how certain people would always socialize together, or how some people would approve of some things. I know, for instance, in a bar,

only people of one ethnicity, or mainly people of one ethnicity, would gather. We never thought about that before. Only right before the Homeland War, we started to notice, or maybe some people, especially these older generations, warned us that we would see who tends to congregate in this or in that place. In principle, it was true, even though before we didn't notice that. But we started noticing that, and to this day, nothing significant changed with respect to that.[21]

In this account, divergent shared memories of the violence from World War II were present in the socialist period throughout Croatia even though they were not openly talked about until the start of the regime changes in the early 1990s. This respondent was cautious and vague regarding the specific ethnicities into which people were divided, perhaps in part because in his community, the local-level ethnicization processes of the exclusion of moderates and the production of borders were never carried out in the same way as in some other regions throughout the war. Nevertheless, based on this account, the evidence of social divisions preceding the war existed even in this community, as family stories gained new significance in the changing national political context.

In contrast to the previous account, which does not include ethnic labels, in the following account, a respondent from Eastern Slavonia refers to the violence in the aftermath of World War II as the "Croatian silence" (*hrvatska šutnja*): "This was until the 1990s the term used to refer to events from World War II in Croatian families, particularly in the families whose members were in the armies of Domobrani or Ustaša. People talked but only inside the family. In my family, this was not the case, or at least, I don't remember. I was never brought up to hate anyone."[22] In other words, these "silent memories" of some Croat families in the aftermath of World War II were not forgotten memories, but the "silence" was not just a political question for this respondent. It was also conceived as a necessary self-preservation, or self-defense, strategy under the previous political regime.[23] Luisa Passerini argues that in analyzing the role of memory in politics, it is essential to take "silence into account" in order to uncover the "links between forms of power and forms of silence" ([2007] 2014, 29). It is precisely when there are interruptions, such as regime changes, that it becomes possible to identify "traces of forgetting and silence" (17).[24] In other words, we would expect the "silenced" memories—those memories that were not part of the dominant narratives of a given political regime and that were preserved within families as a form of self-preservation—to reemerge during political regime transitions.

Given these differences across regions and families in experiences with violence in both historical periods, it is difficult to draw a direct causal link between local memories and intergenerational narratives of World War II violence and the patterns violence in the 1990s. Yet, in places where borders managed to divide communities and political moderates were gradually excluded through violence and threats, memories of World War II violence played a more prominent role in the local narratives, including commemorative practices, as will be shown in the next section.

Ethnicization of Local Memories

With changes in the political regime in Croatia in the 1990s, in addition to the emergence of political discourse calling for the redrawing of political borders in order to make them correspond with ethnic identities, it was both possible and desirable, as another form of political mobilization, to speak about the crimes that were *silenced*, or not officially accepted and permitted, in socialist Yugoslavia.[25] While memories during the post–World War II period may have been used for political purposes by state and local leaders, they represented something else for the survivors and their family members. For those individuals, the literature that revealed the crimes that were silenced by the Yugoslav regime served as a long-awaited acknowledgment of their own losses that they were not able to speak of or commemorate for many years. Indeed, a number of authors of testimonial literature that was published in the early 1990s documenting local World War II crimes were witnesses or family members of survivors. Several books directly linked the violence from World War II, and even the violence in the aftermath of World War II, with the violence in the 1990s (Erjavec 1992; Pelikan 1997; Savić 2007).[26] Some of these publications documenting local violence based on local oral histories and documents served as a source of information for some of my respondents. For a resident of Western Slavonia, the information he found in books about his region helped him make sense of the events he witnessed personally during World War II but did not understand fully.[27]

In the region of Eastern Slavonia and Srijem, the fighting in World War II took place mainly between the Partisans, the opposition movement consisting of both Croats and Serbs, and the army of the NDH, including the Domobrani and the Ustaša. Given that most ethnic Serbs in this region were Partisans, they were less likely to encounter the equivalent of "Croatian silence" during the Yugoslav regime.[28] One respondent described another potential form of World War II silence, which became more "ethnicized" in the 1990s: "The Partisan movement was represented more widely in the population. Later in stories, I heard about the movement from local people.... Based on these stories, allegedly one person from Bogota killed one Ustaša and the [Partisan] movement grew from then on. People often don't talk about the football club Mitnica that was built on the site where the people were killed in World War II. This is where people were brought from Srijem and Slavonia, from Sremska Mitrovica when the NDH was formed. . . . People from Srijem were shot there. This is a taboo topic here and local people rarely talk about that."[29] This respondent's account points to the changing focus of the local leaders and communities regarding commemorative practices in the context of the new political climate in the immediate aftermath of the Homeland War in his region. This also changed in 2014, however, when the plans started for the renovation of the site of the Dudik Memorial in the neighborhood of Mitnica, which commemorated the World War II victims of fascist violence and had been destroyed in the 1990s.[30]

Similarly, in the region of Western Slavonia, a number of new monuments connecting the 1940s and the 1990s were built, renovated, and updated once the violence subsided. While some of these monuments had the positive effect of commemorating some of the previously silenced memories, they also, unfortunately, in some cases introduced new silences or reinforced the narratives of ethnicization in these communities. For example, the memorial in the center of the village of Ivanovo Selo next to the monument commemorating the fallen Partisans of World War II, written in Czech—the language of the predominant ethnic group in the village—includes eight graves and a white monument resembling a chapel with a small cross on the top (figure 4). The inscription on the new monument is in Croatian and includes the names and years of birth of eight people from the village who were killed in 1991:

> Od zločinačkih četničkih ruku iz susjednih sela poginuli su kao nevine žrtve
>
> [Innocent victims who died by the criminal hands of the Četniks from neighboring villages]

The language of the inscription on the monument illustrates that the threat in this case came from the armed forces from the neighboring villages. While the neighboring villages were predominantly Serbian demographically, Ivanovo Selo was predominantly a Czech village. Thus, the threat came from people who were once neighbors but now, following the rocket attacks and the killings of civilians, represented "criminal Četniks," a reference from World War II to create a sense of continuity in the categorization of the enemy. This category, however, is actually a new construction, in the context of the 1990s nationalist exclusivist violence resembling fascist violence from WWII, since, in World War II, most ethnic Serbs from this area joined the anti-fascist Partisan movement, along with the Czech population from Ivanovo Selo. So, the people from these neighboring Serb villages who perpetrated the violence against their neighbors in the 1990s

FIGURE 4. Memorial for victims of rocket attacks in Ivanovo Selo
Source: Author's photograph, June 15, 2014.

were most likely the children of the Partisans who fought on the same side as the victims commemorated by the World War II monument located on the same memorial site. In this community, therefore, there was no connection between the patterns of WWII violence, in terms of the ethnic identities of victims and perpetrators, and the violence in the 1990s. Even during WWII, the relations in this multiethnic community were complex, as some of my interviewees recalled the solidarity in the local multiethnic population of this region, even between ideologically opposed neighbors, during World War II:

> My mother is Czech. . . . And my father was a Serb . . . from a poor family with many children. And when we moved to this village, there were Serbs here. Across from us, there was another Czech woman, and my mother was the other one. During World War II, these two were saving these Serbs. And here across . . . in a neighboring village, there was a German neighbor, who during World War II . . . had a bunker in his village. And when World War II started, my father . . . and the other one from the village were supposed to be killed. The German neighbor then came at night and told them that the two of them cannot wait at home

until the morning. And when the Partisans were coming to attack the Germans, then they were the ones who warned the German neighbor about the arrival of the Partisans. . . . There was such solidarity that if somebody needed a slice of bread, we shared it among each other. Today, there is no such solidarity.[31]

While both the 1940s and the 1990s were two contentious periods in Croatia and Western Slavonia, this respondent viewed the prospect of reconciliation as more challenging after the 1990s because the solidarity that once used to exist among people in the same community was lost, in her view. In the 1940s, in the perspective of this respondent, communities were not defined as strictly by ethnicity.[32] In contrast, in the 1990s, ethnicity became the prominent boundary dividing people within communities in this region. These new divisions that the respondent perceived were, as discussed in the previous chapters, in part a result of violence and the physical separation of the population by the dividing line, which created a constant threat of violence during the four years of the war and transformed former neighbors into deadly enemies.

Another monument in this region that links the violence in the 1940s with the violence in the 1990s is located east of Pakrac, in the predominantly Serb village of Gornji Grahovljani. This is an original World War II monument that was renovated and updated to include civilians who lost their lives in the winter of 1991 (figure 5). The inscription on the monument reads,

> U toku NOB-e iz ovog sela poginuo je 21 borac NOV-a i 107 žrtava fašističkog terora.
> Identificirano je 14 poginulih partizana i 86 žrtava fašističkog terora.
> U toku 1991. godine stradalo je 16 civila koji su ostali kod svojih kuća.
> Znatno oštećeni spomenik 2010. obnovilo je nekoliko stanovnika sela.
>
> [During the National Liberation Struggle, 21 National Liberation Army soldiers and 107 victims of fascist terror died from this village. There were 14 fallen Partisans and 86 victims of fascist terror who were identified.
> During 1991, 16 civilians who stayed in their homes lost their lives.
> In 2010, several villagers renovated the monument, which was significantly damaged.]

However, unlike the inscription on the monument in Ivanovo Selo, this inscription does not include information regarding the identities or ethnicities of the perpetrators and victims. The monument also does not include the names of the persons who renovated it in 2010. The inscription referring to the massacre in 1991 only includes the total number of victims and mentions that the victims were

FIGURE 5. Monument for victims of World War II and the violence in 1991 in Gornji Grahovljani

Source: Author's photograph, June 13, 2014.

those who remained at home, presumably during the attack by armed forces on the village. These ambiguities, particularly regarding the identities of the victims in the 1990s, point to a new wave of silences, or the omission of experiences of survivors or family members of the victims that do not fit in the dominant national narrative in contemporary Croatia, as the victims are most probably Serb civilians (Karačić, Banjeglav, and Govedarica 2012). In the local context, this monument can also be seen as contributing to ethnicization narratives by attempting to draw links not only between the two historical periods but also between ethnicity (albeit more implicitly than the previous monument) and ideology.

In the similar way, about a month after Operation Lightning (Bljesak), the Croatian Army's military operation that ended the war in Western Slavonia in May 1995, a local newspaper, *Pakrački list*, announced the unveiling of a monument in Marino Selo commemorating not only the local victims of the Croatian Homeland War in the 1990s but also the victims in Bleiburg and *Križni put* in 1945 (figure 6), two locations where the perpetrators of violence were Partisans and the victims were members of the Ustaša and the Domobrani from the area.[33] While this monument honors a memory that was silenced under the Yugoslav regime, it also contributes to ethnicization narratives by commemorating victims in a similar way as the previous monuments by attempting to draw links between ethnicity and ideology.

In summary, all three monuments from Western Slavonia, although using different discourses and symbols, attempt to connect the violence against locals in different historical periods and contribute to the discourse that links a particular ethnicity with a particular ideology. The renovated World War II monument in Grahovljani, while explicit about the ideology of the victims and the perpetrators in World War II, is the most ambiguous of the three regarding both the ideology and the ethnic identification of the victims and the perpetrators in the 1990s. The new monument in Ivanovo Selo, located next to the World War II monument, ethnicizes the perpetrators from the 1990s, while the Marino Selo monument's narrative ethnicizes the victims across different historical periods.

In northern Dalmatia, another region with high levels of violence in the 1990s, and where entire villages and families were divided among different armies in World War II, the local memories in different historical periods were also contested. After the 1990s, local commemorations of crimes committed by Partisans in the aftermath of World War II became more common, while Partisan monuments were rarely visited or were not renovated (Schäuble 2014, 144). Official commemorations and silences, whether at the local or the national level, served as political opportunities to frame how victims were represented (137). Yet respondents' accounts of violence on the ground during World War II presented a much more complex story. For example, a respondent from a village in this

FIGURE 6. Monument for victims of Bleiburg, *Križni put*, and the Homeland War in Marino Selo

Source: Author's photograph, June 13, 2014.

region said that, based on his grandfather's stories, both Četniks and Partisans would pass through the village, and that people did not panic as much when Partisans would arrive as when Četniks would arrive.[34] According to his grandfather's stories, the Ustaša were not present for most of World War II, and even in 1945, there were no significant population losses. In the Yugoslav regime, based on his assessment, villages or regions that suffered the most from the fascist violence received more attention from the government.[35] This would be an example not of "silencing" but of forgetting, or simply neglecting, segments of the population and areas that did not fit neatly in the memory discourse promoted by the state.

Different personal experiences and variation in the levels of World War II violence, not only by region but also among cities and villages, were also mentioned in interviews in other regions across Croatia. For instance, memories of World War II violence were quite different in Gorski Kotar from those in other parts of Croatia. In some places, respondents recalled stories from World War II about life that went on normally for the most part, such as in Vrbovsko, while in others, people would be taken from their jobs, never to be found again, as in the case of railroad workers in the city of Ogulin.[36] For the most part, the local Croats and Serbs of Gorski Kotar participated in the resistance against fascism in World War II, which my respondents from this region referred to as the resistance against the "occupation, conquest, and the lack of tolerance."[37] They perceived the struggle of the local population in both periods, the 1940s and the 1990s, as a form of resistance to fascism, and this explains the positive response among the locals to mobilization efforts in the 1990s. Given these inconsistencies in the way memories were interpreted and used over time, as well as the variation in local memories within and across regions independently of the memories of World War II violence, it may not be possible to draw a direct causal link between the memories of violence from the World War II period and the levels or patterns of violence across the regions in the 1990s. While two-dimensional, or *ethnicized*, versions of the narratives of World War II violence figured prominently in the discourse and the media in general in Croatia in the 1990s, the use of symbols and World War II references was associated with significant violence along ethnic lines only in those places where the favorable conditions for it had been created. This was especially the case in the region that corresponded to the RSK, where the use of memories of World War II violence and symbols for political mobilization was prevalent in the 1990s (Pavlaković 2013). The instrumentalization of memories of violence was particularly effective in these regions because the population had already been divided along ethnic lines and physically isolated by wartime dividing lines, and the moderates had already been excluded through threats and violence.

Similarly, in Uganda, the interviews revealed a diverse set of personal observations and interpretations with respect to the causes of conflict and the dynamics of wartime violence. A narrative that emerged repeatedly in the interviews referred to the event in 1966, when the military, under the leadership of Milton Obote, attacked the palace of the king of Buganda, Frederick Walugembe Mutesa II, and forced him into exile. In the view of a number of respondents, particularly from the Nakaseke District, this was perceived as a symbolic attack on the culture and political rights of the population of Buganda, the region of the traditional kingdom of the Baganda people. For a number of individuals in Luweero, the events in the 1980s represented a continuation of the struggle of the Baganda for more political representation in the government that began in 1966 when the king was removed by Obote, who assumed power during his first regime.[38] The poisoning of police officers, as representatives of a "militarized state," and organization of a movement to overthrow the leaders who excluded the Baganda from political power, such as Obote and later Idi Amin Dada Oumee, were, from the perspective of the respondents, forms of resistance that prepared the terrain for the 1980s insurgency.[39] One of the respondents talked about her readiness to walk twenty miles on foot and personally take part in the fight for the king during the 1966 crisis, when his palace was attacked and when several subcounty chiefs were arrested.[40]

Obote's removal of the king of the Baganda in 1966 was not the only prominent historical event that was mentioned in interviews. In other accounts, a respondent traced Obote's dislike of the Baganda even further back historically to the period of British colonialism.[41] He noted that Obote did not even like the name Uganda, because it was how the British referred to the Buganda kingdom. The administrative center remained in Kampala, in central Uganda, and the British did not permit the name to be changed or the administrative center to be relocated due to the high costs associated with such actions.[42] Yet, for respondents in other regions of Uganda, such as the West Nile region, 1962, the year of independence from Britain, was a more memorable year of political upheaval and symbolic significance, one whose memory was worthy of being passed down from the members of an older generation to their children.[43]

Still other respondents who mentioned the importance of historical memory noted other mechanisms that were at work in the 1980s in the region of Luweero and that contributed to the polarization and mobilization of people locally.[44] It was the first instances of violence, such as Yoweri Museveni's attack on the military barracks along with the first twenty-six insurgents and the subsequent killing of the subcounty chief in Luweero by the UPC, that contributed to the locals' awareness that the status quo had been altered.[45] What followed were word-of-mouth accounts of the killing of local prominent people by government soldiers, more news about guerilla activities in the area, and the escalation of indiscriminate violence perpetrated by the government against the local population in the area where the guerrilla forces were active. In the recollection of one respondent, he and others around him were not quite sure what was happening.[46] There was an anonymous letter placed on a building in their community that explained the political goals of the insurgents, but people were still skeptical about participation. As the lives of ordinary people became more and more disrupted by targeted violence and they became isolated from the rest of the country, they started organizing to protect themselves and their communities. These interviews show that while memories of historical violence may have played an important role in recruitment and mobilization, other local factors and conditions related to the processes that facilitated the linking of political and regional identities on the ground, such as the division and isolation of the population and the use of force and threats to exclude moderates and recruit supporters, made the targeted violence against civilians possible in the Luweero region.

In Guatemala, a country where the civil war lasted for more than three decades, most of my respondents shared some memories of violence that occurred before the wave of violence in the 1980s. One person noted that the indigenous population in the highlands of Guatemala continued to suffer the consequences of the war even after it ended.[47] Some people in these regions continued to live in limbo, turning to alcoholism or apathy because they were disillusioned by the lack of results their struggle has produced (McAllister and Nelson 2013, 22). Others saw the war as "something that had ended but could always return" (Nelson 2009, 41). From the perspective of one respondent, the violence in the 1980s in the western highlands regions of the country was not simply a product of the Cold War context, as some scholars have argued.[48] Rather, he believed that the origins of the conflict went further back into history, long before the 1960s, because they were directly connected with inequalities resulting from the distribution of land, the only real resource that indigenous communities relied on for their own survival before colonization. In his view, the ideas that indigenous people in this region received from the liberation theology movement, or from other revolutionary movements, were appropriated simply because they addressed the problems that already existed. He mentioned revolutionary movements long before the 1960s, such as the rebellion in Totonicapán led by Atanasio Tzul, a Quiché leader, in 1820 against the Spanish and the establishment of a short-lasting political autonomy for the region. Yet these views of the historical continuity of violent resistance did not account, for example, for the situations in which different members of the family joined opposite sides in the war.[49]

Different individual and local memories of previous waves of violence were mentioned by most respondents in all three countries. They were not sufficient, however, to trigger ethnicization processes locally across all communities. One of the main reasons was that most local memories and communities were not homogenous across the newly relevant identities. In regions where new conditions were created through the exclusion of moderates and the creation of physical barriers that isolated certain communities, local memories became part of the ethnicization discourse in both the official and the unofficial, or family, narratives.

In the next section, I turn to my respondents as teachers and ask them to present their own interpretations regarding a possible link between the past and the more recent waves of political violence, or the role that the memory of violence may have played in their attempts to understand or explain more recent patterns of violence in their own communities.

Memories of Violence from Individual Perspectives

Respondents in all three countries where interviews were conducted were asked the following question, which was slightly modified to fit each context: "Do you think that previous waves of violence in your region are somehow relevant for understanding the contemporary events, and particularly the events connected with the most recent episodes of violence?" In Croatia, a number of participants mentioned connections between the two wars even before they were asked the question directly. For a couple of respondents in Lika, the changes in political institutions—such as the changes in the Croatian Constitution that declared Serbs "an ethnic minority"—in addition to the first incidents of political violence—such as the incident known as Plitvice Bloody Easter (Plitvički krvavi Usrks), in which a Croatian police officer, Josip Jović, was killed in March 1991—served as warnings that what happened in World War II could possibly "happen again."[50] A respondent in central Croatia who lost close family members in both periods reported that the Homeland War reminded her of World War II since her family members died in similar ways.[51] Individuals in central Croatia also recalled the mass slaughter in the Orthodox church Presvete Bogorodice in the town of Glina.[52] The location of this World War II violence became a site of "contested memories," as the former World War II Memorial Center was replaced with the present-day Croatian Cultural Center (Hrvatski dom).[53] Another respondent from this area connected the Homeland War and World War II by noting that when he was being mobilized, his father told him, "When I went to war, I didn't finish that war, but now you will finish it," suggesting that there were unresolved political issues from the past.[54]

When directly asked about connections, however, several respondents questioned those that were made, especially by political leaders and the media. They provided their own analyses of similarities and differences between these two historical periods of violence in their country. For example, those respondents who did not see any connection between the wars in the 1940s and 1990s believed that those two periods represented entirely different historical and political circumstances, given that World War II was a global war, while the Homeland War was a regional war.[55] A respondent from northern Dalmatia who remembered World War II did not find any similarities or connections between the two periods because the scale of the wars was very different, and not comparable, based on her personal experiences.[56] For her, World War II was much worse because there was more violence, she saw the killing of her neighbor, and they had to flee. The respondent's ability to recall the events that occurred in World War II with more detail than the events in the Homeland War may also be an indication that the violence in World War II left a greater impression on her. In a similar vein, a respondent who was born in 1945 in the region of Western Slavonia also did not find any connection because, according to the respondent, World War II was fought in a different time and by a different generation.[57] Other reasons why respondents thought that the two wars were essentially different included views that the main goal of the last war was robbery;[58] that World War II was a "real" war, whereas the Homeland War was not really a war in the respondent's town;[59] that World War II was a worldwide fight against fascism, whereas the Homeland War took place only within the borders of Croatia;[60] that World War II was a struggle against global imperialism, whereas the Homeland War was a struggle against Serbian imperialism;[61] and that "the political circumstances were different," but that the connection was the desire of the Croats to have their own state.[62] In addition, several respondents simply did not know whether there was a connection or whether they saw one, or they did not think about it in such a way.[63]

Especially interesting were the responses that questioned causal connections and noted that attempts to connect the two periods in any way needed to be seen more critically than they had previously.[64] This was the view of the respondent for whom many of the connections that were made were seen as myths used for political purposes.[65] In her view, the personal experiences of war-related trauma actually made people more open-minded than those who heard about such traumas from other sources. This view was echoed by several other individuals who had personal recollections of World War II violence.[66] Another interviewee noted that myths regarding connections could be even more problematic when used by political leaders for political mobilization.[67] This respondent viewed such connections as fabrications of political leaders used to gain political power during the political regime transition in Croatia in the early 1990s. As seen thus far, this was a view that was shared by many respondents.

Yet there were also respondents who believed that there were some similarities or continuities between the two periods. More specifically, respondents identified many different types of connections between the two wars: nationalism,[68] ethnic stereotyping or the highlighting of ethnic or religious differences,[69] the continuation of unresolved issues related to the rights of ethnic majorities or minorities,[70] the pursuit of independence,[71] territorial disputes,[72] experiences of living in a transit zone and the "irrational fear of attack from the outside,"[73] the perception of danger,[74] intergenerational stories of violence from World War II that contributed to distrust in some communities,[75] symbols from World War II that were used to mobilize people in the 1990s,[76] "something" still present from the previous war,[77] acts of violence that may be motivated by revenge for the violence against members of own group during or after World War II in some communities,[78] regional variations in violence in the war and in the postconflict reconstruction,[79] economic crisis and uneven development,[80] veterans' pensions as an economic burden,[81] economic interests and greed,[82] the role of external world powers,[83] and common experiences of survival, exile, and human loss.[84] For example, one respondent perceived a connection between World War II and the Homeland War in the way that Serb and Croat nationalism contributed to fears among ethnic minorities for their status and survival—for the Croats as minorities in the former Yugoslavia after World War II and for the Serbs as minorities in Croatia after 1991.[85] What made this account somewhat different from other respondents' accounts was the respondent's awareness that stereotypes about the "other group" were actually created in the process of narrating the accounts of violence from World War II, and that these stereotypes contributed to the growing distrust among the majority members of the community, regardless of their ethnic identity. Another respondent saw a connection in the way that morality was defined in national, or ethnic, terms, rather than in a more universal way.[86] This respondent presented a critical view of the association of a national identity with morality in her country. She expressed her strong disagreement with this way of conceptualizing morality and categorizing people, and noted that for that reason, she chose to marginalize herself from society's mainstream, particularly during the 1990s. In sum, the interviews from Croatia show that individual interpretations and analyses varied from person to person even within the same region.

Similarly, in Uganda, even though many former participants in the insurgency, survivors, and witnesses evoked past conflicts as they tried to make sense of the violence in the 1980s, each understanding of these connections was different. For instance, the modern political and religious divide in Uganda was understood, in part, as a direct result of the colonial legacy.[87] In the perspective of one respondent, many of the religious, ethnic, and regional cleavages that were still relevant in a subtle way in the modern politics of Uganda could be traced back to the history of British colonialism.[88] The respondent believed that these cleavages were politicized by the British during the independence process and then institutionalized in the Ugandan political system in the postcolonial period. Unlike several other interviewees, he did not mention the crisis of 1966 specifically as a salient historical grievance or single it out as the main event that created an anti-Obote sentiment among the population of central Uganda. Other respondents attributed the political instability in Uganda from the 1960s through the 1980s to the lack of unity among political leaders and parties in the regime transitions following the independence and the unification of different tribes in the state of Uganda as a legacy of the British colonialism.[89] The lack of preparedness for the political transition, people's inexperience with political parties, and the British influence in joining different tribes of East Africa in the single state of Uganda were among the reasons cited for the subsequent political instability and series of crises following the independence of Uganda in 1962. In the postindependence period, people did not know much about parties' ideologies and programs. They supported parties based on the issues and circumstances that were most relevant to the people at the time. Among the population of central Uganda, the monarchist Kabaka Yekka Party and the Democratic Party were popular, while among the northerners, the UPC was more popular, mainly because the party was not supportive of the institution of kingship in postindependent Uganda, which would give more political power and representation to the population of the central part of the country than the population of the North. The issue of kingship was the most divisive in the 1960s, when the Ugandan population was starting to become politically active in their independent state.[90] These analyses thus emphasized a bottom-up mobilization process among the population in central Uganda in the 1980s as a result of historical grievances and colonial legacies.

Several respondents attributed the successful recruitment of insurgents in the 1980s to the mobilizing activities of political leaders.[91] In one respondent's assessment, Museveni "made use" of the "bitterness" that people in the central region had as a result of Obote's overthrow of the king in 1966: "He knew where to go and win people. He knew they had bitterness. He knew they had bitterness which he could exploit and win fighters and he did."[92] In another account, Museveni's success in mobilizing supporters among the Baganda could be explained by the attention he paid to the traditional institution of kingship both symbolically and substantively when the kingship was reinstituted in Uganda following the war.[93] While there is evidence, in both interviews and secondary sources, that Museveni mobilized political support among the Baganda by appealing both to historical grievances among this population as a result of the 1966 actions of Obote and to the cultural tradition of kingship, the interviews also showed that even within the Luweero region, individuals viewed the role of the memory of previous conflicts in connection with the 1980s violence differently.

In Guatemala, different respondents also understood the connections between historical cycles of violence and the wave of violence in the 1980s differently. In relating the conditions under which the rebellion within the military of Guatemala started in 1960, several respondents emphasized the divergence of interests and preferences within the military regarding the influence of foreign powers—namely, the United States—in Guatemalan politics, as well as disagreements regarding internal governance both within the military and within the country.[94] The involvement of the Guatemalan military in the training of the participants in the Bay of Pigs invasion was, in their view, just an immediate factor that prompted the rebellion of those members of the military who had already disagreed with the status quo and the role that foreign powers were allowed to play in domestic politics. Another respondent did not find a direct connection with any particular event in the country's history, but he discussed economic and political power imbalances as a source of conflicts.[95] Unlike other respondents, this interviewee did not specify a particular historic episode of rebellion that could be connected to the more recent conflict, but he talked in general terms about inequality and manipulation by those who hold political and economic power.

Connections between historical and modern conflict may also be indirect. One respondent, for instance, discussed how those in power, beginning with the Spanish in the colonial period, used the national education system to manipulate and weaken indigenous communities. One of the myths taught through this education system was that the Kaqchikel community betrayed the Quiché community when the Spanish arrived. But even before the colonization, rivalry existed between the two ethnic groups. He interprets the repetition of this myth as a deliberate attempt to create new myths and new conflicts in order to weaken the indigenous population of Guatemala and make it easier to conquer them. In response, the indigenous communities found more value in the "teachings" passed on from generation to generation within communities in order to help younger generations. More specifically, the respondent mentioned finding protection from the natural environment and preserving cultural values through narratives embroidered symbolically on national costumes as two examples of how indigenous communities resisted oppression and loss of cultural identity historically.[96]

While other respondents found indirect connections between historical forms of resistance in indigenous communities and more recent forms of resistance, one respondent discussed the significance of the guerrilla movement of the 1960s.[97] He recounted a conversation with a senior member of the original guerrilla movement that started long before the indigenous population of the western highlands of Guatemala was mobilized for insurgency in later years. The respondent did not know the guerrilla movement had existed for such a long time before he and his villagers had ever known about it. In the view of the senior member of the insurgency, the two movements were different because younger generations were ready to kill without understanding fully the reasons for the armed rebellion. Another respondent did not see a direct connection with any particular event, but, as others did, he discussed the origins of the rebellion in terms of historical socioeconomic inequalities.[98] He talked about the efforts of the dominant groups in the nation to oppress the indigenous population economically as a source of cheap agricultural labor on the south coast, but also to oppress them politically and through violence when they organized the insurgency and tried to resist this exploitation. This respondent believed that the violence was the result of attempts by the political and economic elite in the country to exclude the indigenous people. Hence, in Guatemala, respondents, even those who were from the same region, diverged in their understanding of the connections between past conflicts and more recent conflicts.

In this chapter, I examined the role that memories of past waves of violence may play in understanding the sources and patterns of more recent violence. There is evidence that memories, especially intergenerational and local memories, are present in a number of respondents' narratives and interpretations of modern violence. It is important to understand, however, that such memories, particularly local or community memories, may be linked with mobilization for violence. Given that individual, intergenerational, and local memories varied to a great extent, there was no direct association between the memories of past violence and the likelihood that a similar type of violence would occur in the same communities in the modern period. When asked about any possible historical connections, respondents questioned and analyzed the continuities imposed by previous or current political regimes while searching for those, in their view, genuine connections and discontinuities between the more and the less distant past in an attempt to make sense of their own experiences of political violence. Many different interpretations were presented, and they also varied both across the regions and within regions. Therefore, in order to understand why violence, and specifically targeted violence against civilians, was particularly pervasive in some regions and communities, it is not sufficient to analyze solely how memories of previous waves of violence influence individual perceptions and motivations. What is needed is to identify the local conditions under which memories of historical violence become more powerful tools of political mobilization.

This chapter also showed how collective memories were in some cases connected to personal or intergenerational experiences that were seen as inconvenient truths by political regimes. In societies with silenced memories, as political power cycles from regime to regime, or from party to party, leaders, in their mobilization discourse, may bring out collective memories of past cycles of violence in the process of legitimizing their own power or representation of the previously marginalized sectors of society. Yet they tend to also, in some instances, engage in silencing the memories of those experiences that could potentially harm the dominant regime's reputation. Such cycles of the political use of memory, and possible new waves of violence, can be broken, perhaps, by returning the memories to the local and personal realm and by empowering the people to freely remember and commemorate their communities' experiences in any manner they wish. That is an unlikely course of action, however, for leaders who engage in ethnicization efforts. This is because the political use of the memories of violence constitutes the very content of their mobilizing discourse. In this way, some of these leaders work on creating conditions favorable for the control and mobilization of the population on the local level for their participation in political violence. When violence is used as a political strategy, its aim is to include some groups and exclude others from the states conceptualized in terms of newly defined political ethnicities. I analyze the evidence for the use of violence as a political strategy in Croatia, Guatemala, and Uganda in the next chapter.

6

VIOLENCE AGAINST CIVILIANS AS A POLITICAL STRATEGY

Why are civilians targeted even when they do not represent a realistic military threat to the rival side in the war? The explanations that give more significance to factors related to military strategy do not help us understand, for instance, why attacks against civilians are carried out in territory that is already occupied (Hultman 2007; Kalyvas 2006; Metelits 2010; Weinstein 2007; R. Wood 2010). While studies that emphasize prewar ideological cleavages, political grievances, or emotions provide answers to questions regarding why members of some ethnic or political groups are targeted and not others, they still leave several unanswered questions (Balcells 2010; 2017; Bulutgil 2016; Cederman, Gleditsch, and Buhaug 2013; Petersen 2002). Specifically, why do such acts of violence occur only in some communities, even when they all have had similar prewar social cleavages? Why are these acts more extensive at particular times during a war? Why are civilians subjected to excessive and inhumane acts of violence? I argue that we should understand targeted violence against civilians in amoral communities first and foremost as a political strategy.[1] I draw a conceptual distinction between a *political strategy* and a *military strategy* while recognizing that the two may be complementary and used simultaneously by warring armies, political leaders, and the populations these leaders claim to represent.[2] The main distinguishing feature is that a political strategy is characterized by the targeting of individuals who are defined by their *political ethnicity* and excluded from the envisioned nation-state, or nation-body. Violence used as a political strategy may include individualized tactics, such as the torture, rape, harassment, and arrest of civilians in territory that was already conquered, as well as targeted massacres, looting, the burning of property, the destruction of cultural symbols, and the destruction of infrastructure. From the perspective of military strategy, some of these actions may be considered irrational, unnecessary, and ultimately destructive; however, when analyzed from the perspective of political strategy, a consistent pattern can be seen in the acts that target individuals who are perceived by the perpetrators as "political enemies" based on not only their ethnicity but also their political views.

Patterns of Targeted Violence against Civilians in Croatia

Most cases of mass violence against civilians in Croatia occurred in the beginning of the war, during the fall and winter between 1991 and 1992, around the city of Vukovar in Eastern Slavonia; around Pakrac, Okučani, and Daruvar, among others, in Western Slavonia; around Sisak, Glina, and Petrinja in central Croatia; in Gospić and Široka Kula, among other places in Lika; and in or near Škabrnja, Knin, and Šibenik in northern Dalmatia (see figure 2). In the last months of the war in the spring and summer of 1995, when the borders became contested again, the level of violence increased again in all the regions just listed except for Eastern Slavonia, which underwent a peaceful reintegration into the territory of Croatia.

These general patterns of violence may be explained by the existing theories proposed by scholars of civil wars, most notably Stathis Kalyvas in *The Logic of Violence in Civil War* (2006), who argues that the timing of violence in war is linked with the adversaries' efforts to carve out and control particular territories over the course of warfare. Once military control is attained, violence is expected to subside in the occupied territory (244–245). While many cases of violence against civilians in Croatia can be explained in this manner, the targeted massacres of civilians in territories militarily conquered by the perpetrator, particularly those in which noncombatants were targeted on the basis of their presumed ethnicity, still need to be explained, as I have attempted to do throughout this book.

The first instances of targeted mass violence occurred in the summer of 1991 in Eastern and Western Slavonia, central Croatia, and northern Dalmatia (I. Goldstein 2008, 698). For instance, on June 26, 1991, one day after the declaration of Croatian and Slovenian independence from Yugoslavia, a group of ethnic Serbs in central Croatia, in response to the political mobilization discourse of the leaders of the SDS, attacked the police station in the town of Glina near Sisak (Barić 2005, 120; see figure 2). Following the attack, the Croatian police forces were forced to retreat from Glina toward the town of Petrinja, and, based on the analysis of the historian Ivo Goldstein (2008, 698), this strategy indicated the start of a more aggressive phase in the war in Croatia, in which the insurgents collaborated with the JNA in order to create instability through violence in some ethnically mixed regions of Croatia. Only days after the attack on the police station in Glina, on July 6, 1991, armed units of ethnic Serb rebels committed a mass crime against civilians in Ćelije, an Eastern Slavonian village located between Osijek and Vukovar, by expelling ethnic Croats from their homes and burning the village down (698). From that point until the end of 1991, targeted violence against civilians became more frequent and involved increasingly more victims.

The platforms of the nationalist parties that were competing for power in the territory of the former Yugoslavia had been previously described in the programs that linked the political aim of creating a state with the ethnicity of the new state's desired population.[3] The first steps of the political leaders and their respective armies were to decide on the borders of these states and to enforce them through discourse, threats, and small-scale violence targeting individuals who were visible or prominent in some way. In this manner, they sent a message of who was to be included and who was to be excluded. More specifically, in the case of Croatia, once the wartime borders of the RSK in the territory of Croatia were created and the territories conquered by one army or the other, it was time to reinforce the new political order by removing any potential opposition through a combination of physical elimination and terrorism against the coethnics of the adversary and even against the perpetrators' coethnics who were not considered to be politically loyal. While this pattern was repeated throughout the war, the violence was more extensive in the beginning and at the end of the war. In most cases, the armed forces that occupied a territory carried out violent attacks against the civilian population within the first few days of the occupation and, in fewer cases, several weeks or several months following the occupation.

In the area of Sisak, a month after the attack on the Glina police station, on July 26, 1991, ethnic Serb paramilitary forces used ethnic Croat residents as a human shield.[4] One civilian victim, a Croat woman, was shot from the "hill near the road where Serbian paramilitary forces" were located.[5] Serb paramilitary forces also wounded an ethnic Croat who was a member of the police reserve unit while he was walking with the other fifty residents in the group used as a human shield.[6] He was later killed in front of the local health clinic.[7] A number of locals near Glina from both sides' armed forces also lost their lives during this time. For example, an ethnic Croat who was a policeman in the reserve unit died when the bombs around his belt were set off by shelling near him after he attempted to throw a bomb on the tank that was following the civilians in the human shield along the road.[8] An ethnic Serb who was a member of the TO died along with the other four men who were in a vehicle with him in July 1991.[9] There is no specific information about the perpetrators, but before he and the other four men died, locals were throwing bombs at them while the JNA forces were approaching the area.[10]

While several of the killings in this area occurred over the course of the warfare, the decision of the Serb paramilitary forces to round up local civilians in specific villages and use them as a human shield was an act of violence against individuals who did not pose a military threat and who were selected on the basis of their ethnicity. This strategy, while it could be classified in standard scholarly accounts as a military one, corresponds more closely with the type of violence committed in the context of amoral communities for several reasons. One is that not all civilian human lives counted equally in the eyes of the perpetrating armies. Those civilians who were perceived as the adversary's coethnics were targeted. Because it was not possible to deduce one's ethnicity based on any visible markers and without a conversation revealing one's family background, conclusions regarding ethnicity in the war zone were drawn in this situation based on the territory in which individuals lived after the initial dividing lines were set up. Also, most locals knew which villages in the war zone were predominantly ethnic Croat or ethnic Serb. Given that victims were targeted on the basis of their presumed identities—political ethnicities—these acts of violence are better conceived as acts that are part of political strategies than solely as acts constituting the military strategies of the warring armies.

The methods of subjecting civilians who were the adversary's coethnics to deadly situations were repeated throughout the war. In the massacre in Lovas, a town in Eastern Slavonia near Tovarnik (see figure 2), the ethnic Serb paramilitary volunteer unit Dušan Silni, accompanied by the reservists of the JNA and local residents, forced around eighty local ethnic Croats to walk over landmines (Documenta, n.d.e).[11] At the clover field where the paramilitary forces and the JNA had set up the mines in a series of rows, victims were told that they should "hold hands and mow the grass with their feet" (Pančić et al. 2007, 13).[12] A total of twenty-four people died, whether from the mines or from gunshots, while fifteen were wounded in the minefield (Documenta, n.d.e).[13] One of the survivors described what happened after the occupation of Lovas. They were taken to the minefield on October 19, 1991. Beforehand, one or two days after the Serb forces occupied the village, they ordered the locals to keep the gates of their houses open and wear white armbands in order to be distinguished.[14] This was a small multiethnic community where people knew each other and where there were no visible physical differences between the residents of different ethnicities. The requirement to wear white armbands could be interpreted as an attempt to make social boundaries visible in the community and probably also intimidate the victims. On October 18, one day before the massacre, several local Serb perpetrators whom the victims knew by name told the members of the local cooperative (*zadruga*) to report to the building of the cooperative, supposedly for a work meeting. There, they tortured them psychologically and physically. The next morning, the victims were told that they had to dispose of any valuables in a hat before being taken to an unknown location, which turned out to be the clover field where they were forced to walk over the landmines.[15] In this case, the victims were singled out on the basis of their ethnicity. They did not represent any military threat, given that the Serb forces had already occupied the town when they carried out this massacre.

While the Serb forces primarily targeted ethnic Croats in Lovas, over the course of the war, the victims also included residents of other ethnicities when they took the political or military side of the perpetrator's adversary. For example, a local who was not an ethnic Croat or ethnic Serb and who was a member of the Croat armed forces was killed, possibly by the Serb police, after he was wounded and arrested.[16] In some cases, victims could have been targeted due to their lack of a clear political position toward the coethnic perpetrator or due to some other personal matter. In one instance for which we have limited information regarding the exact circumstances, three men, possibly members of the Serb paramilitary forces, took an elderly ethnic Serb civilian from his house in January 1992 and killed him.[17] Even with limited information about these crimes, it may be observed that in Lovas, Serb forces, after they had already established military control in the area, carried out inhumane and excessive acts of violence against the local population, which included many civilians who were mostly of Croat ethnicity, but there were also cases of violence against people of other ethnicities.

Lovas is only one town among many in the region of Eastern Slavonia, which is highly ethnically diverse and is located near the geographic border with Serbia along the Danube, that experienced mass violence against civilian population. The Serb forces and the JNA shelled to the ground the city of Vukovar in their effort to occupy it during the fall of 1991, and many local civilians lost their lives or were forcibly displaced during the more than three months of armed fighting and bombing (ICTY 2004, 31). While this violence may be classified as part of the military strategy by scholars of political violence, the city of Vukovar and the surrounding area also experienced in this war the most extensive postoccupation targeted violence against those civilians who were perceived as potentially loyal to the adversary, based on their ethnicity, ambiguous ethnicity, or political or personal views that did not align strongly with those of the occupying regime (ICTY 2012a, 11).[18] After the ethnic Serb forces occupied the city of Vukovar on November 18, 1991, "thousands of Croats and other non-Serbs" were expelled, many people who participated in the defense of the city were arrested and tortured, and 35 (or more) were murdered (ICTY 2004, 16–17; ICTY 2012a, 12).[19] Furthermore, around November 20, 1991, 264 people from the Vukovar hospital were taken to the nearby Ovčara farm, where, after beatings and torture, most were executed and buried in a mass grave (ICTY 2004, 15).[20] Before being taken to the Ovčara farm, however, on November 19, the ethnic Serb forces took the victims to the facility of Velepromet near the barracks of the JNA, where they were "separated based on political, racial and/or religious grounds and suspicion of involvement in the Croatian forces" (ICTY 2012a, 11).[21] As is evident, the targeted violence against civilians in this case occurred after the Serb armed forces had already occupied the area. They categorized the victims as "enemies" solely on the basis of their political ethnicities. The case of the Ovčara massacre, therefore, represents another example of the use of violence as a political strategy.

A number of top-level political and military leaders of the Serb forces faced trial for war crimes and crimes against humanity in the territory of Eastern Slavonia and other parts of Croatia in the ICTY in The Hague. Several were sentenced, a few were acquitted, and several high-ranking political and military leaders died before the trial was completed. Specifically, in the case of the crimes committed in Vukovar, three former JNA officers, Mile Mrkšić, Miroslav Radić, and Veselin Šljivančanin, faced trial for crimes "on or about 18 to 21 November 1991 against Croats and other non-Serbs who were present in the Vukovar hospital after the fall of Vukovar," which included the responsibility for the 264 victims who were arrested and murdered near the Ovčara farm (ICTY 2007, 1). In 2007, Mrkšić was sentenced to twenty years and Radić was acquitted, while in 2010, Šljivančanin was sentenced to ten years of imprisonment (ICTY 2007, 289; 2010, 14). A number of the perpetrators of the crimes at Ovčara also faced trial in the Belgrade District Court. In 2005, of the sixteen people who were on trial, fourteen were given prison sentences ranging from five to twenty years and two were acquitted (Documenta, n.d.b; ICTY 2007, 4). The case was reversed in 2006 by the Supreme Court of the Republic of Serbia, and following new trials and appeals, eight perpetrators were sentenced for crimes in Ovčara by the appeals court in Belgrade in 2017.[22] Also, for war crimes in Eastern Slavonia, Goran Hadžić, commander of the Serb TO forces in the first two years of the war and the former president of the RSK, was indicted in 2004, but his trial was terminated following his death in 2016 (ICTY, n.d.a). The highest-ranking person who was indicted by the ICTY in 2001 for crimes against humanity and war crimes in the territory of Croatia, including Eastern Slavonia, was Slobodan Milošević, the former president of Serbia.[23] He died in his prison cell from a heart attack in 2006 before the trial was completed (Parker 2006). For war crimes in other parts of Croatia, Milan Martić, who started as a police chief in Knin and rose to the position of the president of the RSK, was sentenced to thirty-five years of imprisonment (ICTY 2008, 129). Without going into the details of the trials and the reasons for particular sentences, as this would be beyond the scope of this book, it is important to acknowledge that the role of the ICTY in bringing justice for the victims of crimes against humanity committed by various armed forces in the territory of the former Yugoslavia was criticized by scholars for a number of reasons, including the length of time the ICTY took to complete trials, the degree to which justice was served in some cases from the victims' perspectives, and the tribunal's effectiveness in promoting both justice and reconciliation in the regions affected by wars in which not only a lack of justice but also political corruption represented challenges to the development of democratic institutions and the rule of law (Gordy 2013; Subotić 2009). Despite these shortcomings, the work of the ICTY was significant in gathering evidence and, in a number of cases, successfully sentencing people who were responsible for crimes committed against civilians. In other words, there is extensive evidence now that violence against civilians in certain multiethnic communities across Croatia constituted a political strategy because it occurred after the armed forces of the perpetrator had already established military control over the area and people were targeted on the basis of their presumed ethnicity, which, following the exclusion of moderates and the forced division of the local population along the new ethnically defined borders discussed in the previous chapters, served as a marker of potential political loyalty to the new regime.

The use of violence as a political strategy, or targeted violence against civilians after the occupation, rather than as part of military advancement, is one of the key characteristics of amoral communities. To further illustrate this point, I will briefly discuss three different cases of massacres that occurred in central Croatia in the first year of the war: in Novo Glinsko Selo (near Glina), in Baćin (near Košutarica on the border with Bosnia and Herzegovina), and in Joševica (near Glina). In Novo Glinsko Selo, Serb paramilitary formations killed thirty-two civilians in October 1991 (ICJ 2001, 16). There was no military fighting in this location at the time, and only elderly people who were unarmed stayed behind.[24] The perpetrators were believed to be Serb paramilitary armies consisting of people from the neighboring villages, including some people who personally knew the victims, but it is also possible that this act of violence was performed by some people from the outside the community.[25] Even without complete information about this event, it is evident that violence was committed against noncombatants after the fighting was over and the victims did not perceive themselves to be in immediate danger. While it is possible that this crime was committed by nonlocal forces, at least one person on the perpetrator's side was a local who warned one of the people he recognized to escape.[26] As in other cases, victims were specifically targeted on the basis of their ethnicities.

The massacre in the area of Baćin took place in October 1991 when the Serb forces were in control of the territory and Croatian forces had already withdrawn.

Of the roughly 120 civilians who had fled from other war-affected areas to the neighboring villages of Dubica, Cerovljani, and Baćin, 53 were gathered by force and held in the Dubica fire station (ICTY 2004, 13–14; ICTY 2005, 282–283).[27] Ten people were released after it was established that they were ethnic Serbs or "had connections with Serbs," and the next day, after the remaining detained individuals were transferred to another location near Baćin, the detainees were executed along with other individuals who were brought from Baćin, Cerovljani, and Dubica (ICTY 2005, 282–283). There were three ethnic Serbs, however, who remained and were killed along with the ethnic Croats because two refused to vote in the referendum that would make their town part of the SAO Krajina and one refused to join the local Serb leadership.[28] This case shows that individuals were targeted not solely on the basis of their ethnicity but also on the basis of their potential political loyalty to the newly established regime of the RSK. The perpetrators assessed potential loyalty on the basis of family or other personal connections with ethnic Serbs or on the basis of individuals' political preferences. Given that violence was used as a political strategy, the killing of local ethnic Serbs who did not demonstrate support for the RSK regime served both to eliminate possible political opposition and as a threat (i.e., in-group policing) to any other members of the local community who might express criticism toward the new regime.

The crime in Joševica occurred in December 1991, also in the area that was already under the control of ethnic Serbs. On December 16, 1991, twenty-one people were killed (Documenta, n.d.c). A witness stated that he saw two people in camouflage uniforms arriving in the early afternoon at his house and described how he managed to hide when his wife was killed (Pandža Orkan 2012, 77). Unlike in the cases of Novo Glinsko Selo and Baćin, the local Serb authorities in Joševica carried out an investigation and produced a forensics report (78–81). Based on the report, all victims were civilians, including many elderly individuals and four children between the ages of ten and sixteen, and all died from close-range shots to the head (78–81). The possible perpetrators who were identified in these reports were the soldiers in the Reconnaissance-Commando Unit Glina (Izviđačko-diverzantska grupa Glina), who were training in Serbia at the time the report was written (82).[29] This crime was reported, and interpreted locally, as an act of revenge for the military operation in a nearby village in which ethnic Serbs were killed.[30] The targets in Joševica were people, including women and elderly residents, who were not members of the armed forces on either side.[31] This case was different from the others because the local RSK government attempted to carry out an investigation. Yet it was also similar to the others in that the victims were noncombatants who were killed after the territory was already under the control of the Serb forces and the perpetrators were not held accountable for this crime during the war, or even many years after the war (Documenta, n.d.c).

The three cases of Novo Glinsko Selo, Baćin, and Joševica all share certain characteristics. The mass violence did not take place over the course of the military's advancement, and the violence occurred relatively soon after the conquest of the desired territory. The Serb forces carried out the first two crimes only days after the occupation, while in the third case, Joševica, the massacre was perpetrated several months later. Only in Joševica is there evidence that the local authorities investigated and at least demonstrated the intention of holding the perpetrators accountable. The investigation, however, did not result in any legally determined sanctions or even in a trial during the war. Finally, as all three cases occurred in the first year of the war, when the new political regimes were still being consolidated and faced potential challenges from both inside and outside the occupied territory, these acts of violence can be interpreted as part of the political strategy to divide the local population even further than it already had been through the processes of ethnicization discussed in the earlier chapters. As a result of the targeted violence against civilians, people became separated not only by the wartime dividing lines or borders but also by hatred for each other on the basis of ethnicity. As the cases of targeted violence accumulated rapidly in the first year of the war, so did the drive for revenge, and political discourse was used to highlight the victimization of one's own ethnic group while minimizing, or even outright denying, the extent of the crimes one's group committed against the rival group's civilians. This further fueled the distortion of the population's perception of reality, hatred, and the drive for violence, thus permitting the military and political leaders of the new regimes to control the population in amoral communities more effectively.

The next two cases of civilian massacres also took place in the beginning of the war in the regions of Lika and northern Dalmatia. In the village of Široka Kula, located in Ličko-senjska županija, Serb paramilitary forces, among whom were several locals who knew their victims, attacked civilians and killed eight people of Croat ethnicity on October 13, 1991.[32] The Serb armed forces entered the village in the course of the fighting with Croat armed forces in nearby Lički Osik, where Serb forces also committed violence against civilians.[33] Following the harassment of the civilian population in Široka Kula, members of the armed forces directed civilians into the bomb shelter, where they shot and killed them.[34] About a month later, on November 18, 1991, in the northern Dalmatian village of Škabrnja in Zadarska županija, the ethnic Serb armed forces committed another massacre against the civilian population. On that day, Serb forces, including members of the JNA, Martić's police (police force of the RSK under the command of Milan Martić based in Knin), and the TO, went from one house to the next and killed a total of thirty-eight non-Serb civilians, in addition to another seven in the neighboring village of Nadin the following day (ICTY 2004, 14–15).[35] Between November 18, 1991, and February 1992, Serb forces killed another twenty-nine ethnic Croat civilians from Škabrnja (ICTY 2004, 15).[36] One of my respondents interpreted the massacre in Škabrnja as an instance of mass violence that had a strategic purpose of frightening, and controlling, the people of Croat ethnicity across northern Dalmatia.[37] The respondent viewed this act of violence as contributing to the already present sense of fear and, relatedly, the hatred for the perpetrators' ethnic group, resulting in the division of the local population in northern Dalmatia along ethnic lines.[38] Unlike in other examples, the places in which the crimes took place were not already occupied when the ethnic Serb forces committed violence against civilians. As in other examples, however, civilians who clearly did not pose any military threat were targeted exclusively on the basis of their ethnicity or political orientation.

This spiraling of violence along ethnic lines is evident in the next case, as well. Several days after the massacre of ethnic Croat civilians in Široka Kula that occurred on October 13, 1991, a number of ethnic Serb and some ethnic Croat civilians in Gospić, Ličko-senjska županija, were killed by Croat forces on October 17–18, 1991.[39] The victims from the city of Gospić and the surrounding area were first rounded up, then taken to the military headquarters in Perušić, and finally transported to the location where they were killed by shooting.[40] In this case, the victims of Serb ethnicity included some individuals whose family members were in the Croatian armed forces, some who signed statements expressing loyalty to the Republic of Croatia, one who had been a member of the Croatian Army, and even some who participated in the civilian protection of the city of Gospić.[41] The investigation of this case was hindered by the assassination of one of the ICTY's key witnesses, Milan Levar, in 2000. Only twenty-four bodies were found in Lipova Glavica, where the victims were burned and thrown on top of the landfill.[42] Even though the information on this case is limited, it is evident that people were singled out by Croat forces on the basis of their ethnicity primarily, including even ethnic Serbs who demonstrated in some way that they were politically loyal, and on the basis of the political loyalty of ethnic Croats (i.e., as a form of in-group policing). The violence took place in territory that was still under the attack of the Serb forces, but it was under the control of ethnic Croat forces when the violence against civilians was carried out. Therefore, the civilian casualties did not occur over the course of a military operation or a bombing campaign.

These cases from Lika and northern Dalmatia, in addition to the cases mentioned earlier from other regions where mass violence against civilians occurred during the first year of the war, are the most extreme examples of the use of violence as a political strategy. Through direct violence, people were taught to fear expressing personal political views and preferences that may be critical of the newly established regimes. Through this strategic use of violence, people were also taught to hate their former neighbors whose ethnicity corresponded to that of the rival armed forces who committed violence against civilians in their communities. In those regions where the conditions of amoral communities were created, people were discouraged from expressing their personal views and were forced to choose sides, as the foregoing examples illustrate. More importantly, the violence against people perceived as political adversaries, even if they were the perpetrators' coethnics, sent a warning message to other local residents that they should remain politically loyal to the regime in power.

The war in Croatia ended between August 4 and 5, 1995, with the military counterinsurgency operation of the Croatian Army known as Operation Storm (Oluja). On the eve of this military operation, in anticipation of violence and as a result of the warnings received from their neighbors or, in some cases, from their local governments, tens of thousands of residents in the RSK territories left their homes in convoys and headed toward Serbia.[43] The exact number of people who fled their homes in Croatia, for a short period or indefinitely, is not known.[44] Also, the precise number of civilians who lost their lives as a result of Oluja is not known.[45] Even without having the precise number of victims or the exact dates when they were killed, the existing studies show that most victims did not die over the course of the warfare but rather were killed from close proximity though they did not pose a military threat (Graovac 2004a, 2004b).[46] The perpetrators included both members of different armed forces and armed civilians (Graovac 2004a, 144). Thus, the patterns of targeted violence following the military occupation are similar to the cases of violence against civilians committed by the Serb forces against Croat civilians in the first year of the war, and as such, they also constitute the use of violence as a political strategy, as well as a military strategy.

Following eleven years of trial in the ICTY in The Hague, on November 16, 2012, the Croatian Army generals who planned Oluja, Generals Ante Gotovina, Ivan Čermak, and Mladen Markač, were found not guilty of "convictions for persecution, deportation, murder, and inhumane acts as crimes against humanity, and of plunder of public and private property, wanton destruction, murder, and cruel treatment as violations of customs of war" (ICTY 2012b, 55).[47] This judgment of the ICTY constituted a reversal of its earlier decision, on April 15, 2011, when only Čermak was acquitted and Gotovina and Markač were sentenced to twenty-four years and eighteen years of imprisonment, respectively (ICTY 2011, 1339–1341.[48] A number of controversies regarding the role of the ICTY as an institution of justice and the symbolic role of Gotovina in Croatian society and in the reconciliation efforts have already been addressed extensively in the scholarship

(Pavlaković 2008a, 2010). Not surprisingly, Oluja was also interpreted differently by different groups (Žunec 2007, 732). From the perspective of the Croatian government, Oluja constituted a rightful act of reclaiming parts of its national and sovereign territory according to international law, and from the perspective of human rights organizations and the victims, the crimes against the civilians and their property in the aftermath of the military operation should have been prevented, stopped, or investigated by the authorities (732). One of the negative long-term implications of the lack of legal action against the perpetrators of violence against civilians, in general, is that it reduces the likelihood of reconciliation in communities that experienced such violence, because for the people who were taught by the horrific acts of violence described in this chapter to distrust others on the basis of ethnicity, even the perceived lack of justice may continue to feed their growing sense of victimization at the expense of their empathy for *all* civilian victims who suffered or died in the same way, regardless of their ethnicity.

In addition to targeted violence against civilians, the destruction of cultural content and symbols associated with the excluded political ideology or the excluded ethnicity also represents a political strategy. This may be done in preparation for violence, during the violent campaigns, or in the aftermath. In the Croatian context, the monuments that were connected with antifascist ideology or with the former Yugoslavia were systematically destroyed, starting with the political regime transition in the 1990s, by the supporters of the new ethnically defined nationalist regimes among both ethnic Serbs and ethnic Croats (Karačić, Banjeglav, and Govedarica 2012; Pavlaković 2008c, 2011).[49] In the areas that were transformed into amoral communities during the war in the 1990s, both Croat and Serb armed forces participated in the destruction of antifascist monuments commemorating not only the antifascist struggle but also the political motto of Brotherhood and Unity that was employed by Josip Broz Tito and the Yugoslav regime as a post-World War II reconciliation attempt (Dragojević and Pavlaković 2017; Pavlaković 2013, 903). For instance, the monument of Marko Orešković in the town of Korenica, located in the region of Lika, was destroyed by the Serb paramilitary forces (Dragojević and Pavlaković 2017; Pavlaković 2013, 903). Also, there were attempts to change some antifascist monuments by replacing a five-pointed-star with a cross and a Croatian coat of arms (Hrženjak 2002, xiii).[50] An example of the symbolic transformation of the site of memory was the decision of the local authorities in 1995 to rename Glina's Memorial Center (Spomen dom), located on the site of the Presvete Bogorodice Orthodox Church and the massacre of local Serbs by the Ustaša in World War II, as the Croatian Cultural Center (Hrvatski dom), which was originally a building adjacent to the church. This decision to use the actual historical name of a building that had been demolished in 1976 for a place that commemorated a World War II crime committed by the Ustaša regime is highly problematic because it represents a "politics of memory" that promotes "competition in victimization," ethnically defined, instead of interethnic reconciliation in a community with a rich history of interethnic cooperation and tolerance.[51]

In addition to this evidence of the destruction, neglect, or transformation of monuments associated with Croatia's World War II and socialist past, Ante Lešaja also documented the destruction of politically, ideologically, or culturally sensitive literature from the public libraries across Croatia throughout the 1990s "even outside of the areas affected by war atrocities" (2012, 69, 127).[52] In Croatia in the early 1990s, the clearing of the libraries of specific ideological or cultural influences was accompanied by the cleansing, or "purifying," of the language of words with foreign roots, and particularly words that sound Serbian (Kordić 2010, 22–27). The practice of removing from the libraries and textbooks the content that is connected with competing political ideologies, excluded political ethnicities, or alternative narratives of violence was documented not only in Croatia but also in other neighboring ethnically defined states, such as Serbia and Bosnia and Herzegovina, and continued throughout the 1990s, and even through the 2000s (Subotić 2013).

In addition to monuments and books, churches corresponding to the religions of the excluded groups were also damaged or destroyed systematically by armies claiming control over a given territory throughout the war. For instance, Serb armies destroyed 571 Catholic churches, based on the report of the Croatian bishops' conference in 1996 (Perica 2002, 3–4, 248).[53] Just like the targeted violence against civilians, the destruction of cultural symbols connected with excluded political ethnicities could be seen as a political strategy to gain authority and control over the population in the newly occupied territory designated to be part of the state envisioned as a nation-body.

Violence against Civilians as a Political Strategy in Civil Wars

In order to understand why civilians are targeted in civil wars on the basis of their ethnicity, religion, race, or other cultural traits, it is not sufficient to consider only the military strategies of competing armies. As the analysis of several cases of mass violence in Croatia has shown, civilians were targeted when they did not pose any threat to the perpetrators' armed forces. Civilians were singled out on the basis not only of their ethnicity but also of their political orientation. Perpetrators targeted certain individuals or groups in order to eliminate political opposition in the newly conquered territory, which represented to the occupying armies and their political leaders the extension of their nation-body, a new state defined in terms of the politically, socially, and economically dominant ethnicity. In this section, I compare these patterns with the patterns of violence in the cases of Uganda and Guatemala, two countries with different histories and national-level conditions associated with internal conflict compared to Croatia.

As already mentioned in earlier chapters, during the war in Uganda in the early 1980s, the central region was the base of both the NRA insurgents and the predominantly ethnic Baganda population in opposition to the Obote regime and supportive of the NRA insurgency. While civilians and members of various armed forces lost their lives over the course of the war in Uganda in many different situations and for many different reasons, civilians were also targeted on the basis of their suspected political views and their political ethnicities.[54] More specifically, in the area surrounding the town of Semuto in the Nakaseke District, civilians who were seen as supporters of the NRA were targeted by the UNLA and the supporters of the UPC (Mutibwa 2009, 73–74; Kasozi 1994, 147–148; Weinstein 2007, 226–229).

A particular practice of targeting suspected or potential members of rebel forces in public places by government forces in the 1980s was known as *Panda Gari* (Baguma 2009, 68). *Panda Gari* entailed mass arrests of political opponents in urban areas of central Uganda and in public places where young men were picked out from the crowd and taken away on trucks or buses (Kasozi 1994, 147–148). While the general region where these operations took place was the area from which insurgents recruited their followers, the soldiers making arrests were less concerned with identifying the actual insurgents than with sending a message to the local population of the area. In such situations, individuals with weapons at the roadblocks had the ultimate power because they could arrest anyone who looked suspicious for whatever reason without any concrete evidence against them (Kalema 2009, 81). By publicizing and broadcasting the names of those who were arrested, the government aimed to frighten and discourage other citizens from joining the insurgency. Yet the oppressive and arbitrary nature of the victimization of civilians in the *Panda Gari* operations actually had a contrary and politicizing effect, as many young people became motivated to join the antigovernment forces.[55] While presumed political views were the main reason for targeting particular individuals, sometimes ethnic or cultural identities served as a shortcut for identifying political enemies.[56] For example, the Baganda from central Uganda were targeted because the insurgents were based in this region, and many people from this region were assumed to be against the Obote-led government (Kutesa [2006] 2008, 159).[57] Also, the Munyankole from West Uganda were targeted because Yoweri Museveni was from that tribe and that region.[58]

The process of ethnicization through targeted violence was a two-way process throughout the war. Just as the government forces assumed that westerners and the people from the Luweero Triangle were connected with the guerrilla forces, so too the guerrillas assumed that the people from the North and the East supported the government.[59] The social ties among the elites in the government, which were based on their places of origin, and presumably their ethnicities, in the perspective of one respondent, created group cohesion among the government and the pro-government forces.[60] In one case, a person who worked as an electoral officer in an area where no one voted for the ruling party was arrested, probably because the regime in power thought "he had influenced the votes in this area, since there was no vote there for the ruling party."[61] Another respondent confirmed a similar pattern of targeting individuals based on an assumption that political views coincided with a person's ethnicity or a place of origin.[62] This respondent clarified that the link between political and ethnic or regional identities was made during the war not only by various armed forces looking for enemies or political leaders but also by the general population.[63] In situations in which the armed forces did not have a social base of support, as in the case of government soldiers vis-à-vis the population in central Uganda at various checkpoints, individuals' ethnic, linguistic, regional, or tribal identities became a shortcut for identifying political enemies (Mi 2009, 131–132). The soldiers guarding checkpoints sometimes even used body scars to distinguish a potential insurgent, presuming that the scar signifies that a person could have been harmed in a combat situation.[64] In the war-affected areas, and even in urban areas where people did not know each other personally, there were no guarantees of safety during the war, and people used regional or ethnic identities as shortcuts in assessing potential danger or harm in their immediate surroundings.

Targeted violence against people of certain ethnicities or certain geographic origins associated with a particular political allegiance further contributed to divisions along political, ethnic, and geographic lines among the population locally. Once the ethnicization was set in motion, then any members of ethnic groups that were labeled as enemies, whether they were part of an actual political movement or an insurgency, and civilians who were not active politically, as well as anything associated with that group, including their cultural symbols or property, became the target of violence (Kasozi 1994, 158; Kutesa [2006] 2008; 18–19).[65] For example, political and social gatherings in the Luweero Triangle were, in the words of a former NRA commander, "a legitimate target for the UNLA's massacres" (Kutesa [2006] 2008, 122). One military operation took place in June 1983 in the Wakiso District, while another one, in which sixty people were killed and thousands arrested, took place in March 1983 in the Luweero District (Kasozi 1994, 147–148). In those attacks, soldiers engaged in harassing residents, robbing, raping women, and arresting young men who were suspected to be connected with the guerrilla forces (147–148). On one occasion, in the account of one respondent, young men in the village were rounded up by the soldiers and killed by a firing squad.[66] Government soldiers also used civilians in these communities as human shields to protect themselves when moving across the area.[67] One respondent described how on her visit to Luweero during the war, she witnessed for the first time the "deliberate targeted rape of women," and while it was not known with certainty who the perpetrators were, in that case, it was "largely said that Milton Obote's army" was responsible.[68] Other respondents and witnesses also noted that "the national army was raping women and even abducting people" and that those of higher socioeconomic status, as well as "those who belonged to Museveni's political party," were the ones who were targeted.[69]

The government categorized not only the insurgents but also the civilians in this region as political enemies in part due to their mutually protective and supportive relationship with the insurgents.[70] Throughout the war, whenever the guerrillas would receive news that the government soldiers were arriving, entire villages in Luweero would be evacuated.[71] As the government under Obote was not only politically but also militarily challenged by the insurgents, operations such as the *Panda Gari* or attacks on civilians in the insurgent-held territories were seen by the regime in power as legitimate forms of identifying the enemy. The message was that "one would not know when one would be picked up for a guerrilla and sent for ultimate slaughter" like a "hunted animal" (Bahemuka 2009, 64). In other words, being identified as an enemy of the state transformed former citizens into excluded groups that were dehumanized (Derrida 2009, 2010; Haleem 2012). By carrying out a conspicuous performance of violent mass arrests of young men, civilians in these public spaces were made aware that supporting the insurgents made them political enemies, and, in the "state of emergency" declared by the government under Obote, violence against them was used not only as a military strategy but also, ultimately, as a political one.

Among the insurgents, also, there were efforts to identify political enemies using shortcuts such as person's place of origin or personal background (Kutesa [2006] 2008, 122). In some villages and towns across the Luweero area, the communities were so tight-knit that it was possible to identify a potential political opponent by relying on locals to identify people who were not familiar to others or who were not from the area (122). In the words of one of my respondents, the relationship based on trust between the insurgent forces and the local population was the source of the strength of the guerilla forces vis-à-vis the government forces.[72] Instead of the individuals of a particular ethnicity or political view, it was the socially embedded individuals who were assumed to belong to the community politically, as members of the Democratic Party and also as supporters of the insurgents.⁷³ Because most people in these rural communities knew each other, it was possible to use social ties and the town of origin as a shortcut categorization for those who belonged and those who were to be excluded, even if people did not fully trust one another in general under the conditions of war. This is how sympathizers of the Obote regime were singled out by the communities in the insurgent-controlled areas and labeled as traitors, or *ekipinga*, not by the insurgents but by the local population. Then individuals who held different political views from the majority became targets of violence during the war by the members of their own communities.⁷⁴

In Guatemala in the early 1980s, the "extreme repression" of civilians in the predominantly indigenous area of the western highlands, which was associated with political opposition, under the regime of Lucas García, came to be seen as "increasingly counterproductive" (Schirmer 1998, 18). It was during this period that a new leader, Efraín Ríos Montt, assumed power through a coup in March 1982. Montt not only ousted García and his supporters but also "annulled the electoral law and 1965 constitution, dissolved Congress, suppressed political parties and imposed a state of siege" (J. A. Booth, Wade, and Walker 2014, 180; Garrard-Burnett 2010; McAllister and Nelson 2013). Even though it was García who began the scorched-earth counterinsurgency campaign, it was under Montt that violence against civilians escalated: "The most violent month of the entire thirty-six-year civil war was April 1982, during Ríos Montt's first six weeks in power, when in a single thirty-day period 3,330 people died at the hands of their own government" (Garrard-Burnett 2010, 89). This resulted in a devastating loss of life among the civilian population in the specific geographic areas that the army identified with insurgents (Brockett 2005, 123–124). One of this military campaign's phases, known as Fusiles y Frijoles (Beans and Bullets), effectively ethnicized the conflict by targeting noncombatants, predominantly the Mayan population in the western highlands of Guatemala (Garrard-Burnett 2010, 86). While my respondents described some differences in the violence under the two leaders, they confirmed that both leaders essentially engaged in targeted violence against the civilian population where the insurgents were based with a goal to discourage the political and logistical support that local population was providing for the rebels. Specifically, in El Quiché, a group of respondents from the same community described attacks, including looting and destruction of property, by soldiers in their village in 1982 under the regime of García.⁷⁵ The counterinsurgency campaigns under both leaders could, therefore, be classified as both military and political uses of violence.

One of the main reports documenting wartime human rights violations during this period, which was published by Guatemala's Commission for Historical Clarification (La Comisión para el Esclarecimiento Histórico) in 1999, "attributed

93 percent of the war's acts of violence . . . to the army and state security forces" and "described the killings as genocidal because 83 percent of the victims were indigenous, and the attacks on the indigenous population were part of a deliberate strategy to rid the rebels of support" (J. A. Booth, Wade, and Walker 2014, 186–187). The report was criticized both by the military and by human rights activists. The military "criticized the report for political bias" (Sieder 2001, 191). Human rights activists criticized its limited potential for achieving justice for victims since its main purpose was "to investigate human rights violations committed during the armed conflict, clarify the causes and consequences of that conflict, and formulate specific recommendations to prevent future abuses of human rights," though the report did not "individualize responsibility for abuses" (190). The other main report documenting human rights abuses was published by REMHI in 1998. While the first report was only criticized publicly, the second report, also containing extensive evidence of human rights abuses that included victims and perpetrators of all identities, which should have been seen as a genuine effort of the civil society led by the Catholic Church of Guatemala toward reconciliation, was accompanied by the assassination of the head of the REMHI, Bishop Juan Gerardi, near his home only two days after the report was published (191). Gerardi, in a similar way as Milan Levar in Croatia, who was assassinated years after the war had ended following his testimony to the ICTY concerning human rights abuses in his hometown, attempted to delegitimize publicly the political justification for the use of violence against the civilian population.

While the two reports documenting violence during this period, that published by Guatemala's Commission for Historical Clarification and that published by REMHI, estimate the number of victims to be around two hundred thousand, there are a number of controversies with respect to "counting" and categorizing victims (Nelson 2015, 63–64).[76] The findings in both of these reports, in addition to many subsequent testimonies of survivors and families of victims, among the efforts of many other researchers, judges, and activists, contributed to bringing former president Montt to trial for genocide in 2012 (McAllister and Nelson 2013, 23). Even though in 2013 he was "convicted of genocide and crimes against humanity and sentenced to 80 years of prison," a retrial was ordered due to a procedural error (J. A. Booth, Wade, and Walker 2014, 195–196). Montt passed away in 2018 before the trial was completed, however. For human rights advocates, the survivors of the violence that took place in Guatemala in the early 1980s, and the victims' families, just as in the case of the deaths of Milošević and Hadžić before the completion of their trials, the lack of closure is disappointing because these leaders' "responsibility" for the human rights violations that occurred when they held political and military power was not established legally or formally (Gordy 2013). Even though the courts are essential in gathering evidence and sentencing those who are responsible for human rights violations, they are ultimately limited in achieving reconciliation in the communities where violence against civilians has already happened.

At the height of violence during the war in Guatemala in the early 1980s, regions across the country varied in their levels of violence against civilians. Among the most violent regions were the villages considered by the military as "red" because this is where the insurgency was based, and "entire villages... were massacred," including civilians, in "Chimaltenango, northern and southern Quiché, and northern Huehuetenango" (Schirmer 1998, 55). From the perspective of the military, the attacks and killings, including the murders of civilians, in the places associated with insurgency were seen as part of a military strategy and as "unfortunate but necessary consequences in their justified campaign strategy to destroy the guerrillas," while the responsibility for the crimes, in their view, rested with "the guerrilla[s] for using villagers as shields" (56–57). Yet, in those areas labeled as red zones or enemy territory, particularly in the western highlands of El Quiché, "no distinction was made between the *guerrilleros* and their peasant supporters," and entire villages were obliterated as part of the scorched-earth campaigns (48). Entire communities where the population was linked with insurgency were attacked indiscriminately (Garrard-Burnett 2010, 16). In one respondent's experience, a violent campaign against the civilians in his village was carried out, probably as a result of revenge by the military for having suffered attacks by the guerrillas.[77] Another respondent, however, did not know why the military murdered civilians, including children, in her village. People would see cadavers, and just "turn in the opposite direction" silently, afraid to say anything.[78]

In the areas labeled by the military as red, it was almost impossible to remain neutral. Even if a person succeeded in remaining neutral throughout the war, he or she was warned by the guards at the checkpoints to be careful and avoid the red areas.[79] As in the cases of Croatia and Uganda, one's ethnicity did not predetermine which side of the conflict he or she would choose.[80] In one respondent's recollection, "there were very few *ladinos* there," and this could have been a deliberate strategy of the predominantly *ladino* political elites in the state to weaken the population that the guerrillas mobilized politically and used as a base of support.[81] My respondent also could have joined either side, regardless of his ethnicity, but preferred to maintain a neutral stance, given that he had a choice. As a neutral person, he had access to both sides.[82] It was, therefore, after individuals took sides, whether voluntarily or by force, that ethnicity *and* political orientation started to matter in determining who would be the target of violence by the armies.

Part of the training of the army intelligence officers consisted of teaching them how to perceive victims as political enemies first and foremost, rather than as human beings, so that they could be prepared to kill them and, if necessary, to extract information from them by subjecting them to extreme cruelty: "When you arrive at this section, they tell you that if they ordered you to kill your mother, you would have to go and kill her. Or your father, or your uncles, or your brothers, or any friend or relative—you couldn't refuse" (Schirmer 1998, 286). The military of Guatemala, as a professional institution, trained cadets to follow the "rules of engagement" (*reglas de enfrentamiento*) they were given by their officers, and they were not supposed to harm an innocent person or civilians, rape women, or steal property from civilians.[83] In practice, however, in areas designated as enemy territory, the lawlessness was a context that provided "unwritten" permission to loot property and rape women (289). Some individuals who perpetrated violence thought that the "cruelty and savagery" would be rewarded with a "rise in rank in accordance with the number of unfortunates they execute" (Montejo 1987, 39). When a certain community is labeled as enemy territory, then the entire community becomes a target of violence: "We kidnap, we torture. Frankly, we aren't very interested in their identity" (Schirmer 1998, 288). If, over the course of torturing, an innocent person was killed, and that person's family inquired about the crime, they would be told that the intelligence officer who committed the crime in error was punished, but he would only be transferred to another place, where he would not have contact with the victim's family (291). One of my respondents described how his relative, who was innocent, was kidnapped and killed even though the family and the community tried to save him repeatedly while he was in prison.[84] These areas that were categorized as guerrilla or enemy territory during the war had characteristics of amoral communities because the perpetrators did not make a distinction between civilians and combatants, and the violence against the communities categorized as political enemies was extreme and far beyond what would have been necessary to deter the insurgents militarily. Because the local population in those communities was seen as a political and logistical extension of the guerrillas, or the enemy of the state, the use of violence was justified by the armed forces on the basis of the narrative of the "state of exception" or emergency situation and their concern for the security of citizens who did not support the rebellion.

The introduction of civil patrols was an attempt to turn the population politically away from the guerrillas and toward the government. Some civil patrollers were forced to kill their own community members who were accused of being guerrilla supporters (REMHI 1999, 23).[85] Based on my respondents' accounts, some communities literally switched sides, almost from one day to the next, from being guerrilla supporters to being army supporters in exchange for amnesty and access to food and other basic resources they lacked while being isolated by the violence.[86] Based on personal accounts, for men who joined the civil patrols, this was more a strategy of survival than a result of their own convictions. During that time, in this particular village they continued to protect their neighbors by always saying that they had not seen any members of the guerrilla forces in the region.[87]

While the armed units representing the state perpetrated most violence, insurgents also engaged in violence against civilians in the war-affected areas (Garrard-Burnett 2010, 16). The view that the time of war was somehow different due to the state of emergency and, therefore, the use of excessive violence or extrajudicial killings was justified applied not only to the military but also to the guerrillas (Santa Cruz [2004] 2006, 194). For example, members of the military who were not in combat at the time of the attack were also subject to violence by the guerrillas.[88] As it did not occur in the context of defense or combat, this act of violence could also be categorized as a political use of violence. The symbolic and excessive use of violence by the guerrillas as a political strategy was also evident in the act of torturing a victim by carving the name of a guerrilla organization, the EGP, on the victim's skin.[89]

In Guatemala, the regions where insurgents were based became places where wartime conditions made the values of mutual protection and loyalty that had existed between family members, friends, and neighbors in peacetime secondary to fears about survival and anxiety about security. In those regions, violence against civilians constituted not only a military strategy but also a political strategy designed to gain the political support of the population.

The Ethnicizing Role of the Political Use of Violence

Thus far, I have shown how mass violence was used as a political strategy against those who represented opposition, on the basis of their presumed ethnicity or political position, throughout the war with an aim to create new political spaces that would form a foundation for future states. In the case of Croatia, the ethnicizing effects of violence did not end with the war. Rather, the mass violence reinforced the process of ethnicization that had been triggered earlier, "dehumanized"[90] the victims of violence, and created a deeper divide among populations that had previously shared the same territory. Yet it cannot be claimed that even in former amoral communities, these effects were universal. Many people stated that they did not understand the purpose of violence as it was presented to them by political leaders or the media, and, both during the war and afterward, they continued to give greater importance to the human qualities of people in their communities than to their ethnicity or political views.

In the view of a respondent from central Croatia, the ways in which the media framed reports of wartime crimes tended to divide people along ethnic lines in the aftermath of mass violence: "Whatever is done, the media says, 'Četniks did it,' but there is no nation that is criminal in its entirety; rather, each nation has its criminals."[91] In this example, several connections that contributed to ethnicization were made. First, by linking the crimes with Četniks or Ustaša, groups that were named after armed units known for mass violence in World War II, the media messages added to the already present sense of fear and uncertainty among the population due in part to local or family histories that were shared across generations. Second, the assumption that was often made by the audience of these media messages in the context of war, as this respondent's statement illustrated, was that Četniks and Ustaša were automatically linked with entire ethnic groups, or nations, or Serbs and Croats, respectively. All of these associations related to interpreting the incidents of mass violence against civilians contributed, in addition to other factors discussed in the previous chapter, to new divisions and distrust among people of different ethnicities who shared the same communities before the war.

Information about local incidents of mass violence was transmitted through the national and local media, as well through word-of-mouth accounts.[92] Yet the framing and presentation of violent incidents contributed not only to further ethnic divides but also to the expectation of revenge by the perceived members of the group that was victimized.[93] Even intergenerational stories from World War II influenced some individuals' understanding of contemporary violence, as those who experienced violence in the previous war expected, on the basis of their personal observations, that ethnically targeted violence would cause a boomerang effect, leading to more violence in the form of revenge—an ethnic Croat village for an ethnic Serb village.[94] In some cases, the ethnic categorization of the perpetrators and victims of violence, and the ethnic divisions that ensued following cycles of violence, linked various historical periods in the same geographic region.[95] In that context, one respondent mentioned the genocide trial that was taking place at the time of the interview in 2014 as an event that she perceived as harmful for reconciliation because it served to remind everyone about the crimes from the past.[96] This comment shows this respondent's critical stance toward the trial between Croatia and Serbia. As I mentioned in the introduction, this genocide trial, from the start, did not contribute to the reconciliation effort in communities affected by war. Rather, observers believed that the states should direct the resources toward rebuilding both the communities and the lives of their citizens who were victims of war, regardless of their identity or political views. Yet, based on the experience of one of my respondents, the decision to deny her financial assistance, to which most residents of her city were entitled, was seen as justified by the local state representatives because her ethnicity was associated with the "enemy" in the war and because her property was bombed by members of her own ethnic group.[97] Even years after the Croatian government reconstructed and returned property to the predominantly Serb population that fled during Oluja, and the number of houses that were occupied by the Croat returnees was successfully reduced from 20,000 to 1,400 in November 2004, there was no significant permanent return of the population to the war-affected regions (Leutloff-Grandits 2013, 140–144). There could be many reasons for this outcome, including the length of time it took to address any requests, the adverse economic situation in these communities, and the state of local politics (Leutloff-Grandits 2013, 140–144). Yet such evidence is worrisome for the long-term prospect of reconciliation in these communities.

As mentioned earlier, the violence did not produce the same effect across the entire territory of Croatia, even in former amoral communities. Generally, in communities with higher levels of targeted mass violence, there is some evidence that the violence had a detrimental effect on interethnic social relations. For instance, based on the survey conducted by Dragutin Babić in 2004 across Eastern and Western Slavonia including 442 respondents who were represented based on their ethnicity and migration status, the majority of residents from 213 who responded, including local Croats, local Serbs, and newcomers (from Bosnia and Herzegovina, Serbia, or Montenegro), of Eastern Slavonia stated that they lived in peace and were respectful toward one another before the war (Babić 2008, 89–94). After the war, most from 185 who responded in Eastern Slavonia, including members of all three groups of survey participants, reported that if they came across a person of the other ethnicity, they would "wait before greeting them to see how the other side would react first" (143). Only a little over 20 percent of the sixty-four Croats and sixty-nine Serbs interviewed would behave in a similar way as before the war and "stop and talk about everything" (143). Furthermore, based on in-depth interviews with six high school students, three Croats and three Serbs, conducted in a Vukovar in 2004, young people had limited interethnic contact and were cautious about forming close friendships with people of another ethnicity (196–198). Yet even in the regions where the highest rates of civilian killings occurred, people questioned—and continue to question—the divisions based on ethnicity and the political strategy of violence.[98] One of my respondents shared his personal pain as a result of the killings that he witnessed, as well as other extreme acts of violence that he heard about, observed, and experienced as a former prisoner during the war.[99] His own experience made him realize the futility of violence as a political strategy; violence ultimately does not divide people by identities. Rather, violence destroys all who are found in its path, including those who participated, whether willingly or unwillingly, and those against whom the violence was directed, as in the case of an ethnic Croat victim and a Serb soldier, both heavily wounded, who tried to make sense of the events around them and what happened to them while lying in adjacent hospital beds.[100] At that point, and not only because it was still not certain that they would survive, both of their lives were already irreparably destroyed by the violence. In some cases, people continued to recognize each other's human qualities and engaged in generous and, during the war, risky acts of extending a helping hand across the dividing line.[101] In one case, a respondent helped an elderly Serb woman after Oluja when she remained alone at home.[102] These examples illustrate the range of consequences of the political use of violence on the local level, even in communities that were affected by war. Some people who were mobilized in war did not have strong feelings, or "hate," as one respondent called it; others closed themselves in and locked their doors; some people fled; and still others resumed normal relations with family members who had been ethnicized by the war.[103]

Based on the examples from Croatia, Uganda, and Guatemala considered in this chapter, the use of violence as a political strategy had both intended and unintended consequences. Its aim was to teach individuals that they should be guided not by their own personal views but rather by concerns for the collectivity, defined by a political ethnicity. In the cases in which the use of violence as a political strategy ethnicized everyday life, this created new challenges for reconciliation and postconflict reconstruction in the communities in which the most extreme forms and levels of violence against civilians occurred. These reconciliation efforts were further hindered by the countereffort of perpetrators who continued to justify the use of violence as a political strategy during the "state of emergency" in order to protect and secure their own communities against threats and enemies, defined politically and ethnically. Another unintended consequence of targeted violence against civilians, as evident in the examples in this chapter, was that it provided a motivation for revenge and caused a subsequent spiraling of violence (Balcells 2017; Petersen 2002).

Targeted violence against civilians is used as a political strategy to divide people who share the same community and to establish political power over the occupied territory and the remaining population by force. The perpetrators attempt to justify it by invoking the security myth that particular culturally defined members of the community represent a political threat and, by extension, a threat to one's own survival. This type of violence, however, destroys not only individual lives and entire communities but also the very political regimes that advocate its use, as they gradually self-destruct through the loss of legitimacy when they continue to govern not by gaining political support through successful policies but by constantly searching for, and seeking to eliminate, the threat of political opposition from within.

Conclusion
PREVENTING COLLECTIVE CRIMES

Two sounds remained in his memory. After hearing the "drrrr" of the gun, there was silence, then the breathing out, "Whoo . . . when the soul comes out."[1] Killing another person cannot be explained. It cannot be justified. What I hoped to accomplish in this book was to identify conditions that made this type of violence possible in some places, so that it can be prevented in the future. Before the war, my respondents, many of whom witnessed wartime violence firsthand, talked about their normal lives with their neighbors, who were normal people. How, then, did violence against civilians become possible in some places while peace was possible in others? I considered political and social changes across different communities by reaching out to people who witnessed or experienced wartime violence personally and who had had some time since the end of the war to reflect on these events, which possibly had a profound effect on their own beliefs and values over time. In addition to examining these local-level factors, I also asked how the political goals, particularly with respect to different, and competing, conceptions of statehood, became points of contention only in certain communities. In my research in Croatia, I included communities, both urban and rural, with similar demographic compositions but different levels of violence against civilians. As the research progressed, I realized that there were two interrelated questions that I was trying to address—the why and the how. While the question of why may be important from the perspective of a social scientist, given that the patterns of wartime violence against civilians are not random, the question of how is more important from the perspective of the witnesses of violence because it can lead to knowledge about the processes that make this type of violence possible but not inevitable. Such processes can be stopped or reversed in time, and as a result, the targeted mass violence against civilians can be prevented.

In order to assess whether some of the state- or local-level conditions and processes that were present in Croatia existed in cases that were historically, culturally, and geographically different, in my analysis, I also considered the 1980s violence in Uganda and Guatemala. In both countries, I conducted a small sample of interviews with people who could provide diverse perspectives. There were important differences in the dynamics and the patterns of violence across the three cases. In Guatemala and Uganda, the state armies and insurgents clashed. Throughout the war, most violence was perpetrated by the state against the civilian population supporting insurgents. In Croatia, the army of the former Yugoslavia, the collapsed state from which Croatia fought to secede, as well as various paramilitary organizations, supported the insurgents and clashed with the army of Croatia and several paramilitary organizations on the other side. Most of the violence against civilians in Croatia was perpetrated by insurgents, particularly in the first years of the war. In Guatemala and Croatia, the state either excluded the political ethnicities associated with the insurgents or limited their access to political power. In Uganda, the insurgents consolidated the regime that either excluded or limited access to political power for the opposition. Yet, in all three countries, one or both of the warring sides at different times systematically targeted not only the adversary army but also civilians of certain groups or in certain geographic areas under the justification that they represented a threat to the nation-body, as conceived by the group aiming to gain or preserve political, and socioeconomic, dominance in the state.

In those communities where state-level and local-level processes of ethnicization coincide, conditions conducive for wartime collective crimes are created. State-level processes of ethnicization, defined as the linking of a single political goal with a single ethnic, religious, or racial identity, begin most commonly in the discourse of political leaders who give more or less explicit permission, framed as a necessity, to use violence not only as a military strategy but also as a political one. It is a process through which political leaders conceptualize the state as a nation-body by identifying those who belong to it and those whose political loyalty is perceived as ambiguous. The latter, in the leaders' political discourse, then begin to be represented as a threat to the state's survival and, by extension, to those defined as rightful members of the given state. Local-level processes of ethnicization, in turn, are triggered by two complementary mechanisms. The first one is the exclusion of moderates, or those whose loyalty is considered questionable due to their opposition of the processes of ethnicization, through threats, selective targeted violence, social ostracism, and various forms of in-group policing. The second mechanism is the production of borders, usually initially in the form of barricades, checkpoints, or roadblocks, and later in the form of wartime dividing lines, with the aim to control the civilian population. In communities where the exclusion of moderates and the production of borders occurred, and where newly engineered identities were established, defection by members of the in-group became more difficult and any ambiguity in identifying members of the out-group was increasingly reduced. As a result, in those communities, which I call amoral communities, individuals were not able to act safely in accord with their own values if those values departed from those imposed on them through the state- and local-level processes of ethnicization. It is in such communities that the conditions conducive to collective crimes, or violence against civilians who were targeted on the basis of their identities, emerged during times of war.

Understanding that wartime events are conditioned by specific historical trajectories, particular geopolitical and international conditions, and many other factors that are unique to each place, my goal from the outset was not to develop a generalizable explanation of wartime collective crimes; instead, my aim was to identify some similarities in local conditions, as well as compare different interpretations of respondents with diverse backgrounds who were witnesses of war, so that such atrocities may be anticipated and possibly prevented. This book thus offers several insights for scholars of violence against civilians and genocide research across disciplines. Specifically, it highlights how two specific processes—the exclusion of moderates and the production of borders—link state-level political mobilization and ethnicization attempts with local conditions that make targeted violence against civilians more probable in some communities. The role of state leaders, and political leaders' narratives, in creating conditions favorable to the exclusion of certain members of the nation-body on the basis of ethnicity, race, religion, or another cultural trait has already been recognized in the literature on nationalism and political violence (Bulutgil 2016; Mamdani 2001; Mann 2005; Straus 2015; Wimmer 2001, 2013). Many scholars of political violence, in explaining the patterns of violence in wars, have questioned the automatic link between top-down mobilization and local-level mobilization for violence by starting to focus more on explaining local-level variations in violence against civilians and emphasizing the role of the military strategy over political explanations for such violence (Hultman 2007; Kalyvas 2006; Metelits 2010; R. Wood 2010). A number of scholars, however, have shown that political cleavages—and other nonmilitary explanations, such as a desire for revenge—account for the local-level variation in the levels of violence against civilians in many cases (Balcells 2017; Cederman, Gleditsch, and Buhaug 2013; Petersen 2002). This book complements the growing scholarship in this area by showing that while the use of violence as a military strategy explains some cases of violence against civilians, the analysis that relies heavily on military strategy as an explanation does not address many research questions that cases of targeted violence against civilians raise.

When used as a political strategy, usually in addition to being used as a military strategy, violence against civilians may reinforce the processes of ethnicization that begin as standard political discourse but end with communities that are deeply divided along the new identities (Bergholz 2016; Fujii 2009; Gagnon 2004). Consequently, in those places where violence was used as a political strategy, we would expect that the processes of postconflict reconciliation may be hindered both by the ethnic (or other identity-based) divides that endure as a result of the violence and by the perpetrators' reliance on the myth that violence against civilians was a necessary and justifiable part of the struggle for the security of the included political ethnicities under the "state of emergency." Despite these challenges, there are mixed findings even in communities that experienced violence against civilians, leaving some room for hope for the processes of reconciliation. In other words, while there is evidence that violence magnifies divisions that were not as relevant before the war, there is also evidence that this is not an inevitable outcome. It depends, in large part, on the national-level political conditions, including the discourse of political leaders, and the local-level conditions that make room for divergent voices. Just as past waves of violence do not inevitably lead to long-lasting divisions, the memories of the more recent waves of violence are also not automatically linked with persisting divisions along the identities created by the violence. The outcome depends on the coordinated efforts and genuine commitment of political leaders at all levels of government to create peace.

There are several implications of my research for the efforts to prevent violence against civilians. Given the local constraints imposed by the production of borders and the exclusion of moderates, an internal, or community-level, *nonviolent* resistance, even if mounted despite the odds, would be unlikely to succeed unless linked strategically with other resisting communities to form a countermovement. Therefore, one implication of this research is that a more probable path toward the prevention of wartime collective crimes would be external diplomatic efforts to put a stop to any attempts to physically divide the local population, or segregate people territorially on the basis of their presumed political ethnicities or other identities. In other words, people need to be free to choose where they want to live independently of their ethnic, religious, racial, or other social identities. Their respective states and local governments should protect their basic human rights. Taking into account the evidence in this book, as well as in other studies of political violence, that violence creates and deepens social and political divisions, it is essential that any international effort of mediation does not imply or include violence or the threat of violence; therefore, care should be taken when the first signs of possible conflict are observed (Zartman 2005). Another implication of my research is that the current system of peacekeeping, which relies on militarized responses that reinforce the very conditions that are conducive to wartime collective crimes, such as relocating the population to "safe zones" or refugee camps, may not be adequate in preventing further cycles of violence. Instead of attempting to control the movement of people fleeing violent conflict through increasingly more restrictive refugee laws, states should allow all those affected by such violence the freedom to decide whether they wish to integrate socially, economically, and politically into their new communities, return to their homes in the future if and when it is safe for them to do so, or settle in another country altogether.

As scholars who are researching how to prevent the formation of amoral communities, we must cross disciplinary boundaries more intentionally as we learn about particular conditions that may influence people's ability to make decisions. The research on political violence entails listening to the voices of those with first-hand experiences who are in the position to offer lessons for future generations.

Appendix

AN EXCERPT FROM THE FIELD NOTES BY HELGA PAŠKVAN

This is an opportunity to gather my impressions from my trip to the part of North Dalmatia that was affected by war.[1] I started in the morning on a nine o'clock bus, just as we ended our phone conversation while I was buying a return ticket. The return ticket carries some weight that I did not realize until later—it had a certain meaning for this entire trip. I love to travel along the seacoast, but unfortunately we did not take that road for too long. In Senj, we had to take the back road, because of the storm, and we continued on that road all the way through Lika and the hinterland near Paklenica and Obrovac. We passed through a portion of Zrmanja Canyon, which was beautiful. I immediately started thinking about this landscape, which had been horribly violated during the Homeland War. Even if one's view accidentally and in passing falls on some graffiti or on the remnants of a destroyed building, a person immediately imagines the atmosphere of these horrors. It is not the same to pass through this area in person and to talk about it in class at the university. Out there, there is always something that remains in the atmosphere; something that one comes to collect in order to speak about it in the classroom. After passing more roads, pine trees, fragmented streamlets very close to the view, and pine trees that were turned into a blackened ruin, from the distance I can still hear your voice. It is because of that voice that these efforts make sense, to speak with people about war in order to seek peace. These people with whom I will speak experienced loss both consciously and unconsciously, and the caution I read between the lines of emails of our contacts are certainly justified: "Would this be yet another researcher arriving to elicit manipulated answers from the participants [in the war] from 1991 to 1995?" I already had to explain everything to him even before the summer, when we first considered getting in touch with him regarding his assistance with identifying possible respondents. In other areas, like in Rijeka and Gorski Kotar, that process was much quicker and simpler, and the work with people from these different areas simply cannot be compared. Luckily, he became familiar with your work, and finally he met you personally, and even before he met you, right after reading your work, he decided to help.

I felt somewhat disoriented, both hot and cold at the same time, when I arrived after six hours on the bus. I decided to get a room for myself at the hostel near the station, even though it was louder than the other, more modern hotel nearby. The woman from the reception desk and I went for a walk after I settled in. We were guiding each other; she had not yet had a chance to have a real walk through the city after having studied there for several months. Based on the map, we could not figure out where the organization I was looking for was located, as if it was an hour away, even though everything was nearby, behind a corner or two. A woman standing at the open door of her house talks to us. People trust each other here. She tells us where to go to see a view from the hill. Thick drops of darkness started falling while we tried to take a look. Darkness fell all around us. We entered a gallery of an old church (from a multitude of churches in that stone puzzle of a city on the thousand-and-first step) where one of the sculptresses from the city had her exhibit. Since I wouldn't be able to stay until the opening on Friday, she let us in. A beautiful experience. Some relaxation before work.

I think that I will never forget the gestures of one of the respondents. She was tired from her headache, and the fresh air in the park suited her so it took longer. But this was not the only reason. Then her relative passed by, and she almost left with her in the middle of the sentence. The church bells rang noontime, and I had a new appointment set up an hour ago, but I could not stop this conversation, full of emotions and brutal honesty, which started with a cautious exposition of personal experiences. This woman's husband stayed on the other side of the dividing line. She took him for a weekend there, and then he simply stayed on the other side. She said it somehow gesturing and saying, "He stayed over there." I remember that I paused the audio recorder and exchanged with her only a sentence or two, nothing special, but I must have said something right because she started from the beginning and said, "Who cares, since I already started talking about it, I'll tell you everything," and she freed herself to proceed telling me, with a clear talent for storytelling, her story full of emotions.

I barely made it to the next interview. I realized in that basement room, overfilled with books and hot despite the open window, that I was very tired. I drank half a liter of water and nibbled on the chocolate offered to me just to stay awake.

At one moment, after the respondent answered his phone and I left the audio recorder on pause, I forgot to turn it back on. But nothing essential was missed, something about an olive tree growing on the seacoast that started to develop after the war. A message arrived from a colleague concerning where I would stay in the next place. She asked when I was arriving. I had already decided—tonight. Half an hour of sunshine on the coast, and some bread and milk until the next respondent. With the previous respondent, I spent more time than planned, and I so wanted to go out in the sun. But to make it simpler, we stayed inside in the dark and damp space.

On my way to the next interview, I stopped near the first hosts, I don't even know why, but probably to recharge my batteries until the next destination, which was half an hour away. The oldest host was happy to see me because for her, meetings and these types of stories are food for the soul, as she said it herself. She was very disappointed we had to stop after only half an hour. These women are precious sources; I don't know if I still have their contact information. At the end, the last woman respondent waited for me in front of the hostel. The image I remember, her looking back and waving, had a sound of emptiness—beginnings of the ends, the eighties and the nineties, the period about which she spoke with deep nostalgia from the angle of her family. And then back to the bus and toward the village I had never visited before.

Traveling at night didn't permit me to see the landscape, and I lost myself in the warm sounds of high school students returning home from the city and in the joy that I am going to be in the countryside soon. I had a sensation that there was a lot of open land around us and vastness. I was not wrong even when I arrived to her home. It was a warm place, dogs barking and running by the car until it stopped, the cow bells and mooing, of course, then an explanation of her father that calves would be loud that night because they were hungry since it was the first day that they were separated from their mother. Meeting with her mother, and my first contact in the area, gave me an even better feeling that I would rest well here after the urban chase from one interview to the next. "Eat, drink, as if you were at home," a vegetarian dinner was served right away, and fresh milk. My colleague was fasting these days and was not eating meat, so it felt good that I was not the only vegetarian at that big table. Afterward in bed, I covered myself with two wool blankets and two quilts; it was freezing in the room of my colleague that she let me use during my visit. We have a similar style of arranging the room, except hers was a bit more organized. Even the books are somewhat familiar. Her studies in sociology and art history filled her shelves with more books than my sad photocopies and scripts in the boxes, and I concluded that I have only a few important and dear books. Her room displays icons of Jesus and Maria, and has an incense burner hanging from the ceiling. This was new for me, but it felt somehow pleasant and warm. We exchanged two or three words about the power of a prayer, and then went to sleep.

The next day, I took photos and recordings of the mooing of calves, which I needed for a play, so maybe you'll accidentally also get some of the mooing in my transfer of the audio files. On the way to the interview in the car, we went over her thoughts on the structure of the interviews, and how she could have also found Bosniaks, or Muslims, but I had told her that it was not necessary. Maybe that was a misunderstanding, a couple would have been good. She asked if it mattered whether respondents were from rural or urban areas, and I said that it mattered, of course, and that is why we looked for respondents in both areas. "Don't take out all these papers right away," she said wisely. "You'll scare them." An older, thin, and hunched woman received us into her little house that was barely twenty squared meters large. It was sad inside, a small kitchen with a bed, and with sadness hanging in the air. We explained about the study, and as we started with the first question about the war, I also shook because the woman literally started trembling. In that trembling, which lasted almost to the end, until the part when we talked about Yugoslavia in the heart and how she started reading the Bible, and how we were all from Adam and Eve, we are not different—our twenty or so minutes were over.

We bravely continued to the next neighbor. On our way, we discussed how people there don't live like people on the seacoast, one on top of another, so you have to walk a bit between houses. An old woman and her tall and handsome son in a smallish residence, a home that had some unpleasant smell, without importance. She turned off the television, which was playing folk music. My colleague wanted to help out, so you have a few of her questions, as well, on the recordings. I thought she was a bit too direct, and then later on our way to the third house, we had a discussion regarding whether subquestions were needed in such a direct tone that she had. Her approach was to ask how they would say it in such and such way, and my approach was little by little, as I was careful that I didn't compromise the situation or try to influence specific moments in their stream of remembering. This is always a disagreement in the literature, too, whether the culture of memory is a poetically informative free narrative where I don't give importance to the most provocative questions but I let them open up as if they were seashells in the tide, or if it is a journalistic interview, in which a respondent talks a bit, and then the interviewer asks, "What do you think about . . . ?" Of course, sometimes, you have to ask subquestions. Memories stifle intimate spaces, and when memories are blocked, all that is needed for people is more space and trust. How can trust be formed at first? Is it blind, and therefore irrational, or does it, precisely because of it, justify hope in humanity?

Our respondent prepared the third neighbor with a joke that neither of us is married. As I was relaxing and noticing spring in the gardens and around me in the nature on my way to the car, just thirty meters away, to get more papers and statements, I ran into the first respondent, who was talking with the neighbor we just interviewed. He added something about how people during the period when they were under Maria Theresa converted without any problems in a village where a mostly ethnic Croat population lived in order to reduce their taxes. And he added how he heard of some cases of how people in this last war converted from an Orthodox faith to a Catholic faith so that they would not lose their jobs. I said that I left the audio recorder in the house and asked if I could add this note in my report, and he agreed.

Our first respondent walked us to the house, and she said, "I would like to say something for recording about the tenancy rights and moving into peoples' houses." I was already bravely waving with my papers and explaining to everyone about my colleague, about you, and about a book where their story would be written. I think that all three took the papers about participation. I was not even aware at first how both you and my colleague have good last names for moving around in this part of the country, in contrast to the city.

After these unusual meetings, where I understood the depth of the issues while protected by the remoteness of the villages, without offending dear people, we arrive at another, similar place. A neighbor lets us in. A mother and a son, again, different from the first ones, both physically and in their articulation. She spoke quickly in a dialect; I hope you'll be able to understand her. He, with a mild speech defect, adds to her statement, and she adds to his. They gave us a lot of time, given that the old woman was in the middle of cleaning fish for lunch when we arrived. Then a little break at the house of the relatives of my colleague, where it was interesting how the woman at first didn't want to participate at all, and then started talking about her case in detail, while repeating, "Please don't mind me." I noticed that she was honored and content when I said, both in the beginning and at the end, that everyone can choose whether they want to participate or not. Even I was content because I said that in such a relaxed manner as if I was speaking about the clouds in the sky.

Then, rushing toward the house, we stopped for a quick meal, and continued further. We picked up a respondent in front of the office of my colleague's mother. She pointed to a stone near the road—an ancient sediment from I don't know when, but after the war nobody returned the sign with that information. That is where Ustaša (or Četnik) gallows were located. Layers of history, all in some fog of remembrance, noted, but publicly unmarked. In the break from the interview, the woman expressed her concern that she was perhaps not talking about important things, but I was content because she was giving a realistic picture that she managed to put together from moments that figured most prominently in her memory, and those were facts that nobody until now mentioned.

    The next respondent was a young man who waited with his girlfriend in the dark living room with television and tea. His girlfriend left us with a promise that when she returns from her walk, she can also give us her story. It sounded interesting because she arrived from Bosnia after the war. However, she was too young for the interview, and she didn't even return in time, so it was better in the end. I am very sorry though that we don't have any Bosniaks and we have only one Croat woman in this village. But we have interethnic marriages, and our respondent was a child from such a marriage. Finished for today? No, the colleague planned one more respondent in the village, but in the end I was glad that he asked us to come tomorrow since the old man was watching a soap opera. His story was a very historical one of someone with a lot of personal experiences.

    Mother and daughter were getting ready quickly before my departure and talking about the shopping in the city, and in that bustle, we talked about how it was difficult to find respondents and how it would have been difficult if I went alone, but I don't know, I would not have gone alone anyway. The colleague mentioned how it was difficult to find men even though he asked them, and how people declined when they saw your last name. It was difficult to find new respondents because the interviews were not precisely structured in terms of the sample, like two with such and such age, two of that category, and so on. You preferred some flexibility because it was not easy to meet all those criteria for such a topic, you told me. I understood that it was difficult to find respondents, but maybe they exaggerated in some part, in which one, I wonder. I am rewinding the film. I leave with an intuition that probably there is a lot of truth in that. At that moment, my colleague's text message arrives in response to my objection that there were no more male respondents. He said, "Men, believe it or not, got scared. When they hear about the research they think they would not be good enough to help." Exactly that, "I really don't know how much I could help you," was something that one of my respondents repeated many times. I don't know if that was avoidance or just a saying.

    In the bus on our way to the next town, now in daylight, I saw something—red, heart-shaped graffiti on the bus station: "Serbia and Russia" in Cyrillic. Oh my God, how gullible. The front door of the bus could not close all the way and kept sliding. The driver talked on the cell phone in an angry voice. "I call them for a month already, and now I call them, but they don't respond. I have a wrong last name, so they won't [help me]." I started to feel slightly nauseous. I arrived and dropped my bag quickly in my hostel, and then rushed to the park to talk with a mother whose baby was sleeping in the stroller. The place of encounter was better than a café or their apartment; even though the most important thing was that we were lucky the baby didn't wake up. After everything, I want to say that there were one or two pieces of information I was asked specifically to leave out because, as much as they were public secrets already, this was politically sensitive information.

Some chaos entered my mind, and if the bus for Rijeka were leaving later, I would have gone for a walk. But this way, I was sitting near the station, lost in my thoughts and half in tears, with my bag, and I waited for a more proximate choice, a trip to something familiar, home. While the mountain Dinara, covered with snow on the hottest spring day in Croatia, was somewhere in front of us and behind us, near the road, I asked my colleague, "How is it that people return when the atmosphere of uncertainty is still here?" She said, "You cannot understand that, a person wants to return home, a person is pulled by home." I can understand that very well, except that this instinct in me gets on my nerves. I would like to fly everywhere, but I have a hard time moving away from a place that is my home, even though I am currently unhappy that I don't have my more independent home. The return ticket does not guarantee a sense of security; maybe that is why it is cheaper.

This trip has changed me somehow, and I cannot explain how exactly. It broke something in me, and I hope to realize what soon. I only see that I don't want to lose time anymore. After this experience, I have to start believing again in the light side of humanity, on every step. I also understand more now why people are angry, frowning, and why they repeat mistakes. But there are no excuses. As my host mother would say, "If you cannot forgive yourself, then you cannot forgive others." And every light that is even slightly present in the room is something that I will notice more from now on. That is also sad, but the sunset behind the Maslenica Bridge soothes me.

Notes

INTRODUCTION

1. In response, the Republic of Serbia also filed a genocide lawsuit against Croatia, but for the violence from World War II.

2. The official narratives that denied both the public recognition of loss and responsibility for crimes on a human level, regardless of a person's ethnicity, clashed with the post-conflict peace and reconciliation efforts of the nongovernmental sector in the region.

3. Author's interviews, Sisak-Moslavina 2.1, 3.1, June 24, 2014.

4. As shown by scholars who collect and analyze personal narratives in their research, these individual stories' "analytic value rests on their ability to reveal something new about a social position defined by and of interest to the analyst but more legible through an insider's view" (Maynes, Pierce, and Laslett 2008, 6). Relying on individual narratives and extended field research, Tone Bringa's (1995) work, for example, illustrates the meaning of Muslim identity for the residents of a central Bosnian village during the latter part of the 1980s. Similarly, the work of scholars employing political ethnography approaches seeks to uncover meaning from the perspective of people with direct experience by analyzing interviews, text, symbols, narratives, or observations from field research (Schatz 2009; Wedeen 2009).

5. They also include "counternarratives that dispute misleading generalizations or refute universal claims," and may provide information crucial for understanding any connections between the personal and the social context, as argued by scholars who employ personal narratives in their research (Maynes, Pierce, and Laslett 2008, 1–3). For the study of violence in local communities, this approach makes it possible not only to identify new perspectives or counternarratives but also to explore any links between the conditions identified at both the micro level and the macro level that made violence possible in some communities during a particular time (Autesserre 2010; Bergholz 2016; Fujii 2009; Schatz 2009; E. Wood 2003).

6. See, for example, Autesserre 2010, 2014; Balcells 2017; Ballinger 2003; Bergholz 2016; Brass 1997; Bringa 1995; Cammett 2013; Das 2007; Fujii 2009; Gagnon 2004; Jambrešić Kirin and Povrzanović 1996; Jansen 2007; Schatz 2009; Scott 1985; Straus 2015; Subotić 2013; Wedeen 2009; E. Wood 2003.

7. Author's interview, Primorje-Gorski Kotar 17, June 3, 2014.

8. The disconnect between two sets of scholarly studies has already been noted and bridged in the literature by a number of scholars (Bergholz 2016; Finkel 2012; Fujii 2009; Straus 2012).

9. See, for example, Blattman and Miguel 2010; Cederman, Gleditsch, and Buhaug 2013; Downes and Cochran 2010; Hultman 2007; Humphreys and Weinstein 2006; Kalyvas 1999, 2005, 2006; Metelits 2010; Weinstein 2007; R. Wood 2010; Zahar 2001.

10. Balcells (2010, 2017) builds on earlier work of Roger Petersen (2002) showing that emotions, such as a desire for revenge, also may play a role in explaining why some civilians may be targeted. Revenge is thus both a cause and a consequence of targeted violence, especially when occurring in response to the first rounds of violence.

11. Throughout the book, I define an *ethnic group* both as a group of people and as the system of symbols representing a social identity based on a belief in the group's common descent (Barth 1996; Calhoun 2003; Horowitz 1985; Jenkins 2008; Weber [1922] 1996).

12. The exclusion of moderates by local or national elites in the social or political process of radicalization, or polarization, has been recognized by a number of scholars investigating different historical periods and geographic contexts (Bergholz 2016; Bermeo 2003; Gagnon 2004; Hajdarpašić 2015; Heberle [1940] 1970; Straus 2012, 2015).

13. Building on recent historical research on nationalism, I conceptualize ethnicization as a potentially "open-ended" and "impossible to complete" process, as the guardians of the emerging identities, or the political ethnicities, remain prepared to act against any perceived threat to the territorially demarcated nation-body, even after the wartime violence ends (Hajdarpašić 2015, 201).

14. See, for example, Cohen 1993, 2007; Djokić 2003; Dragović-Soso 2007; Gagnon 2004; Glaurdić 2011; Jović 2009, 2017; Lampe 1996; Perica 2002; Petersen 2002; Ramet 1992; Woodward 1995.

15. Other major parties that did not make such a strong case for linking ethnicity and a political goal of independence or autonomy were less successful in this election. For example, another contender in that election was the centrist Coalition of the Popular Compromise (Koalicija narodnog sporazuma), which lacked a unified program and consisted of the Croatian Social-Liberal Party (Hrvatska socijalno-liberalna stranka), Croatian Peasant Party (Hrvatska seljačka stranka), Croatian Christian Democratic Party (Hrvatska kršćanska demokratska stranka; HKDS), and Social Democratic Party of Croatia (Socijaldemokratska stranka Hrvatske). The Coalition of the Popular Compromise, led by Savka Dabčević-Kučar and Miko Tripalo, won 15 percent of the votes and only three representatives in the parliament (I. Goldstein 2008, 648). The communist successor party, represented by the Social Democratic Party (Socijaldemokratska partija) under the leadership of Ivica Račan, won second place in the elections, securing 35 percent of the votes and twenty seats in the Socio-Political Council (649). The relatively strong standing of the Social Democratic Party may be explained in part by the votes of ethnic Serbs in Croatia and in part by those of ethnic Croats who were skeptical of the other parties' programs, particularly of the populist nationalist program of the HDZ (Barić 2005; I. Goldstein 2008, 649).

16. Given the ethnic composition of the JNA, which in the 1980s was dominated by ethnic Serbs who constituted 57 percent of the active army staff, 60 percent of officers, and 30 percent of recruits, this shift in the political strategy of the JNA was not surprising (Bieber 2007, 306).

17. Based on Documenta's report from December 13, 2017, there were 16,080 victims of war registered in the organization's database as of that date when 70 percent of the Croatian territory was accounted for. More specifically, in the report from Sisak-Moslavina County, there were 2,224 victims, and 55 percent of the total victims were civilians. Most, or 689, of the civilian victims in this region were ethnic Croats, while 417 were ethnic Serbs, and there was no ethnic identity information for 118 civilian victims. Men constituted around 74 percent of 2,224 victims, or 1,643 persons (Documenta 2017).

In Western Slavonia, Documenta accounted for 2,183 victims, and of that number 85 percent were men and 15 percent were women, while around 37 percent were civilians, 50 percent were soldiers, 7 percent of victims had an ambiguous status, and for 6 percent, there was no information about the status. Ethnicity was known for 1,588 victims, and among that number, there were 872 ethnic Croats, 641 ethnic Serbs, 29 Czechs, 18 Hungarians, 14 Italians, 6 Yugoslavs, 3 Bosniak Muslims, and several individuals of other ethnicities (Documenta, n.d.d). The estimates published by the Croatian historian Ivo Goldstein (2008, 751), which do not include missing persons, show that 22,283 persons died in the war, and among that number, there were 8,147 soldiers and 6,605 civilians on the Croat side, while 6,222 persons died on the Serb side, of which about two-thirds were soldiers and about a third were civilians. Based on the data from the Croatian Ministry of Health and the Ministry of Croatian Defenders (Ministarstvo branitelja), Andrija Hebrang (2013, 102) estimated that 7,263 civilians and 6,891 members of armed forces died or were missing on the Croat side. Furthermore, based on incomplete data listing civilians who died in the territory of Croatia from August 17, 1990, through March 25, 1999, Ante Nazor (2011, 376), director of the Croatian Memorial Documentary Center for the Homeland War, estimated that a total of 4,737 civilians died, and of that number the most, or 2,587, were in the territory of Eastern Slavonia.

18. Some of the issues with current publications were pointed out in the round-table discussion, entitled "Documenting Events in the Homeland War," held in Zagreb on February 9, 2006. Historian Igor Graovac noted that there was an error of considering demographic losses—based on census numbers, for instance—as "real losses" (Roginek 2011, 26–27). Similar challenges existed in other places of mass violence in the region. For instance, in the neighboring Bosnia and Herzegovina, where the death toll in the 1990s' war was much higher than in Croatia, the publication of the Bosnian Book of the Dead, prepared by the Sarajevo-based Research and Documentation Center, was controversial because the number of individuals who were identified in the center's database (over 97,000) was smaller than the estimates published in the media previously (between 150,000 and 250,000) (Nettelfield 2010).

19. Žunec also mentioned the importance of figuring out whether some of the soldiers were not citizens of Croatia but rather volunteers from Serbia or members of the JNA forces from Serbia or other republics, so they would not be counted by both states. Žunec added that when talking about the victims of the war, in the case of Croatia, it is important to conceptualize who the victims were, especially since the number of individuals who were displaced by violence is significantly greater than the number of individuals who lost their lives (Roginek 2011, 53).

20. The number of disappeared based on the 2012 ICRC report: 610, or 27 percent of the total number of 2,269, in Vukovarsko-srijemska, and 607, or 27 percent, in Sisačko-moslavačka. Combined, these two counties make up a little more than half, or 54 percent, of the total number of disappeared across Croatia in the 1990s.

21. In this sample from Croatia, in 131 interviews, 69 respondents self-identified as Croats, 52 as Serbs, and 9 as other. The majority of respondents, or 66, were women. The average age was fifty-seven, though the age of respondents ranged from twenty-five to eighty-six. The respondents' education varied widely, too, with 22 respondents with less than a high school education, 56 with a high school education, and 53 with a university or graduate-level education. Furthermore, 44 were employed, 29 were unemployed, 52 were retired, and the remaining respondents were students or had other status. The average number of members in a household was three, and, on average, there was one member of the household without any income (ranging from zero to seven). In regions like Podravina and Gorski Kotar, where war-related violence was limited, most individuals were open to talking at length and readily volunteered to take part in the study, while in regions like Slavonia, central Croatia, Lika, and northern Dalmatia, where people experienced significant personal losses, it was more difficult for respondents to open up or recall some of their traumatic experiences. In those regions, additional interviews from Documenta and the Institute of Ethnology and Folklore were particularly valuable.

22. See the excerpt from research assistant Helga Paškvan's field journal in the appendix for more information about fieldwork experience and challenges that we faced in the field.

23. There were a total of thirty-six respondents. The average age was fifty-eight, the youngest respondent was forty-one, and the oldest was eighty-five. The educational backgrounds of respondents varied, as well. Of thirty-six respondents, twelve had university or graduate-level education, four had trade school, eight had high school, seven had elementary school, and five had some elementary school education. Only ten respondents had full-

time employment, three had part-time jobs, fifteen were agricultural workers, four were retired, and four unemployed. Most, or twenty-seven, respondents were married, six were widowed, and three were single. The average size of the household was eight members, and households had on average five members without any income. Finally, of thirty-six respondents, most, or thirty, self-identified as Muganda ethnically, while others identified with other ethnic groups. There were twenty-six men and ten women among the respondents.

24. In eighteen interviews, twelve respondents self-identified as Quiché, three as members of other indigenous groups, and three as Ladino. The average age of respondents was fifty-five, and the ages ranged from thirty-four to seventy-five. Only four respondents were women, while the remaining fourteen were men. Six respondents had university or graduate-level education, two had high school education, and four had some elementary education. There was one respondent who was literate without any formal schooling, and there were five respondents who were illiterate with no formal schooling. Seven respondents were employed primarily in agriculture, while eleven had full-time employment. All respondents were married. The average size of the household was seven, and on average two members did not have any income.

1. THE MAKING OF AMORAL COMMUNITIES

1. In line with the recent genocide and political science literature, my underlying assumption is that collective crimes are not random or irrational acts (Balcells 2017; Bergholz 2016; Bulutgil 2016; Cederman, Gleditsch, and Buhaug 2013; Eck and Hultman 2007; Fagerlund 2011; Fujii 2009; Harff 2003; Hultman 2007; Humphreys and Weinstein 2006; Kalyvas 1999, 2006; Lemkin 2012; Mamdani 2001; Mann 2005; Petersen 2002; Sanford 2009; Shaw 2007; Staub 2001; Straus 2007, 2012, 2015; Valentino, Huth, and Balch-Lindsay 2004; Weitz 2003; Wimmer 2013; R. Wood 2010; Zahar 2001).

2. The concept of amoral communities is also related to the concept of the condition of *statis*, which is also the title of Giorgio Agamben's book (2015, 16), in the sense that it refers to a set of conditions that are specific to the state of war and in which all members of a community take part in the conflict in some form during the period of war.

3. This is in line with other scholarship that focuses on the processes that make ethnicity a prominent dividing factor in multiethnic states and communities (Bergholz 2016; Gagnon 2004; Mamdani 2001; Žarkov 2007).

4. "Its nature is primarily sociological, since it means the destruction of certain social groups by other social groups or their individual representatives. . . . We are here concerned with particular types of social groups, namely racial, religious, national, linguistic and political groups. We have also pointed out that such groups are exposed to genocide only when they constitute a minority or subjected majority within the community or sphere of control in which they are destroyed" (Lemkin 2012, 33–34).

5. This approach is similar to the approaches of other scholars who are conceptualizing links between ethnicity and political identities in explanations of violence against civilians (Bergholz 2016; Bulutgil 2016; Cederman, Gleditsch, and Buhaug 2013; Cederman, Weidmann, and Gleditsch 2011).

6. The "collective intention," which some studies of genocide attempt to account for, is especially difficult to prove (Shaw 2007, 83). As Michael Mann shows in his study, the "murderous cleansing," or, as I refer to it in my study, a wartime collective crime, "is rarely the initial intent of perpetrators" (2005, 7). Some acts of mass violence against civilians may sometimes occur over the course of war as conflict escalates, necessitating changes in warfare tactics and strategies (Mann 2005; Shaw 2007, 84). For these reasons, I prefer to define *collective crimes* as targeted rather than intentional acts of violence.

7. Balcells also mentions other forms of direct violence in the discussion of qualitative evidence of the kind of direct violence perpetrated by the Left and the Right during the Spanish Civil War (2017, 69–70).

8. Recognizing that definitions of war and types of war are also problematic, for the purpose of this book, I assume that the start of the war is marked by the start of mass violence, including both combatants and noncombatants, while the signing of the peace treaty between the warring sides marks the end of the war.

9. Nationalism, a movement for statehood or self-determination defined in terms of a dominant ethnic group of the given state, has been recognized as a modern phenomenon by many scholars in this field (Anderson 1983; Cederman, Gleditsch, and Buhaug 2013; Gellner 1983; Hobsbawm and Ranger [1983] 1992; D. Horowitz 1985; Malešević 2006; Perica 2002; Ramet [1984] 1992; Wimmer 2001, 2013). Building on this scholarship, Andreas Wimmer identifies two processes that led to the rise of the nation-state globally: "First, the appearance of the nation-state out of absolutism in Western Europe; secondly, the globalization of the model through the break-up of empires and the reordering of the political landscape on a worldwide scale" (2001, 74). It is in the second process, or the stage of nation-state formation, that the existing states serve both as "models" and as "impostors" for the formation of new states (74). The new states may borrow or copy elements of existing states, but also a domino effect takes place in new states, as the self-determination and independence of one group that forms its state entails a creation of ethnic minorities, who, in turn, may also desire independence and self-determination in the form of their own state (Bulutgil 2016; Wimmer 2001, 78). However, not all new states follow a process of nation-state building that entails, according to Wimmer, "ethnicization of the state," or the formation of an ethnic exclusivist nation-state where ethnicity becomes politicized, with minorities excluded in some form (Wimmer 2001, 79). This ethnicization occurred only in those states that were "too weak to overcome indirect rule and communal self-government to penetrate society or override other bonds of loyalty and solidarity, and where a network of civil society organization had not yet developed" (79). In a related fashion, H. Zeynep Bulutgil (2016) argues that the key macro-level conditions conducive to ethnic cleansing include territorial revisions and ethnicity, rather than socioeconomic or other political cleavages, as the dominant dimension of sociopolitical division in the state. Scott Straus (2015) places emphasis on the states' "founding narratives" that include one group and exclude other groups, which are represented as threats, as the main factor explaining the occurrence of genocides in some countries and their absence in other countries. Given that these factors would lead to the exclusion of groups categorized as ethnic minorities, they could also potentially constitute conditions explaining why amoral communities are more likely to form in certain historical periods of the lives of nations.

10. A number of scholars link the state regime or institutions to the occurrence of genocide or ethnic cleansing (Esposito 2010; Foucault [1978] 1990, 2003; Mann 2005; Shaw 2007). For instance, Martin Shaw, who builds on theoretical connections that Mann makes between the formation of democracies and "ethnic cleansing," proposes that "regimes," or "radical party-states," rather than "state institutions," are critical for converting "states into genocidal instruments" (2007, 141). More specifically, Mann begins his analysis by pointing out that democracy, or rule by the people, may have a different meaning in the context of "modern" nation-states, in which "the people" may mean both the *demos*, or "the ordinary people, the mass of the population," and the *ethnos*, or "an ethnic group—a people that shares a common culture and sense of heritage, distinct from other peoples" (2005, 3). The national-level conditions that are most likely to be associated with "murderous ethnic cleansing," according to Mann, include the situations in which

"powerful groups within two ethnic groups aim at legitimate and achievable states 'in the name of the people' over the same territory, and the weaker is aided from the outside," while "the presence of unstable, factionalized party-states" exacerbates such situations (33). A factor that makes such situations more common now than historically, according to Mann, is the "process of capturing and channeling classlike sentiments toward ethnonationalism" in states in which "ethnicity trumps class as the main form of social stratification" (5).

11. Many scholars of nationalism, however, theoretically overemphasize conditions associated with the modernization of societies that initiate state formation, or assume as a given the desire of nations or people to have a political, territorially limited state correspond to a nation. As James C. Scott (2009) shows, there are also cases, specifically in Zomia, the highland region of Southeast Asia, where the phenomenon of "antistate nationalism" is more pervasive than the drive of populations to create their own state. Scott argues that the essence of differentiation between the hill people in Zomia was "competition for power and resources" (244), which motivated the highlanders to differentiate themselves ethnically in order to resist assimilation into the lowland states. Since such cases are rare, however, what causes people to delegate their power to the sovereign, the state, to govern in their name? One possible answer is that people may prefer statehood over various forms of "antistatism" when "they are forced to by some threat or by need" and when they see statehood as a way "to protect their lives" (Foucault 2003, 241).

12. The concept of amoral communities, therefore, complements other studies of collective crimes in the 1990s across the former Yugoslavia and the aftermath that examine the notion of "collective responsibility" for the crimes committed in the name of a particular ethnic or national group (Gordy 2013).

13. People who are targeted in such states are those who represent the equivalent of a classical *homo sacer* (sacred man)—"individuals who may be killed but not sacrificed"— or individuals who are "so completely deprived of their rights and prerogatives that no act committed against them could appear any longer as a crime" (Agamben 1995, pt. 3, chap. 7). How could some individuals be deprived of the right to life in a given community? Roberto Esposito argues that a drive to protect the "life of a community" necessitates "immunization" against any imminent dangers or threats to the community (2011, 5). While members of a community are defined by their obligation or duty to that community, "immunization" releases certain individuals from the obligation and "places" them "outside the community" (Esposito 2011, 5–6).

14. While my concept of political ethnicity is related the concept of "politicized ethnicities" that scholars of ethnic conflict and political violence employ, it is distinct in my emphasis that these are primarily political identities, rather than ethnic groups, that become "ethnicized" through particular local-level processes (Cederman, Gleditsch, and Buhaug 2013; Posner 2004; Wimmer 2001).

15. Those are among the most direct mechanisms that may also trigger emotions, such as fear or rage, that in turn lead ordinary people to make decisions that would have been inconceivable for them under different circumstances (Petersen 2002).

16. Or the "multidimensionality of political cleavages," in Bermeo's words (2003, 224–229). Building on Bermeo's study of polarization, I show that it is the collapse of multidimensionality into a two-dimensional space, where a particular ethno-cultural identity is linked with a particular dominant political goal.

17. As an example of the long-lasting effects of the division of the population by wartime dividing lines and the subsequent distribution of population, see Stef Jansen's (2007) study of postconflict "clashing memories" in the Bosnian town of Tuzla.

2. EVIDENCE OF AMORAL COMMUNITIES

Unless otherwise noted, all translations are my own.
1. Referring to internal enemies, or ethnic Serb rebels, in the context of Croatia.
2. Author's interview, Koprivnica-Križevci 1, June 10, 2014.
3. Even before the actual war began in Croatia, "ethnicity was produced through the representational practices of the media war as much as through the violent practices of the ethnic war" (Žarkov 2007, 2).
4. Author's interview, Eastern Slavonia 10, February 7, 2014.
5. Author's interview, Eastern Slavonia 7, February 6, 2014.
6. Author's interview, Koprivnica-Križevci 6, June 11, 2014.
7. Author's interviews, Sisak-Moslavina 1.1, 2.1, June 24, 2014.
8. Author's interviews, northern Dalmatia 4.1, 4.2, March 12, 2014.
9. Author's interview, northern Dalmatia 7, March 13, 2014.
10. Daily newspaper from Serbia.
11. President of the Party of the Democratic Action (Stranka demokratske akcije), a political party with a program aimed at attracting the Muslim Bosniak population in Bosnia.
12. Author's interview, northern Dalmatia 10, March 13, 2014.
13. Author's interview, Koprivnica-Križevci 7, June 12, 2014.
14. Author's interviews, Primorje-Gorski Kotar 6–13, June 2, 2014.
15. Author's interview, northern Dalmatia 16, March 11, 2014.
16. A singer songwriter from Serbia who was publicly critical of nationalism and is popular across the territory of the former Yugoslavia.
17. Author's interview, Koprivnica-Križevci 15, June 20, 2014.
18. Author's interview, Koprivnica-Križevci 19, June 22, 2014.
19. Other cultural symbols of this period, such as souvenirs of a tree log used by the first rebels in the Krajina regions and postcards of "the sunset on the Serbian Adriatic," also represented an example of how the national-level politics trickled down to the everyday life of the residents in the war-affected areas of Croatia (Kale 2016, 130–131).
20. Author's interview, Primorje-Gorski Kotar 2, June 2, 2014.
21. Author's interview, Sisak-Moslavina 3, March 9, 2014.
22. Other respondents in this region also described how people divided at work: "Then they all of a sudden stopped coming to work. Then they were already probably ready to create that Krajina of theirs. Then that started." Author's interview, Sisak-Moslavina 1, March 9, 2014.
23. Author's interview, Sisak-Moslavina 3, March 9, 2014.
24. Author's interview, Sisak-Moslavina 11, March 26, 2014.
25. Author's interview, Sisak-Moslavina 2, March 9, 2014.
26. Author's interview, Sisak-Moslavina 13, March 26, 2014.
27. Author's interview, Sisak-Moslavina 8, March 17, 2014.
28. Author's interview, northern Dalmatia 23, May 15, 2014.
29. Author's interview, Sisak-Moslavina 4, March 9, 2014.
30. Ethnically and linguistically, present-day Uganda may be divided into the northern region, where Nilotic tribes, including the Langi, Acholi, Alur, Jophadhola and Jonam, and others, lived, and the southern region, where Bantu tribes, including the Baganda, Basoga, Batoro, Banyoro, Banyankore, Bakiga, and others, were based (Nsibambi 2014, 41). During the colonial period, the southern tribes had greater educational opportunities and occupied mostly white-collar jobs, while the northern tribes tended to enlist in the military and police (41).
31. Author's interviews, Uganda 36, June 3, 2015; Uganda 6–20, May 27, 2015.
32. Author's interview, Uganda 33, June 2, 2015.

33. Author's interview, Uganda 2, May 25, 2015.

34. Museveni's son Muhoozi Kainerugaba, major general in the Ugandan Army, cited his father's words in his book, *Battles of the Ugandan Resistance: A Tradition of Maneuver*, in response to a journalist's asking whether his movement was "pro-east or pro-west": "We are pro-ourselves" (Kainerugaba 2010, xiii).

35. Author's interviews, Uganda 21–30, May 28, 2015.

36. Author's interview, Uganda 33, June 2, 2015.

37. García's appointments of Álvarez Ruíz as interior minister and Germán Chupina as the National Police director-general signaled the "decided turn toward mass violence" in the state leadership's counterinsurgency strategy (Weld 2014, 127). The new operations cut off communication between the urban and the rural guerrilla operations (Santa Cruz [2004] 2006, 48). Based on the conditions at that time—recounted in the memoir of Comandante Santiago Santa Cruz Mendoza, a member of the Revolutionary Organization of the Armed People (Organizacíon del Pueblo en Armas de Guatemala) and later a member of the organization under which the guerrillas unified in 1982, the Guatemalan National Revolutionary Unity (Unidad Revolucionaria Nacional Guatemalteca)—due to the new wave of persecutions and arrests, and the introduction of military agents (*orejas* [spies]), military commissioners, and civil patrols, the previous strategies of obtaining supplies and food from local peasants and markets were no longer possible: "We had to be more creative, and more importantly, incorporate the people in the war in order to resolve the problem" (Santa Cruz [2004] 2006, 49). Soon after the Guatemalan National Revolutionary Unity formed, the insurgents planned "to declare a portion of Guatemala liberated territory (*territorios liberados*), with an insurgent government (the EGP handed out its own identity cards), and prepared for a major offensive in the departments of Huehuetenango, Quiché, and Chimaltenango" (Schirmer 1998, 42). These plans were perceived by the military as "a great threat to Guatemala" (Schirmer 1998, 42). This is consistent with other evidence that at this time (i.e., 1980s), "the army came to identify indigenous people as the internal enemy" (Rothenberg 2012, 65).

38. Both the military officials and the government believed that people in this area were tricked by the insurgents (Nelson 2009, 11). From the perspective of the political and economic elites, it was easy to mislead people who lacked education and had limited resources, and in the view of the former military members, that is why the leaders of these communities, including the insurgency leaders, resisted the government's attempts to develop these regions economically Author's interviews, Guatemala 16–18, June 2, 2016. However, this perspective does not take into account the fact that the first insurgents were former members of the military who rebelled against the corruption within the military, among other things. The insurgency then spread from eastern Guatemala to the western highlands, where the indigenous population was recruited by both the military and the insurgents. Author's interviews, Guatemala 10–12, May 31, 2016.

39. In a number of cases, as in the village in the municipality of Cotzal, the military tortured and killed individuals only because they were suspected to be insurgents based on their place of origin, "without any prior verification as to whether the accusation of being a member of the guerrilla or a collaborator was true" (Rothenberg 2012, 10).

40. The National Police was one of the numerous elements of the state's intelligence system that were "subordinated to the armed forces" (Archivo Histórico de la Policía Nacional 2013, 271). Even the Civil Defense Patrols (Patrullas de Autodefensa Civil), which were reinstituted under Montt as part of the counterinsurgency strategy in 1982, were part of this government's extensive intelligence network (REMHI 1999, 105). Additionally, part of the government's strategy was to develop a "wide network of informants" among civilians (Archivo Histórico de la Policía Nacional 2013, 307).

41. Documents in the archives of the National Police provide evidence that "broad sectors of the popular protest movement," including "students, professionals, union members, rural workers' organizations, religious groups, political parties with social and democratic agendas, relatives of the victims of repression," and "the armed opposition and the rebel or guerrilla movement," were under systematic surveillance by the government (Archivo Histórico de la Policía Nacional 2013, 267). Documents identifying political threats (i.e., "the subversion" or "clandestine factions") were sent to the National Police by the state security already from the period of the late 1960s (314). Individuals from the lists would receive death threats whether directly, in person or by phone, or indirectly, in the form of "notes left at the school or at work, lists distributed by death squads sentencing individuals to death for being guerrillas or communists; and messages painted on the walls of houses and offices" (Rothenberg 2012, 11). Locations that were suspected as "guerrilla strongholds" following the surveillance were raided by the National Police, and residents were "on many occasions" killed in these operations (Archivo Histórico de la Policía Nacional 2013, 268). "Generalized terror" attacks, such as the targeting of the staff of the University of San Carlos, even those who were not politically active, contributed to the spread of fear, with the goal of potentially dissuading individuals from joining the political opposition movements (Rothenberg 2012, 12). Student and political leaders were targeted, such as Oliverio Castañeda de León and Manuel Colóm Argueta, who were killed after being identified as political threats as a result of the surveillance (Archivo Histórico de la Policía Nacional 2013, 267; Rothenberg 2012, 12). When individuals who were identified as a political threat could not be found, then their family members would be considered as legitimate targets (REMHI 1999, 5). In short, "the strategy of forced disappearances and murders of leaders or social organizations" became more prominent during particular periods of the war, especially from 1965 to 1968 and from 1978 to 1983, and in the latter period, it followed the "consolidation of the Left" in 1977 (REMHI 1999, 5; Weld 2014, 125). Given the increase in targeted repression during these particular periods, it may be concluded that the state leaders justified the repression as a response to the rising political threat.

42. Author's interviews, Guatemala 10–12, May 31, 2016.
43. Author's interview, Guatemala 13, June 1, 2016.
44. Author's interview, Guatemala 5, May 28, 2016.
45. Historically, however, the "pan-Mayan" identity was not as strong as the local linguistic identities (Short 2004, 52).
46. Author's interviews, Primorje-Gorski Kotar 6–13, June 2, 2014.
47. Author's interviews, Primorje-Gorski Kotar 3–5, June 2, 2014.
48. Author's interview, Primorje-Gorski Kotar 20, June 4, 2014.
49. Author's interview, Primorje-Gorski Kotar 16, June 3, 2014.

3. THE EXCLUSION OF MODERATES

1. Author's interviews, Primorje-Gorski Kotar 14–15, June 3, 2014.
2. Author's interviews, Primorje-Gorski Kotar 14–15, June 3, 2014.
3. Drago Pajić, "Postrojba koja je obranila Rijeku i preuzela vojarne: Prisjećamo se uloge prve riječke vojske" [The unit that defended Rijeka and reclaimed the JNA headquarters: Remembering the role of the first Rijeka forces], *Novi List*, November 27, 2016, http://www.novilist.hr/Vijesti/Rijeka/Postrojba-koja-je-obranila-Rijeku-i-preuzela-vojarne-Prisjecamo-se-uloge-prve-rijecke-vojske.
4. Author's interview, Koprivnica-Križevci 2, June 10, 2014.
5. Documenta interview 306, Eastern Slavonia, February 5, 2013.
6. Author's interviews, Eastern Slavonia 16–17, June 9, 2014.

7. Author's interview, Eastern Slavonia 3, February 6, 2014.
8. Author's interview, Eastern Slavonia 10, February 7, 2014.
9. Author's interview, Primorje-Gorski Kotar 16, June 3, 2014.
10. Author's interview, Western Slavonia 1, May 1, 2014.
11. Author's interview, northern Dalmatia 5, March 12, 2014.
12. Author's interview, northern Dalmatia 6, March 12, 2014.
13. Author's interview, northern Dalmatia 9, March 13, 2014.
14. This was pointed out by Tam Parker and Shana Minkin following my presentation at the University of the South on February 5, 2016.
15. Author's interviews, Eastern Slavonia 2, February 6, 2014; Eastern Slavonia 6, February 6, 2014; Eastern Slavonia 8, February 7, 2014; Eastern Slavonia 9, February 7, 2014; Eastern Slavonia 10, February 7, 2014.
16. Author's interview, Eastern Slavonia 8, February 7, 2014.
17. Author's interview, Eastern Slavonia 2, February 6, 2014.
18. Author's interview, Eastern Slavonia 9, February 7, 2014.
19. Even though the main perpetrator was sentenced to twenty years in prison, he never served his prison sentence (I. Goldstein 2008, 674).
20. Author's interview, Eastern Slavonia 3, February 6, 2014.
21. Author's interview, Eastern Slavonia 1, February 5, 2014.
22. Author's interview, Eastern Slavonia 2, February 6, 2014.
23. Author's interviews: Eastern Slavonia 3, February 6, 2014; Eastern Slavonia 4, February 6, 2014; Eastern Slavonia 5, February 6, 2014; and Eastern Slavonia 6, February 6, 2014.
24. Author's interview, Eastern Slavonia 4, February 6, 2014.
25. Author's interview, Koprivnica-Križevci 2, June 10, 2014.
26. Author's interview, Sisak-Moslavina 4, March 9, 2014.
27. "People, and I was among them, didn't really understand what was happening. We saw what was happening but we didn't want to accept it. If you live in one society for years, and then all of a sudden you realize that that is not it, all of a sudden you are in a situation that you no longer know who you are or what you are. That is the opinion of most people. A small number of people already knew what would happen and they accepted it in a different way." Author's interview, Sisak-Moslavina 5, March 17, 2014.
28. Author's interview, Sisak-Moslavina 5, March 17, 2014.
29. Author's interview, Sisak-Moslavina 10, March 17, 2014.
30. Author's interviews, Eastern Slavonia 19–20, June 9, 2014.
31. Author's interviews, Lika-Senj 1–2, October 18, 2014.
32. Another respondent expressed powerlessness and a sense that political decisions were made by those at the top of the political leadership and by those who ended up gaining from the war and that the options of civilians were limited: "Civilians were in the basement. I was in the center of the town in a basement. I was afraid, together with my neighbors. We were afraid for our lives. Fear of tanks. A tank was in front of my building. What do I have to think?" Author's interview, Sisak-Moslavina 6, March 17, 2014.
33. Author's interviews, Lika-Senj 1–2, October 18, 2014.
34. Author's interview, Uganda 1, May 24, 2015.
35. Author's interviews, Uganda 21–30, May 28, 2015.
36. Author's interview, Uganda 32, May 29, 2015.
37. Author's interviews, Uganda 21–30, May 28, 2015.
38. Author's interview, Uganda 33, June 2, 2015.
39. "Now it is very difficult to know who was against civilians and who was for civilians. Rebels themselves wanted the support from the civilians. And the government at that time also wanted the support from the civilians. The rebels actually had to do something,

which was to turn the population against the government. . . . So you would find actually that civilians were caught in between the government forces and the guerrillas. So essentially that is what happened." Author's interview, Uganda 33, June 2, 2015.

40. Author's interview, Guatemala 5, May 28, 2016.
41. Author's interview, Guatemala 14, June 1, 2016.
42. Author's interview, Guatemala 14, June 1, 2016.
43. Author's interviews, Guatemala 1–4, May 27, 2016; Guatemala 5, May 28, 2016.
44. Author's interviews, Guatemala 1–4, May 27, 2016.
45. Author's interviews, Guatemala 10–12, May 31, 2016.
46. "The population that is not a part of the targeted group needs to acquiesce. They must remain passively supportive or indifferent. Should they not, the authorities would face a substantial hurdle given that mass categorical violence is sustained over time and through space and given that within any regime there will be opposition to the policy. Without popular compliance, the authorities would face a significant obstacle that would limit their ability to extend the categorical violence across a large territory and over time" (Straus 2015, 83).
47. Author's interviews, Lika-Senj 1–2, October 18, 2014.
48. Author's interviews, Primorje-Gorski Kotar 14–15, June 3, 2014.
49. Minutes from the local government meeting held on August 15, 1991, located in Petrinja archives 611.6, Box 1, "Zapisnici sjednica Skupština opštine" [Minutes of the meetings of the county parliament], HR-DASK-SAPC-611, 1990–1996, Zapisnik [Minutes], 15.8.1991, p. 21.
50. Minutes from the local government meeting held on August 15, 1991, p. 21.
51. Documenta interview 173, Eastern Slavonia, October 9, 2012.
52. Author's interviews, Lika-Senj 3–5, October 18, 2014.
53. Author's interview, Eastern Slavonia 15, June 9, 2014.
54. The friend applied a stereotype that all Serbs were Četniks, members of an army from World War II that used the recognizable symbols of beards among men and a *kokarda*, or a coat of arms, with the letters SSSS and the crown of the Serbian king.
55. Author's interview, Western Slavonia 17, May 31, 2014.
56. Author's interviews, Western Slavonia 21, June 14, 2014; Eastern Slavonia 2, February 6, 2014.
57. See the minutes from the local government meeting held on July 28, 1991, located in Petrinja archives 611.12, Box 7, "Zapisnici sjednica Skupština opštine" [Minutes of the meetings of the county parliament], HR-DASK-SAPC-611, 1990–1996, Zapisnik [Minutes], 28.7.1991. Also confirmed in author's interview, June 12, 2014 in Zagreb.
58. Sven Milekic, "Murdered Croatian Serb Peace Advocate Commemorated," *Balkan Insight*, August 3, 2015, http://www.balkaninsight.com/en/article/1990s-croatian-serb-fighter-for-peace-commemorated-08-03-2015.
59. "They would fight for warlords. You asked him, 'To what faction do you belong?' He can't tell you the names because they were in English, so he would just say, 'I am fighting for Kawanga [Paul Kawanga Ssemongere, leader of the Democratic Party and one of the candidates in the 1980 elections].' The man called Kawanga, he had a faction. The other would say, 'I am fighting for Kayiira [Andrew Lutaakome Kayiira, leader of the Uganda Freedom Movement, an anti-Obote rival movement of the National Resistance Movement].' Or, 'I am fighting for Museveni.' Or, 'I belong to the government troops.' You see." Author's interview, Uganda 1, May 24, 2015.
60. "Everyone knew what we were fighting for and why and how we were going to win the war. Up to today, more than two decades after we left the bush, most Ugandans still wonder how we were able to view Uganda's problems in such an analytical and uniform way. People think we were brainwashed. It was not brainwashing, it was systematic analy-

sis of the situation and coming up with a logical conclusion, given the circumstances. The first lesson was to identify and isolate the enemy. The next was to try and persuade as many Ugandans as possible to join our cause.... The most crucial question was whether the war was winnable. It was through this analysis that we adopted the code of operation and the code of conduct of the NRA" (Kutesa [2006] 2008, 120).

61. Author's interviews, Uganda 21–30, May 28, 2015.
62. Author's interview, Uganda 4, May 26, 2015.
63. Author's interview, Uganda 4, May 26, 2015.
64. Author's interview, Uganda 4, May 26, 2015.
65. Author's interviews, Uganda 6–20, May 27, 2015.
66. Author's interviews, Uganda 6–20, May 27, 2015.
67. In one case, however, a former insurgent survived because he managed to convince the government soldiers who captured him that he was surrendering to them, but he later had a hard time reestablishing trust with his fellow insurgents, who suspected that he was alive only because he agreed to serve as a spy for the government. Author's interviews, Uganda 6–20, May 27, 2015.
68. Author's interview, Guatemala 15, June 2, 2016.
69. Author's interview, Guatemala 13, June 1, 2016.
70. Author's interview, Guatemala 7, May 30, 2016.
71. Author's interview, Guatemala 6, May 30, 2016.
72. Author's interviews, Guatemala 10–12, May 31, 2016.
73. Author's interviews, Guatemala 8, May 30, 2016; Guatemala 10–12, May 31, 2016.
74. Author's interview, Guatemala 6, May 30, 2016.
75. The first Civil Defense Patrol (Patrulla de Autodefensa Civil) was actually organized by Lucas García in 1981 (Schirmer 1998, 83).
76. Author's interview, Guatemala 6, May 30, 2016
77. Author's interview, Guatemala 9, May 31, 2016. "There was great fear in those days. We had to take turns patrolling but with tremendous fear. At the same time, the guerrillas also came to say that we should please not patrol. And so you were really afraid; because one came to organize the patrols, and the other came to block it; so you had a serious problem. From that time on, we began to understand that it was not going to be possible to live in that place anymore." Case 2267, Aldea Nojoyá, Huehuetenango, 1980 (REMHI 1999, 8).
78. Author's interview, Guatemala 5, May 28, 2016.
79. Author's interview, Guatemala 5, May 28, 2016.

4. THE PRODUCTION OF BORDERS

1. These new borders further reinforce the formation of new social identities on the local level (Ballinger 2003).
2. Author's interview, Primorje-Gorski Kotar 14, June 3, 2014.
3. Ibid.
4. Ibid.
5. Author's interviews, Primorje-Gorski Kotar 16, June 3, 2014; Koprivnica-Križevci 16, June 20, 2014.
6. Author's interview, Western Slavonia 7, May 1, 2014.
7. Author's interviews, Western Slavonia 11–12, May 1, 2014; Western Slavonia 14, May 31, 2014.
8. Author's interview, Sisak-Moslavina 9, March 17, 2014.
9. Ibid.
10. Author's interview, Western Slavonia 10, May 1, 2014.

11. Author's interview, Eastern Slavonia 1, February 5, 2014.
12. Author's interview, Eastern Slavonia 6, February 6, 2014.
13. Author's interviews, Eastern Slavonia 16–17, June 9, 2014.
14. Author's interview, Western Slavonia 14, May 31, 2014.
15. "We had created a nation within a nation. We went about establishing our own administration known as Resistance Council (RC) system. Owing to the size of the area under our control, the civilian population was big and we could not be everywhere to police them. We asked them to elect from among themselves whom they trusted as their leaders" (Kutesa [2006] 2008, 121).
16. "Hospitals were not working, there was no movement, all the services were down. The government soldiers spent a full month looking for [Yoweri] Museveni. After one month, they opened the roads again." Author's interviews, Uganda 6–20, May 27, 2015.
17. Author's interview, Uganda 3, May 25, 2015.
18. Author's interview, Guatemala 5, May 28, 2016.
19. Author's interviews, Guatemala 10–12, May 31, 2016.
20. Ibid.
21. Author's interview, Western Slavonia 16, May 31, 2014.
22. HR-DASB-70, HR-DASB/AJ 13401, Republika srpska krajina, Srpska oblast zapadne Slavonije, Oblasno vijeće Okučani [Serbian Republic of Krajina, Serbian district of Western Slavonia, District Council of Okučani], 1992–1995, Slavonski Brod, 70.26, Box 3, "Daruvarski sporazum" [The Agreement of Daruvar].
23. HR-DASB-70, HR-DASB/AJ 13401, Republika srpska krajina, Srpska oblast zapadne Slavonije, Oblasno vijeće Okučani [Serbian Republic of Krajina, Serbian district of Western Slavonia, District Council of Okučani], 1992–1995, Slavonski Brod, 70.14, Box 1, "Minutes from the Meeting of the Fifth Regular Session of the People's Parliament on March 21, 1993," p. 1.
24. "Minutes," 3.
25. "Minutes," 4.
26. "Minutes," 6.
27. "Minutes," 9.
28. HR-DASB-70, HR-DASB/AJ 13401, Republika srpska krajina, Srpska oblast zapadne Slavonije, Oblasno vijeće Okučani, 1992–1995, Slavonski Brod, 70.42, Box 6, "Report on the Situation on the Territory of Western Slavonia," March 24, 1995, Document Number 020-8/95-II-01.
29. "Report on the Situation," 1.
30. This connection was highlighted by Richard Apgar following my presentation of my research findings at the University of the South on February 5, 2016.
31. Based on the report of the United Nations High Commissioner for Refugees (UNHCR) and the Serbian Commissariat for refugees published in 1996, there were 183,031 people who registered as refugees in Serbia in the second part of 1995 from the war-affected areas of Croatia (i.e., the RSK territory that corresponded to the UN sectors at that time), and another 9,997 from other regions of Croatia (UNHCR and Commissariat 1996, 20).
32. Author's interview, northern Dalmatia 24, June 16, 2014.
33. Documenta interview 122, northern Dalmatia, June 21, 2011 (video transcribed by the author).
34. Author's interview, Sisak-Moslavina 11, March 26, 2014.
35. Author's interview, Uganda 5, May 27, 2015.
36. Ibid.
37. Author's interviews, Uganda 6–20, May 27, 2015.
38. Author's interviews, Guatemala 10–12, May 31, 2016.
39. Author's interview, Guatemala 8, May 30, 2016.

40. Author's interview, Guatemala 14, June 1, 2016. The control of movement and commercial activity "often preceded collective murders and community destruction" (REMHI 1999, 43).

41. Author's interview, Guatemala 6, May 30, 2016.

42. Author's interview, Guatemala 9, May 31, 2016.

43. There were not only other communities in the war-affected areas that were split ideologically but also families that were divided between support for the guerrillas and the military. Author's interview, Guatemala 15, June 2, 2016.

44. Author's interview, Guatemala 13, June 1, 2016.

5. MEMORIES AND VIOLENCE

1. Author's interviews, Eastern Slavonia 19–20, June 9, 2014.

2. Also, a recent study on ethnic cleansing in Bosnia and Herzegovina shows no association between the levels of violence in World War II and "patterns of ethnic cleansing" in the 1990s (Bulutgil 2016, 137).

3. See the following scholarship addressing the role of memory in collective identity formation: Apfelbaum 2010; Assmann 2006; Ballinger 2003; J. W. Booth 2006; Brown 2003; Frazier 2007; Halbwachs 1992; Hayden 1994; Hirsch 2008; Lemarchand and Niwese 2007; Malkki 1995; Nora 1989; Passerini [2007] 2014; Pavlaković 2013; Petersen 2005; Posen 1993; Schiemann 2007; Todorova 2004; Waterston and Rylko-Bauer 2006; Winter 2010; Wolfgram 2007; Woolf 2005.

4. See, for example: Dragojević 2013; Frazier 2007; Hobsbawm and Ranger [1983] 1992; Lemarchand and Niwese 2007; Makdisi and Silverstein 2006; Pavlaković 2013; Verdery 1999; Wilmer 2002, 163. In the context of Croatia, for example, Dunja Rihtman-Auguštin has shown how the monument of Ban Jelačić in the central square in Zagreb was used historically by political and state leaders, as well as the educational institutions, as a "motor of the myth of an autonomous and independent national state" (Rihtman-Auguštin 2004, 195).

5. I draw on the approaches of scholars who use oral histories as "historical documents . . . actively and creatively generated by memory and imagination in an effort to make sense of crucial events and of history in general" (Portelli 1991, 26). Also, I build on scholarship that considers remembrance processes as primarily "local" social discourses that "have helped shape the way individuals and communities came to understand themselves both locally and in relation to the state" (Bucur 2009, 3).

6. Interviews were critical for this portion of research because, in some cases, local and family histories or memories of violence may exist only in private and intimate circles, particularly if the account clashes with an official political regime's narrative, in which case it becomes a "suppressed or deliberately hidden histor[y]" (Maynes, Pierce, and Laslett 2008, 8).

7. Author's interview, Sisak-Moslavina 6, March 17, 2014.

8. Jadovno was a concentration and extermination camp during World War II located near Gospić in the county of Ličko-senjska.

9. Author's interview, Western Slavonia 1, May 1, 2014.

10. Author's interview, Koprivnica-Križevci 11, June 19, 2014.

11. Author's interview, Primorje-Gorski Kotar 20, June 4, 2014.

12. Author's interview, Koprivnica-Križevci 2, June 10, 2014.

13. Author's interview, Koprivnica-Križevci 1, June 10, 2014.

14. Author's interview, Koprivnica-Križevci 4, June 11, 2014.

15. Author's interview, Koprivnica-Križevci 9, June 19, 2014.

16. Author's interview, Koprivnica-Križevci 13, June 20, 2014.

17. Author's interview, Koprivnica-Križevci 13, June 20, 2014. A local Croat testified on behalf of a prisoner in Danica in his favor. HR-HDA-1514, 1941–1942, Box 1, "Minutes, May 30 and May 31, 1941," document 1514.7, p. 1.

18. Author's interview, Koprivnica-Križevci 5, June 11, 2014. As a person interested in the study of local history and culture, she mentioned how before World War II, relations among the local populations were harmonious, as evidenced in the presence of local singing groups in which the directors, conductors, and singers were of different religious and ethnic backgrounds, and she noted that all of that changed abruptly after 1941 with the new political regime and the establishment of Danica.

19. Author's interview, Koprivnica-Križevci 17, June 21, 2014.

20. Author's interview, Koprivnica-Križevci 12, June 19, 2014.

21. Author's interview, Koprivnica-Križevci 10, June 19, 2014.

22. Author's interview, Eastern Slavonia 11, June 7, 2014.

23. I thank my panel discussant Nadine Akhund-Lange for the term *self-defense*, which further explains the motivations of people to keep some memories exclusively within a close family circle.

24. "We know that certain silences are observable only when they are broken or interrupted" (Passerini [2007] 2014, 17).

25. "Memory silences" have been examined extensively in the literature: Ballinger 2003; Bergholz 2016; S. Goldstein 2007; Hayden 1994; Jambrešić Kirin 2000, 2006; Jansen 2002; Karge 2009; Pavlaković 2008b, 2008c, 2013; Perica 2002; Verdery 1999; Žerjavić 1992.

26. Tonči Erjavec writes about the history of the village of Španovica in Western Slavonia (1992). According to Erjavec, twelve residents of Španovica joined the Ustaša movement and, forming part of the unit consisting of thirty-six soldiers in total who were stationed in the village, attacked and killed much of the civilian population in the predominantly Serbian villages in the area (108–109, 113–116). The village of Španovica paid a high price for these acts when the Partisans burned it down in the autumn of 1942 (130–147). In the latter part of the book, Erjavec (187–205) discusses briefly the local political context preceding the violence in the 1990s, emphasizing the political and, in large part, ethno-national divisions, which were similar to local divisions from World War II. Another book presenting a history of the village Bujavica and connecting these two periods of wartime is Gligorije-Glišo Savić's *The Past That Repeats Itself* (2007), which recounts, among other events, the experiences of the victims of fascism and the participants in the resistance movement organized by the Partisans in the region during World War II in the village of Bujavica, some thirty kilometers away from Španovica. Savić describes how in the latter part of August 1990, the TO of the self-proclaimed SAO Krajina cut off the village from the "rest of the world" by setting up barricades and limiting the movement of residents (84). Similar to Erjavec, Savić drew on the personal stories of witnesses.

27. Documenta interview 220, Western Slavonia, December 14, 2011 (video transcribed and translated by the author).

28. With the exception of people who might have been part of the Četnik movement in other regions and who migrated after WWII to Eastern Slavonia during the period of the agrarian reforms in the 1960s. A number of respondents who migrated, or whose families migrated, in this period, including both Croats and Serbs, discussed "memories" from their families about Ustaša, Četnik, or Partisan violence during World War II. Author's interviews, Eastern Slavonia 9, February 7, 2014; Eastern Slavonia 3, February 6, 2014; and Eastern Slavonia 17, June 9, 2014.

29. Author's interview, Eastern Slavonia 1, February 5, 2014.

30. As pointed out by Vjeran Pavlaković, plans for the renovation of Dudik started in 2014. Dragan Bošnjak, "Počinje obnova Dudika" [Starting of Dudik renovations], *Novosti*, December 24, 2014, http://www.portalnovosti.com/pocinje-obnova-dudika.

31. Author's interview, Western Slavonia 9, May 1, 2014.
32. I would like to thank Sarah Marhevsky for highlighting this distinction between the two wars.
33. "Spomen ploča žrtvama" [Memorial for victims], *Pakrački list*, June 16, 1995, 3.
34. Author's interview, Northern Dalmatia 10, March 13, 2014.
35. Author's interview, Northern Dalmatia 16, March 11, 2014.
36. Author's interview, Primorje-Gorski Kotar 16, June 3, 2014.
37. Author's interviews, Primorje-Gorski Kotar 3–5, June 2, 2014.
38. Author's interviews, Uganda 21–30, May 28, 2015.
39. Author's interviews, Uganda 21–30, May 28, 2015.
40. Author's interview, Uganda 4, May 26, 2015.
41. Author's interview, Uganda 36, June 3, 2015.
42. Author's interview, Uganda 36, June 3, 2015.
43. Author's interview, Uganda 2, May 25, 2015.
44. Author's interviews, Uganda 6–20, May 27, 2015.
45. Author's interviews, Uganda 6–20, May 27, 2015.
46. Author's interviews, Uganda 6–20, May 27, 2015.
47. Author's interview, Guatemala 14, June 1, 2016.
48. Author's interview, Guatemala 13, June 1, 2016.
49. Author's interview, Guatemala 13, June 1, 2016.
50. Author's interviews, Lika-Senj 4, 6, October 19, 2014.
51. Author's interview, Sisak-Moslavina 2.1, June 24, 2014.
52. This World War II event in the Glina church was described in Documenta interview 260, central Croatia, April 26, 2012 (video transcribed and translated by the author).
53. Author's interview, Sisak-Moslavina 4.1, June 24, 2014. The Croatian Cultural Center was constructed in 1911 as a place for the "meetings of local associations, where cultural work would connect, and where Croatian peasant interests would be promoted." In the 1950s, during the period of modernization, the Croatian Cultural Center becomes known as the Cultural Center (Dom kulture), and it was expanded to include a library and People's University (Narodno sveučilište). After World War II, it became known as the Memorial (Spomen dom), where the memory of the 1941 massacre in the Orthodox church in Glina committed by the Ustaša would be commemorated, but without mentioning the ethnicity of the victims or perpetrators. Igor Mrkalj, "Zloupotreba časnog imena 'Hrvatski dom'" [Misuse of the honorable name "Croatian cultural center"], *Novosti*, January 2015, 4–5.
54. Author's interview, Sisak-Moslavina 5, March 17, 2014.
55. Author's interviews, Koprivnica-Križevci 1, June 10, 2014; Koprivnica-Križevci 9, 10, 11, 12, June 19, 2014; Koprivnica-Križevci 13, 14, 15, June 20, 2014; Koprivnica-Križevci 8, June 15, 2014; Sisak-Moslavina 6, 9, March 17, 2014; northern Dalmatia 1, 6, March 12, 2014; northern Dalmatia 11, 17, March 11, 2014; Eastern Slavonia 19, June 9, 2014; Eastern Slavonia 5, February 6, 2014; Western Slavonia 15, 18, May 31, 2014; Western Slavonia 5, 8, May 1, 2014.
56. Author's interview, northern Dalmatia 17, March 11, 2014.
57. Author's interview, Western Slavonia 18, May 31, 2014.
58. Author's interview, Western Slavonia 5, May 1, 2014.
59. Author's interview, Koprivnica-Križevci 8, June 15, 2014.
60. Author's interview, Koprivnica-Križevci 14, June 20, 2014.
61. Author's interviews, Primorje-Gorski Kotar 6, 7, 8, 9, 10, 11, 12, 13, June 2, 2014.
62. Author's interview, Koprivnica-Križevci 18, June 22, 2014.
63. Author's interviews, Koprivnica-Križevci 19, June 22, 2014; Eastern Slavonia 20, June 9, 2014; Western Slavonia 3, 6, 10, 11, 12, 13, May 1, 2014; Western Slavonia 16, 17, May 31, 2014.

64. Author's interviews, Koprivnica-Križevci 5, June 11, 2014; Primorje-Gorski Kotar 6, 7, 8, 9, 10, 11, 12, 13, June 2, 2014; Primorje-Gorski Kotar 20, June 4, 2014; Sisak-Moslavina 10, March 17, 2014; Sisak-Moslavina 11, March 26, 2014; Sisak-Moslavina 3, March 9, 2014; northern Dalmatia 10, March 13, 2014; Eastern Slavonia 11, June 7, 2014; Western Slavonia 1, May 1, 2014.
65. Author's interview, Primorje-Gorski Kotar 20, June 4, 2014.
66. Author's interviews, Primorje-Gorski Kotar 7, 8, 9, 10, 11, 12, 13, June 2, 2014.
67. Author's interview, northern Dalmatia 10, March 13, 2014.
68. Author's interviews, Primorje-Gorski Kotar 2, 6, 7, 8, 9, 10, 11, 12, 13, June 2, 2014; Sisak-Moslavina 8, March 17, 2014; northern Dalmatia 12, March 11, 2014; northern Dalmatia 2.2, March 12, 2014; Western Slavonia 2, 4, 7, 9, May 1, 2014.
69. Author's interviews, Primorje-Gorski Kotar 1, June 2, 2014; Primorje-Gorski Kotar 19, June 4, 2014; Sisak-Moslavina 1, March 9, 2014; Sisak-Moslavina 14, April 21, 2014.
70. Author's interviews, Sisak-Moslavina 13, March 26, 2014; northern Dalmatia 19, March 14, 2014; Eastern Slavonia 14, June 8, 2014; Eastern Slavonia 16, 17, June 9, 2014, Eastern Slavonia 7, February 6, 2014; Eastern Slavonia 9, February 7, 2014; Western Slavonia 4, May 1, 2014.
71. Author's interviews, Koprivnica-Križevci 4, June 11, 2014; Sisak-Moslavina 13, March 26, 2014.
72. Author's interviews, Koprivnica-Križevci 17, June 21, 2014; Western Slavonia 2, May 1, 2014.
73. Author's interview, Koprivnica-Križevci 7, June 12, 2014.
74. Author's interview, Sisak-Moslavina 7, March 17, 2014.
75. Author's interviews, Sisak-Moslavina 1.1, June 24, 2014; Primorje-Gorski Kotar 18, June 3, 2014; northern Dalmatia 24, June 16, 2014; Eastern Slavonia 10, February 7, 2014; Western Slavonia 1, May 31, 2014; Western Slavonia 7, May 1, 2014.
76. Author's interviews, Eastern Slavonia 1, February 5, 2014; Western Slavonia 20, May 31, 2014.
77. Author's interview, Koprivnica-Križevci 2, June 10, 2014.
78. Author's interview, northern Dalmatia 23, May 15, 2014.
79. Author's interview, Primorje-Gorski Kotar 16, June 3, 2014.
80. Author's interview, Primorje-Gorski Kotar 15, June 3, 2014.
81. Author's interview, Lika-Senj 1, October 18, 2014.
82. Author's interview, northern Dalmatia 9, March 13, 2014.
83. Author's interview, Primorje-Gorski Kotar 19, June 4, 2014.
84. Author's interview, northern Dalmatia 15, March 11, 2014.
85. Author's interview, Eastern Slavonia 7, February 6, 2014.
86. Author's interview, Primorje-Gorski Kotar 2, June 2, 2014.
87. Author's interview, Uganda 31, May 29, 2015.
88. Author's interview, Uganda 31, May 29, 2015.
89. Author's interviews, Uganda 6–20, May 27, 2015.
90. Author's interviews, Uganda 6–20, May 27, 2015.
91. Author's interviews, Uganda 1, May 24, 2015; Uganda 3, May 25, 2015; Uganda 34, June 2, 2015.
92. Author's interview, Uganda 1, May 24, 2015.
93. Author's interview, Uganda 35, June 2, 2015.
94. Author's interviews, Guatemala 16–18, June 2, 2016.
95. Author's interview, Guatemala 13, June 1, 2016.
96. Author's interview, Guatemala 5, May 28, 2016.
97. Author's interview, Guatemala 6, May 30, 2016.
98. Author's interview, Guatemala 9, May 31, 2016.

6. VIOLENCE AGAINST CIVILIANS AS A POLITICAL STRATEGY

1. Similarly, Laia Balcells (2017) argues that political rather than purely military reasons explain the patterns of violence against civilians in the Spanish Civil War. My work complements the findings of Balcells and other scholars who bring political factors back into the analysis of violence against civilians.

2. I would like to thank Max Bergholz for posing a question that led me toward making this conceptual distinction more clearly.

3. See the related concept of the "founding narrative" that Scott Straus (2015) developed to explain why, in some African states, civilians may be targeted and excluded politically on the basis of ethnicity.

4. Victim questionnaire 1, 2, and 3, Glina municipality, provided by Documenta to the author in 2014.

5. Victim questionnaire 1, Glina municipality, provided by Documenta to the author in 2014.

6. Victim questionnaire 3, Glina municipality, provided by Documenta to the author in 2014.

7. There is no specific information about the perpetrator of this crime, but most probably it was a member of the Serb paramilitary force that had used civilians as a human shield.

8. Victim questionnaire 2, Glina municipality, provided by Documenta to the author in 2014.

9. Victim questionnaire 4, Glina municipality, provided by Documenta to the author in 2014.

10. Victim questionnaire 4, Glina municipality, provided by Documenta to the author in 2014.

11. Based on the First Level Judgment on February 2, 2012 in Vukovar County Court, one of the accused was found not guilty, and this judgment was later confirmed by the Supreme Court (Documenta, n.d.e). The other fourteen perpetrators were put on trial and found guilty in the judgment, which was not legally binding in the Belgrade District Court (Documenta, n.d.f). Other sources list fifty persons, including one person who was killed on the way to the minefield (ICTY 2004, 16; ICTY 2012a, 10).

12. "Upon reaching the minefield, the detainees were forced to enter the minefield and sweep their feet in front of them to clear the field of mines" (ICTY 2004, 16; ICTY 2012a, 10). See also the reports of the Belgrade Circuit Court proceedings that took place from 2008 to 2012 (Documenta, n.d.f).

13. Other sources list one person killed on the way to the minefield and twenty-one persons killed at the minefield (ICTY 2004, 16; ICTY 2012a, 10).

14. Minutes of the Proceedings in the Vukovar County Court, June 30, 2004, 2, provided by Documenta to the author in 2014.

15. Minutes of the Proceedings in the Vukovar County Court, June 30, 2004, 2–3, provided by Documenta to the author in 2014.

16. Victim questionnaire 1, Lovas municipality, provided by Documenta to the author in 2014.

17. Victim questionnaire 2, Lovas municipality, provided by Documenta to the author in 2014.

18. See nos. 30, 31, 32, and 33 (ICTY 2012a, 11).

19. See no. 55 (ICTY 2004, 16–17) and no. 33 (ICTY 2012a, 12).

20. See no. 49 (ICTY 2004, 15).

21. See no. 31 (ICTY 2012a, 11).

22. Documenta, n.d.b; Filip Rudic, "Serbian Court Sentences Eight for Ovcara Massacre," *Balkan Insight*, January 15, 2018, http://www.balkaninsight.com/en/article/serbian

-court-sentences-eight-in-ovcara-massacre-case-01-15-2018; Hina, "Ovčara, Vukovar: Serbia Acquits 4, Upholds 8 Sentences," *Total Croatia News*, January 16, 2018, https://www.total-croatia-news.com/politics/24478-ovcara-serbia-acquits-4-upholds-8-sentences.

23. Additionally, Milošević was indicted for crimes in Kosovo in 1999 and for crimes in Bosnia and Herzegovina in 2001 (ICTY, n.d.b).

24. Documenta interview 279, central Croatia, December 5, 2012, lines 562–619.

25. Documenta interview 279, central Croatia, December 5, 2012, lines 562–619.

26. Documenta interview 279, central Croatia, December 5, 2012, lines 562–619.

27. See no. 40 (ICTY 2004, 13–14).

28. Minutes from the Witness Testimony outside of the Trial Proceedings, Hrvatska Kostajnica Municipal Court in the name of Rijeka County Court, June 12, 2012, No. 220.2.2012, p. 2, provided by Documenta to the author in 2014.

29. Mate Piškor, "Optužnica protiv šestorice državljana Srbije, ubojica iz Gline 1991" [Charge against six citizens of Serbia, killers from Glina in 1991], *Slobodna Dalmacija*, June 11, 2008, http://urednik.slobodnadalmacija.hr/novosti/crna-kronika/clanak/id/10206/optuznica-protiv-sestorice-drzavljana-srbije-ubojica-iz-gline-1991.

30. Piškor; author's interview, Sisak-Moslavina 5.1, June 24, 2014.

31. Piškor.

32. For crimes in Široka Kula, see First Level Judgment, Gospić County Court, June 16, 1994. Seven perpetrators were sentenced to imprisonment ranging from fifteen to twenty years. They were sentenced in absentia, however. This judgment was confirmed by the Supreme Court on October 25, 1994, provided by Documenta to the author in 2014.

33. Members of the police forces of SAO Krajina committed violence against civilians whom they suspected to be cooperating with the Croat armed forces in Lički Osik in October 1991. Four perpetrators were sentenced by the courts in Belgrade to imprisonment ranging from ten to twelve years (Documenta, n.d.a).

34. First Level Judgment, Gospić County Court, June 16, 1994, 2.

35. See nos. 45, 46, and 47 (ICTY 2004, 14–15).

36. See no. 47 (ICTY 2004, 15).

37. Author's interview, northern Dalmatia 15, March 11, 2014.

38. Based on the respondent's observation, before the mass violence started, people did not divide along ethnic lines in this ethnically diverse region.

39. The court document mentions that there were at least thirty-nine victims who were killed on the location of Lipova Glavica, but the exact number is not known. See First Level Judgment, Rijeka County Court, March 24, 2003, 2–3, 353, provided by Documenta to the author in 2014. Three perpetrators were sentenced to imprisonment ranging from twelve to fifteen years (3). This judgment was confirmed by the Supreme Court on June 2, 2004, provided by Documenta to the author in 2014.

40. First Level Judgment, Rijeka County Court, March 24, 2003, 2–3, 14.

41. First Level Judgment, Rijeka County Court, March 24, 2003, 353.

42. First Level Judgment, Rijeka County Court, March 24, 2003, 353.

43. Author's interview, northern Dalmatia 19, March 14, 2014. Once the population was divided along the Krajina borders and the violence was already taking place, it was easier for rumors to be perceived as credible warnings of a life-threatening danger. People like this respondent recognized, however, that rumors were more believable during the time of war precisely because it was not a "normal life."

44. Based on the existing data from the UNHCR and the Commissariat for Refugees of the Republic of Serbia, the largest number of refugees arrived in Serbia from July through December 1995, even though the refugees began arriving in 1991. From July 1 until December 31, 1995, a total of 181,010 arrived from the Croatian UN protected areas and 12,349 from other parts of Croatia, amounting to a total of 193,359 people who arrived in

Serbia and were registered as refugees in this period (UNHCR and Commissariat 1996, 34, table 17a, "Refugees Based on Prior Residency and Time of Arrival"). In order to provide a point of comparison, the total number of refugees from Croatia who were registered by the UNHCR in Serbia in 1996, and who arrived in the period from 1991 until June 6, 1996, amounted to 290,667, and 67 percent of those refugees arrived in the second part of 1995, within a month before and four months after the military operation Oluja (UNHCR and Commissariat 1996, 34). The total number of registered refugees in Serbia in 1996 was 537,937, and the refugees from Croatia amounted to 54 percent, while the refugees from Bosnia and Herzegovina amounted to 43 percent (UNHCR and Commissariat 1996, 34).

45. One of the few scholarly studies, although even this study was based on disputed data (which the author, Croatian historian Igor Graovac, corrected throughout his work), showed that in the UN Protected Sector South, including Lika and northern Dalmatia, 414 civilians died in 1995 (2004a, 134, 140). Among the victims, two-thirds were male, two-thirds were over sixty years of age, and 97 percent were ethnic Serbs (Graovac 2004a, 138–140). The cause of death of these victims varied, and the report listed the following categories: "burned to death," "found dead," "thrown into a water well, pit, or fire," "shot," "slaughtered," "missing," "died by hanging," and "died from bombings and grenades" (141–142).

46. There are several questions raised by the circumstances of this military operation that remain. Why did most civilians in the RSK territory flee even though they were not part of the insurgency and presumably had nothing to fear? Also, why did many of them not return soon after the military operation ended, as evidenced by their registration in Serbia as refugees a year afterward? While it is beyond the scope of this book to answer these questions systematically, it is relevant to pose them because they point to the long-term consequences of the use of violence as a political strategy throughout the four years of the war. Given that the processes of ethnicization had already started in the local communities of the RSK territory, where the exclusion of moderates, the production of violence, and the mass crimes previously outlined had already created enemies of former neighbors, civilians in these communities represented the extension of the various armed forces and also a potential political threat to the new regime.

47. On November 16, 2012, Ante Gotovina and Mladen Markač were acquitted of all charges following the appeal (ICTY 2012b, 55–56).

48. See vol. 2 (ICTY 2011, 1339–1341).

49. The Alliance of Anti-Fascist Veterans of Croatia (Savez antifašističkih boraca Hrvatske) documented the destruction of 731 monuments and 2,233 other commemorative markers from 1990 to 2000 (Hrženjak 2002). For instance, some of the monuments that were destroyed entirely commemorate "the killing of Serbs by Ustaša," "the killing of Jews," or "murders or other crimes against Croats committed by fascist occupiers (Italians or German)"; "speak about the role of the Communist Party and particular notable organizers of the People's Anti-Fascist Struggle, members of the Communist Party"; "promote Tito as an organizer of the anti-fascist forces and victory over fascism"; or "promote the brotherhood and unity of Croat, Serb, and other ethnicities as a role in their victory over fascism" (xii). The attempts to change the names of public spaces associated with the former regime occurred all across Croatia, even in the capital city of Zagreb and other areas that were not directly affected by war (Rihtman-Auguštin 2000). For example, in December 1990, the local government in Zagreb changed the name of the Square of the Anti-Fascist Struggle (Trg žrtava fašizma) to the Square of the Prominent Croats (Trg hrvatskih velikana) (Karačić, Banjeglav, and Govedarica 2012; Pavlaković 2011; Rihtman-Auguštin 2000). In this case, however, as a result of the organized protests of the city residents, the

name of the square was changed back to the original name, which it is still known by today (Pavlaković 2011).

50. Unlike the violence against civilians, however, as noted already, the destruction of monuments occurred not only in times of war but also in some cases many years after the war had ended. In 2001, a grave commemorating national heroes from World War II in the Mirogoj cemetery in Zagreb was partially destroyed with an explosive, while a monument commemorating the victims of Ustaša violence in 1941 in the village of Prkos was destroyed in its entirety (Karačić, Banjeglav, and Govedarica 2012, 101).

51. Igor Mrkalj, "Zloupotreba časnog imena 'Hrvatski dom'" [Misuse of the honorable name "Croatian cultural center"], *Novosti*, January 2015, 4–5.

52. In this study, Lešaja (2012, 73–90) showed that while the destruction of literature during the war was documented particularly in the two most violent years of the war—1991 and 1992—in 56 newspaper articles, two monographs, six books, and 9 other sources, the evidence of the general destruction of literature in the areas outside the war zones, and even after the war had ended, is more extensive, as it spans decades, from 1990 through 2009, and includes 140 newspaper articles, three monographs, nine books, fifteen manuscripts, and 124 other sources.

53. Also, the mosques and Serb churches were destroyed across Croatia and Bosnia and Herzegovina in the 1990s (Perica 2002, 3–4, 248).

54. For example, wartime conditions, the lack of work, and adverse living conditions contributed to the recruitment of minors into various armies and to higher rates of mortality. Author's interviews, Uganda 1, May 24, 2015; Uganda 34, June 2, 2015.

55. Author's interview, Uganda 35, June 2, 2015.

56. Author's interview, Uganda 35, June 2, 2015.

57. Author's interview, Uganda 35, June 2, 2015.

58. Author's interview, Uganda 35, June 2, 2015.

59. Author's interview, Uganda 4, May 26, 2015.

60. Author's interview, Uganda 4, May 26, 2015.

61. Author's interview, Uganda 4, May 26, 2015.

62. Author's interview, Uganda 31, May 29, 2015.

63. Author's interview, Uganda 31, May 29, 2015. Another respondent mentioned that the northern tribes had more power in the government, while the Baganda "felt bitter . . . against government because of atrocities which had been committed against the fellow Baganda and against the people who belonged to the Democratic Party." Author's interview, Uganda 32, May 29, 2015. This statement illustrates how the ethnic and political identities began to merge on the local level and resonate among ordinary citizens, not just among the political or military elites.

64. Author's interview, Uganda 36, June 3, 2015.

65. Author's interview, Uganda 32, May 29, 2015.

66. Author's interview, Uganda 32, May 29, 2015.

67. Author's interviews, Uganda 6–20, May 27, 2015.

68. Author's interview, Uganda 2, May 25, 2015. In the view of this witness, "rape was used to dehumanize people," or, more specifically, women and other civilians, during the war.

69. Author's interviews, Uganda 21–30, May 28, 2015.

70. This would explain why some of my respondents considered civilians to be not targets but rather "casualties of war" or victims of government soldiers "because of what happens in war," such as when they fell under suspicion of being "traitors" or "informers." Author's interview, Uganda 34, June 2, 2015.

71. Author's interviews, Uganda 21–30, May 28, 2015.

72. "The guerrillas advanced, they knew that they needed to befriend other people . . . local people, while the government army was against the local people. We were supporting the guerrillas. That was their major weapon, forming the relationships with local people. They trusted the local people. And when the government soldiers were oppressing us, for us, we saw saviors in the guerrillas. Whenever we had something to eat, we would share it with them. Friendship was the major weapon of the guerrillas." Yet this contradicts the statement of another respondent, who noted that under wartime conditions people did not even trust their own family members: "Your very brother could betray you. . . . We were told not to trust even your very shadow, even your very shadow. Be careful of everybody, even your brother, and even your shadow. That was the motto during that time when we were being trained." Author's interviews, Uganda 21–30, May 28, 2015.

73. Author's interviews, Uganda 21–30, May 28, 2015.

74. Author's interview, Uganda 1, May 24, 2015.

75. Author's interviews, Guatemala 1–4, May 27, 2016. They did not understand why some people in their community were killed, but they knew that in order to survive, they had to flee with their children when they heard that the army was coming. When Montt came to power, the situation calmed down in their own village because people had to join the civil patrols, the organization that served as a buffer between the guerrillas and the military, even though killings continued in neighboring villages.

76. Some of the problems with categorization that have already been noted, such as distinguishing between civilians and participants, are not unique to the case of Guatemala. In her study of how Guatemalans dealt with their losses, entitled *Who Counts? The Mathematics of Death and Life after Genocide*, Diane M. Nelson writes that "Guatemalans used to guesstimate the toll . . . by saying every extended family had lost at least one person—so everyone is minus one" (2015, 2). She writes that some cases of collective crimes, such as those in Joyabaj, were not "counted" in the report by Guatemala's Commission for Historical Clarification, even though they were a "public secret" until "a landslide revealed human remains" in 2000 (Nelson 2015, 76). But there are also damages that do not lend themselves easily to counting, such as the psychological effects of having endured the war and having to live "side-by-side with the men responsible for their suffering" (86). Even qualitatively, it is difficult to demonstrate the effect of war on people. The translated transcriptions generally do not reveal the full extent of the intimate, personal, and deep emotions that my respondents shared with me over the course of the interviews. For example, a person who was arrested and tortured did not wait for me to ask the first interview question. He started telling me his story right after the introductions because, as he said after the interview, he had a need to "get it off of [his] chest." Author's interviews, Guatemala 1–4, May 27, 2016. His pain did not pass with the years. Another respondent, whose words I could not understand because she spoke only Quiché and her husband was translating into Spanish, was looking directly in my eyes during the entire interview. Author's interview, Guatemala 7, May 30, 2016. As she was telling me how she lost her child and father while fleeing from the army and hiding in the ravines, her eyes were full of tears. Her sadness remained the same even though many years have passed since the deaths of her loved ones. Therefore, acknowledging that we, as social scientists, cannot fully capture, either quantitatively or qualitatively, the experiences of people who endured the war is an important point of departure when considering the effects of the war.

77. Author's interview, Guatemala 7, May 30, 2016.

78. Author's interview, Guatemala 14, June 1, 2016.

79. Author's interview, Guatemala 5, May 28, 2016.

80. Author's interview, Guatemala 5, May 28, 2016.

81. Author's interview, Guatemala 5, May 28, 2016. For example, in a massacre at Finca San Francisco Nenton in 1982, most of the soldiers who perpetrated violence against the

indigenous community were of indigenous identity themselves and were recruited from "neighboring villages, such as nearby San Miguel, Jacaltenango; the survivors could tell by their manner of speaking" (Garrard-Burnett 2010, 96).

82. Author's interview, Guatemala 5, May 28, 2016. As a result, he was able to learn about survival methods of communities that were isolated during the war and to observe that, as in the time of peace, there were individuals who were initially motivated to improve the conditions of their respective communities but over time became more concerned with their personal interest.

83. Author's interviews, Guatemala 16–18, June 2, 2016.

84. Author's interview, Guatemala 9, May 31, 2016.

85. In several cases, though, civil patrollers were not simply forced, but they looked as if they were killing "with the full intention of wiping out 'the ones from the mountains'" (Montejo 1987, 62). According to a testimony by a former insurgent, one army officer only verified that the patrollers carried out the execution: "From that day I knew the attitude of this new officer who had washed his hands of the crime, so that he could claim that the army does not kill, that it is the Indian defenders who are doing the butchering. . . . How astute of him!" (67).

86. Author's interview, Guatemala 5, May 28, 2016.

87. Author's interviews, Guatemala 1–4, May 27, 2016.

88. Author's interviews, Guatemala 16–18, June 2, 2016.

89. Author's interviews, Guatemala 16–18, June 2, 2016.

90. In the words of Irm Haleem, when talking about her research on terrorist political violence (2012, 5).

91. Author's interview, Sisak-Moslavina 4.1, June 24, 2014.

92. Author's interview, northern Dalmatia 12, March 11, 2014.

93. Author's interview, northern Dalmatia 12, March 11, 2014.

94. Author's interview, northern Dalmatia 12, March 11, 2014.

95. Author's interview, northern Dalmatia 12, March 11, 2014.

96. Author's interview, northern Dalmatia 12, March 11, 2014.

97. Author's interview, Sisak-Moslavina 11, March 26, 2014.

98. Author's interview, Eastern Slavonia 15, June 9, 2014.

99. Author's interview, Eastern Slavonia 15, June 9, 2014.

100. Author's interview, Eastern Slavonia 15, June 9, 2014.

101. Author's interview, Eastern Slavonia 8, February 7, 2014.

102. Author's interview, northern Dalmatia 12, March 11, 2014.

103. Author's interview, Sisak-Moslavina 12, March 26, 2014.

CONCLUSION

1. Author's interview, Eastern Slavonia 15, June 9, 2014.

APPENDIX

1. Helga Paškvan, who holds a master's degree in cultural studies, was a student at the University of Rijeka when she worked as the research assistant for this project. I am including her excerpt to provide a glimpse into the ethnographic research process for this book and highlight its transforming effects on the researchers, the participants, and, hopefully, the readers. This is also a form of recognition to Helga, as I am indebted to her for contributing both her time and her talent for ethnography to this project. Helga wrote the original text in Croatian and removed respondents' identifying information, and I translated it.

References

Agamben, Giorgio. 1995. *Homo Sacer: Sovereign Power and Bare Life*. Stanford, CA: Stanford University Press. Kindle.
——. 2005. *State of Exception*. Translated by Kevin Attell. Chicago: University of Chicago Press.
——. 2015. *Stasis: Civil War as a Political Paradigm (Homo Sacer II, 2)*. Translated by Nicholas Heron. Stanford, CA: Stanford University Press.
Amoureux, Jack. 2015. *A Practice of Ethics for Global Polities: Ethical Reflexivity*. New York: Routledge.
Anderson, Benedict. 1983. *Imagined Communities: Reflections on the Origin and Spread of Nationalism*. London: Verso.
Apfelbaum, Erika. 2010. "Halbwachs and the Social Properties of Memory." In *Memory: Histories, Theories, Debates*, edited by Susannah Radstone and Bill Schwarz, 77–92. New York: Fordham University Press.
Archivo Histórico de la Policía Nacional. 2013. *From Silence to Memory: Revelations of the AHPN*. Foreword by Carlos Aguirre. Preface to the English translation by Kate Doyle. Eugene: University of Oregon Libraries.
Arendt, Hannah. (1963) 2006. *Eichmann in Jerusalem: A Report on the Banality of Evil*. New edition with an introduction by Amos Elon. New York: Penguin Books.
——. 1998. *The Human Condition*. Chicago: University of Chicago Press.
Assmann, Jan. 2006. "Kultura sjećanja" [The culture of memory]. In *Kultura pamćenja i historija* [The culture of remembering and history], edited by Maja Brkljačić and Sandra Prlenda, 45–78. Zagreb: Golden Marketing–Tehnička knjiga.
Autesserre, Séverine. 2010. *The Trouble with Congo: Local Violence and the Failure of International Peacebuilding*. New York: Cambridge University Press.
——. 2014. *Peaceland: Conflict Resolution and the Everyday Politics of International Intervention*. New York: Cambridge University Press.
Babić, Dragutin. 2008. *Suživot Hrvata i Srba u Slavoniji: (Re)konstrukcija multietničkih lokalnih zajednica nakon ratnih sukoba* [Coexistence between Serbs and Croats in Slavonia: (Re)construction of multiethnic local communities after the war]. Zagreb: Golden Marketing–Tehnička knjiga.
Baguma, Yosam. 2009. "*Panda Gari* Experience." In *Looking Back: Personal Memories of Uganda's Troubled Past, 1970–2000*, edited by Patricia Haward, 68–71. Kampala: Fountain Publishers.
Bahemuka, T. L. Kisembo. 2009. "Cookie Night." In *Looking Back: Personal Memories of Uganda's Troubled Past, 1970–2000*, edited by Patricia Haward, 64–67. Kampala: Fountain Publishers.
Balcells, Laia. 2010. "Rivalry and Revenge: Violence against Civilians in Conventional Civil Wars." *International Studies Quarterly* 54:291–313.
——. 2017. *Rivalry and Revenge: The Politics of Violence during Civil War*. New York: Cambridge University Press.
Balcells, Laia, and Patricia Justino. 2014. "Bridging Micro and Macro Approaches on Civil Wars and Political Violence: Issues, Challenges and the Way Forward." *Journal of Conflict Resolution* 58 (8): 1343–1359.

Ballinger, Pamela. 2003. *History in Exile: Memory and Identity at the Borders of the Balkans*. Princeton, NJ: Princeton University Press.
Banac, Ivo. 1984. *The National Question in Yugoslavia: Origins, History, Politics*. Ithaca, NY: Cornell University Press.
Barić, Nikica. 2005. *Srpska pobuna u Hrvatskoj, 1990–1995* [Serbian rebellion in Croatia, 1990–1995]. Zagreb: Golden Marketing–Tehnička knjiga.
Barth, Fredrik. 1996. "Ethnic Groups and Boundaries (1969)." In *Theories of Ethnicity: A Classical Reader*, edited by Werner Sollors, 294–324. New York: New York University Press.
Batović, Ante. 2017. *The Croatian Spring: Nationalism, Repression and Foreign Policy under Tito*. New York: I. B. Tauris.
Benhabib, Seyla. 2002. *The Claims of Culture: Equality and Diversity in the Global Era*. Princeton, NJ: Princeton University Press.
Bergholz, Max. 2016. *Violence as a Generative Force: Identity, Nationalism, and Memory in a Balkan Community*. Ithaca, NY: Cornell University Press.
Bermeo, Nancy. 2003. *Ordinary People in Extraordinary Times: The Citizenry and the Breakdown of Democracy*. Princeton, NJ: Princeton University Press.
Bieber, Florian. 2007. "The Role of the Yugoslav People's Army in the Dissolution of Yugoslavia: The Army without a State?" In *State Collapse in South-Eastern Europe: New Perspectives on Yugoslavia's Disintegration*, edited by Lenard J. Cohen and Jasna Dragović-Soso, 301–332. West Lafayette, IN: Purdue University Press.
Bilić, Bojan. 2012. "'Movementising' the Marginal: Recruitment to the Anti-war Campaign of Croatia." *Narodna umjetnost* 49 (1): 41–58.
Blattman, Christopher, and Edward Miguel. 2010. "Civil War." *Journal of Economic Literature* 48 (1): 3–57.
Booth, James W. 2006. *Communities of Memory: On Witness, Identity, and Justice*. New York: Cornell University Press.
Booth, John A., Christine J. Wade, and Thomas W. Walker. 2014. *Understanding Central America: Global Forces, Rebellion, and Change*. 6th ed. Boulder, CO: Westview.
Brass, Paul R. 1997. *Theft of an Idol: Text and Context in the Representation of Collective Violence*. Princeton, NJ: Princeton University Press.
Bringa, Tone. 1995. *Being Muslim the Bosnian Way: Identity and Community in a Central Bosnian Village*. Princeton, NJ: Princeton University Press.
Brockett, Charles D. 2005. *Political Movements and Violence in Central America*. New York: Cambridge University Press.
Brown, Keith. 2003. *The Past in Question: Modern Macedonia and the Uncertainties of Nation*. Princeton, NJ: Princeton University Press.
Buckley-Zistel, Susanne. 2008. *Conflict Transformation and Social Change in Uganda: Remembering after Violence*. New York: Palgrave Macmillan.
Bucur, Maria. 2009. *Heroes and Victims: Remembering War in Twentieth-Century Romania*. Bloomington: Indiana University Press.
Bulutgil, H. Zeynep. 2010. "War, Collaboration, and Endogenous Ethnic Polarization: The Path to Ethnic Cleansing." In *Rethinking Violence: States and Non-state Actors in Conflict*, edited by Adria Lawrence and Erica Chenoweth, 57–81. Cambridge, MA: MIT Press.
———. 2016. *The Roots of Ethnic Cleansing in Europe*. New York: Cambridge University Press.
Calhoun, Craig. 2003. "'Belonging' in the Cosmopolitan Imaginary." *Ethnicities* 3 (4): 531–568.

Cammett, Melani. 2013. "Using Proxy Interviewing to Address Sensitive Topics." In *Interview Research in Political Science*, edited by Layna Mosley, 125–143. Ithaca, NY: Cornell University Press.

Cederman, Lars-Erik, Kristian Skrede Gleditsch, and Halvard Buhaug. 2013. *Inequality, Grievances, and Civil War*. New York: Cambridge University Press.

Cederman, Lars-Erik, Nils B. Weidmann, and Kristian Skrede Gleditsch. 2011. "Horizontal Inequalities and Ethnonationalist Civil War: A Global Comparison." *American Political Science Review* 105 (3): 478–495.

Cohen, Lenard J. 1993. *Broken Bonds: The Disintegration of Yugoslavia*. Boulder, CO: Westview.

———. 2007. "Disintegrative Synergies and the Dissolution of Socialist Federations: Yugoslavia in Comparative Perspective." In *State Collapse in South-Eastern Europe: New Perspectives on Yugoslavia's Disintegration*, edited by Lenard J. Cohen and Jasna Dragović-Soso, 365–396. West Lafayette, IN: Purdue University Press.

Das, Veena. 2007. *Life and Words: Violence and the Descent into the Ordinary*. Oakland: University of California Press.

Derrida, Jacques. 2005. *Rogues: Two Essays on Reason*. Translated by Pascale-Anne Brault and Michael Naas. Stanford, CA: Stanford University Press.

———. 2009. *The Beast and the Sovereign*. Translated by Geoffrey Bennington. 2 vols. Vol. 1. Chicago: University of Chicago Press.

———. 2010. *The Beast and the Sovereign*. Translated by Geoffrey Bennington. 2 vols. Vol. 2. Chicago: University of Chicago Press.

Dević, Ana. 1997. "Anti-war Initiatives and the Un-making of Civic Identities in the Former Yugoslav Republics." *Journal of Historical Sociology* 10 (2): 127–156.

Djokić, Dejan, ed. 2003. *Yugoslavism: Histories of a Failed Idea, 1918–1992*. Madison: University of Wisconsin Press.

Documenta. 2017. "Poimenični popis poginulih i nestalih / Sisačko-moslovačka županija." ["List of the deceased and missing individuals / Sisak Moslavina County"] December 13, 2017. Accessed November 20, 2018. https://www.documenta.hr/hr/poimeni%C4%8Dni-popis-poginulih-i-nestalih-sisa%C4%8Dko-moslova%C4%8Dka-%C5%BEupanija.html.

———. n.d.a. "Crime in Lički Osik." Accessed November 20, 2018. https://www.documenta.hr/en/crime-in-lički-osik.html.

———. n.d.b. "Crime in Ovčara (Miroljub Vujović et al. Case)." Accessed November 20, 2018. https://www.documenta.hr/en/crime-in-ovčara-miroljub-vujović-et-al.-case.html.

———. n.d.c. "Gornje Jame i Joševica—zločini nad hrvatskim civilima." Accessed November 20, 2018. https://www.documenta.hr/hr/gornje-jame-i-joševica-zločini-nad-hrvatskim-civilima.html.

———. n.d.d. "Istraživanje ljudskih gubitaka / Zapadna Slavonija." Accessed November 20, 2018. https://www.documenta.hr/en/istra%C5%BEivanje-ljudskih-gubitaka-zapadna-slavonija.html.

———. n.d.e. "Zločin u Lovasu." Accessed November 20, 2018. https://www.documenta.hr/hr/zločin-u-lovasu.html.

———. n.d.f. "Zločin u Lovasu." Accessed November 20, 2018. https://www.documenta.hr/hr/zločin-u-lovasu-1.html.

Downes, Alexander B., and Kathryn McNabb Cochran. 2010. "Targeting Civilians to Win? Assessing the Military Effectiveness of Civilian Victimization in Interstate War." In *Rethinking Violence: States and Non-state Actors in Conflict*, edited by Adria Lawrence and Erica Chenoweth, 23–56. Cambridge, MA: MIT Press.

Dragojević, Mila. 2013. "Memory and Identity: Intergenerational Narratives of Violence among Refugees in Serbia." *Nationalities Papers* 41 (4): 1065–1082.
———. 2016. "Violence and the Production of Borders in Western Slavonia." *Slavic Review* 75 (2): 422–445.
Dragojević, Mila, and Vjeran Pavlaković. 2017. "Local Memories of Wartime Violence: Commemorating World War Two in Gospić." *Suvremene teme* 8 (1): 66–87.
Dragović-Soso, Jasna. 2007. "Why Did Yugoslavia Disintegrate? An Overview of Contending Explanations." In *State Collapse in South-Eastern Europe: New Perspectives on Yugoslavia's Disintegration*, edited by Lenard J. Cohen and Jasna Dragović-Soso, 1–39. West Lafayette, IN: Purdue University Press.
Driscoll, Jesse. 2015. *Warlords and Coalition Politics*. New York: Cambridge University Press.
Eck, Kristine, and Lisa Hultman. 2007. "One-Sided Violence against Civilians in War: Insights from New Fatality Data." *Journal of Peace Research* 44 (2): 233–246.
Erjavec, Tonči. 1992. *Španovica: Kronika nastajanja i nestanka* [Španovica: The chronicle of creation and disappearance]. Zagreb: Novi liber.
Esposito, Roberto. 2010. *Communitas: The Origin and Destiny of Community*. Translated by Timothy Campbell. Stanford, CA: Stanford University Press.
———. 2011. *Immunitas: The Protection and Negation of Life*. Translated by Zakiya Hanafi. Cambridge, UK: Polity.
Fagerlund, Emilia. 2011. "The Tigers' Roar: Insurgent Violence against Civilians in Sri Lanka." *Psychology and Society* 4 (1): 96–116.
Falla, Ricardo. 1994. *Massacres in the Jungle*. Boulder, CO: Westview.
Fein, Helen. 1979. *Accounting for Genocide: National Responses and Jewish Victimization during the Holocaust*. New York: Free Press.
Finkel, Evgeny. 2012. "Mass Killing and Local Context." *Comparative Politics* 45 (1): 107–124.
Forti, Simona. 2015. *New Demons: Rethinking Power and Evil Today*. Stanford, CA: Stanford University Press.
Foucault, Michel. (1978) 1990. *The History of Sexuality*. Vol. 1, *An Introduction*. Vintage Books edition. New York: Vintage Books.
———. 2003. *"Society Must Be Defended": Lectures at the College de France, 1975–76*. New York: Picador.
Frazier, Lessie Jo. 2007. *Memory, Violence, and the Nation-State in Chile, 1890 to the Present*. Durham, NC: Duke University Press.
Fujii, Lee Ann. 2009. *Killing Neighbors: Webs of Violence in Rwanda*. Ithaca, NY: Cornell University Press.
Gagnon, V. P. 1995. "Ethnic Nationalism and International Conflict: The Case of Serbia." *International Security* 19:130–166.
———. 2004. *The Myth of Ethnic War: Serbia and Croatia in the 1990s*. Ithaca, NY: Cornell University Press.
Garrard-Burnett, Virginia. 2010. *Terror in the Land of the Holy Spirit: Guatemala under General Efraín Ríos Montt, 1982–1983*. New York: Oxford University Press.
Gellner, Ernest. 1983. *Nations and Nationalism*. Oxford: Blackwell.
Girard, Rene. 1972. *Violence and the Sacred*. Baltimore: Johns Hopkins University Press.
Glad, Nada. 2017. *Goranski MIR-ovi* [Peace activism in Gorski Kotar]. Delnice, Croatia: Matica Hrvatska Čabar.
Glaurdić, Josip. 2011. *The Hour of Europe: Western Powers and the Breakup of Yugoslavia*. New Haven, CT: Yale University Press.
Goldhagen, Daniel Jonah. 1996. *Hitler's Willing Executioners: Ordinary Germans and the Holocaust*. New York: Alfred A. Knopf.

Goldstein, Ivo. 2008. *Hrvatska, 1918–2008* [Croatia, 1918–2008]. Zagreb: EPH Novi Liber.
Goldstein, Slavko. 2007. *1941: Godina koja se vraća* [1941: The year that keeps returning]. Zagreb: Novi Liber.
Goldstein, Slavko, and Ivo Goldstein. 2011. *Jasenovac i Bleiburg nisu isto* [Jasenovac and Bleiburg are not the same]. Zagreb: Novi Liber.
Gordy, Eric. 2007. "Destruction of the Yugoslav Federation: Policy or Confluence of Tactics?" In *State Collapse in South-Eastern Europe: New Perspectives on Yugoslavia's Disintegration*, edited by Lenard J. Cohen and Jasna Dragović-Soso, 281–299. West Lafayette, IN: Purdue University Press.
——. 2013. *Guilt, Responsibility, and Denial: The Past at Stake in Post-Milošević Serbia*. Philadelphia: University of Pennsylvania Press.
Graovac, Igor. 2004a. "Civilne žrtve u Sektoru Jug u Oluji i neposredno nakon Oluje (osnovni pokazatelji)" [Civilian victims in Sector South during and immediately after the Operation Storm (key indicators)]. *Polemos* 7 (13–14): 129–145.
——. 2004b. "Pokazatelji o civilnim žrtvama u bivšem, pod zaštitom Ujedinjenih naroda, Sektoru Sjever u Oluji i nakon nje" ["Characteristics of civilian victims in the former Sector North, under the protection of the United Nations, during the Operation Storm and after"]. In *Dijalog povjesničara/istoričara*, edited by H.-G. Fleck and I. Graovac, 449–466. Zagreb: Zaklada Friedrich Naumann.
Graovac, Igor and Dragan Cvetković. 2005. *Ljudski gubici Hrvatske 1941–1945. Godine: pitanja, primjeri, rezultati . . .* [Human losses in Croatia, 1941–1945: Questions, examples, results . . .]. Zagreb: Dijalog and Friedrich Naumann Stiftung.
Gurr, Ted. 1969. *Why Men Rebel*. Princeton, NJ: Princeton University Press.
Hajdarpašić, Edin. 2015. *Whose Bosnia? Nationalism and Political Imagination in the Balkans, 1840–1914*. Ithaca, NY: Cornell University Press.
Halbwachs, Maurice. 1992. *On Collective Memory*. Chicago: University of Chicago Press.
Haleem, Irm. 2012. *The Essence of Islamist Extremism: Recognition through Violence, Freedom through Death*. New York: Routledge.
Harff, Barbara. 2003. "No Lessons Learned from the Holocaust? Assessing Risks of Genocide and Political Mass Murder since 1955." *American Political Science Review* 97 (1): 57–73.
Hayden, Robert. 1994. "Recounting the Dead: The Discovery and Redefinition of Wartime Massacres in Late- and Post-Communist Yugoslavia." In *Memory, History, and Opposition under State Socialism*, edited by Rubie S. Watson, 167–184. Santa Fe: School of American Research Press.
Heberle, Rudolf. (1940) 1970. *From Democracy to Nazism: A Regional Case Study on Political Parties in Germany*. First Published by Louisiana State University Press. New Edition with Preface by Rudolf Heberle. New York: Howard Fertig.
Hebrang, Andrija. 2013. *Zločini nad civilima u Srpsko-crnogorskoj agresiji na Republiku Hrvatsku* [Crimes against civilians in Serbo-Montenegrin aggression on the Republic of Croatia]. Zagreb: Udruga hrvatskih liječnika dragovoljaca 1990–1991; Zadar, Croatia: Ogranak Matice Hrvatske u Zadru.
Hechter, Michael. 2000. *Containing Nationalism*. Oxford: Oxford University Press.
Hilberg, Raul. 1992. *Perpetrators, Victims, Bystanders: The Jewish Catastrophe, 1933–1945*. New York: HarperCollins.
Hirsch, Marianne. 2008. "The Generation of Postmemory." *Poetics Today* 29 (1): 103–128.
Hobsbawm, Eric, and Terence Ranger, eds. (1983) 1992. *The Invention of Tradition*. Canto ed. New York: Cambridge University Press.
Hockenos, Paul. 2003. *Homeland Calling: Exile Patriotism and the Balkan Wars*. Ithaca, NY: Cornell University Press.

Horowitz, Donald. 1985. *Ethnic Groups in Conflict.* Berkeley: University of California Press.
Horowitz, Irving Louis. 1976. *Genocide: State Power and Mass Murder.* New Brunswick, NJ: Transaction Books.
Hrženjak, Juraj, ed. 2002. *Rušenje antifašističkih spomenika u Hrvatskoj, 1990–2000* [Destruction of antifascist monuments in Croatia, 1990–2000]. Zagreb: Savez antifašističkih boraca Hrvatske [Alliance of Anti-Fascist Veterans of Croatia].
Hultman, Lisa. 2007. "Battle Losses and Rebel Violence: Raising the Costs for Fighting." *Terrorism and Political Violence* 19 (2): 205–222.
Humphreys, Macartan, and Jeremy M. Weinstein. 2006. "Handling and Manhandling Civilians in Civil War." *American Political Science Review* 100 (3): 429–447.
ICJ (International Court of Justice). 2001. *Memorial of the Republic of Croatia: Case concerning the Application of the Convention on the Prevention and Punishment of the Crime of Genocide (Croatia v. Yugoslavia).* Vol. 5, *Appendices.* ICJ, March 1, 2001. Accessed December 4, 2018. https://www.icj-cij.org/en/case/118.
ICRC (International Committee of the Red Cross), Croatian Red Cross, and Ministarstvo branitelja Uprava za zatočene i nestale. 2012. *Book of Missing Persons on the Territory of the Republic of Croatia.* Zagreb: ICRC (International Committee of the Red Cross), Croatian Red Cross, and Ministarstvo branitelja Uprava za zatočene i nestale.
ICTY (International Criminal Tribunal for the Former Yugoslavia). 2004. Second Amended Indictment "Croatia" (including Annexes), *Slobodan Milošević,* Case No. IT-02-54. July 28, 2004. Accessed December 2, 2018. http://www.icty.org/x/cases/slobodan_milosevic/ind/en/040727.pdf.
———. 2005. Transcript, *Milan Martić,* IT-95-11. December 13, 2005. Accessed December 4, 2018. http://www.icty.org/x/cases/martic/trans/en/051213IT.htm.
———. 2007. Public Judgment, *Prosecutor v. Mile Mrkšić, Mirslav Radić, and Veselin Šljivančanin,* Case No. IT-95-13/1-T. September 27, 2007. Accessed December 4, 2018. http://www.icty.org/x/cases/mrksic/tjug/en/070927.pdf.
———. 2008. Judgment, *Milan Martić,* Case No. IT-95-11. October 8, 2008. Accessed December 4, 2018. http://www.icty.org/x/cases/martic/acjug/en/mar-aj081008e.pdf.
———. 2010. Review Judgment, *Prosecutor v. Veselin Šljivančanin,* Case No. IT-95-13/1-R.1. December 8, 2010. http://www.icty.org/x/cases/mrksic/acjug/en/101208_review_judgement.pdf.
———. 2011. Judgment, Vols. 1 and 2, *Ante Gotovina et al.,* Case No. IT-06-90. April 15, 2011. Accessed December 4, 2018. http://www.icty.org/x/cases/gotovina/tjug/en/110415_judgement_vol1.pdf and http://www.icty.org/x/cases/gotovina/tjug/en/110415_judgement_vol2.pdf.
———. 2012a. Second Amended Indictment, *Goran Hadžić,* Case No. IT-04-75-PT. March 22, 2012. Accessed December 2, 2018. http://www.icty.org/x/cases/hadzic/ind/en/120322.pdf.
———. 2012b. Appeals Chamber Judgment, *Ante Gotovina et al.,* Case No. IT-06-90. November 16, 2012. Accessed December 4, 2018. http://www.icty.org/x/cases/gotovina/acjug/en/121116_judgement.pdf.
———. n.d.a. "Hadžić (IT-04-75)." Accessed December 4, 2018. http://www.icty.org/case/hadzic/4 and http://www.icty.org/en/action/cases/4.
———. n.d.b. "Milošević, Slobodan (IT-02-54)." Accessed December 4, 2018. http://www.icty.org/case/slobodan_milosevic/4.
Irvine, Jill A. 1993. *The Croat Question: Partisan Politics in the Formation of the Yugoslav Socialist State.* Boulder, CO: Westview.

———. 2007. "The Croatian Spring and the Dissolution of Yugoslavia." In *State Collapse in South-Eastern Europe: New Perspectives on Yugoslavia's Disintegration*, edited by Lenard J. Cohen and Jasna Dragović-Soso, 149–178. West Lafayette, IN: Purdue University Press.

Jakovina, Tvrtko, ed. 2012. *Hrvatsko proljeće 40 godina poslije* [Croatian spring 40 years later]. Zagreb: Centar za demokraciju i pravo Miko Tripalo, Filozofski fakultet sveučilišta u Zagrebu, Fakultet političkih znanosti u Zagrebu, Pravni fakultet sveučilista u Zagrebu.

Jambrešić Kirin, Renata, ed. 2000. *The Politics of Memorizing and Forgetting: Reminiscences of the Second World War in Croatia*. Prague: Research Support Scheme.

———. 2006. "Politička sjećanja na Drugi svjetski rat u doba medijske reprodukcije socijalističke kulture" [Political memories of World War II in time of the media reproduction of the socialist culture]. In *Devijacije i promašaji: Etnografija domaćeg socijalizma* [Deviations and faults: Ethnography of the autochthonous socialism], edited by Lada Čale Feldman and Ines Prica, 149–178. Zagreb: Institute of Ethnology and Folklore.

Jambrešić Kirin, Renata, and Maja Povrzanović, eds. 1996. *War, Exile, Everyday Life: Cultural Perspectives*. Zagreb: Institute for Ethnology and Folklore Research.

Jansen, Stef. 2002. "The Violence of Memories: Local Narratives of the Past after Ethnic Cleansing in Croatia." *Rethinking History* 6 (1): 77–94.

———. 2007. "Remembering with a Difference: Clashing Memories of Bosnian Conflict in Everyday Life." In *The New Bosnian Mosaic: Identities, Memories and Moral Claims in a Post-war Society*, edited by Xavier Bougarel, Elissa Helms, and Ger Duijzings, 193–208. Burlington, VT: Ashgate.

Jenkins, Richard. 2008. *Rethinking Ethnicity*. Los Angeles: SAGE.

Jović, Dejan. 2007. "The Slovenian-Croatian Confederal Proposal: A Tactical Move or an Ultimate Solution?" In *State Collapse in South-Eastern Europe: New Perspectives on Yugoslavia's Disintegration*, edited by Lenard J. Cohen and Jasna Dragović-Soso, 249–280. West Lafayette, IN: Purdue University Press.

———. 2009. *Yugoslavia: A State That Withered Away*. West Lafayette, IN: Purdue University Press.

———. 2017. *Rat i mit: Politika identiteta u suvremenoj Hrvatskoj* [War and myth: Identity politics in contemporary Croatia]. Zagreb: Fraktura.

Kainerugaba, Muhoozi. 2010. *Battles of the Ugandan Resistance: A Tradition of Maneuver*. Kampala: Fountain.

Kale, Jadran. 2016. "Sjevernodalmatinski nacrt etnologije rata" [Ethnology of war in Northern Dalmatia]. *Ethnologica Dalmatica* 23:115–151.

Kalema, Roy Golooba. 2009. "Escaped Escorting a Corpse." In *Looking Back: Personal Memories of Uganda's Troubled Past, 1970–2000*, edited by Patricia Haward, 81–89. Kampala: Fountain Publishers.

Kalyvas, Stathis. 1999. "Wanton and Senseless? The Logic of Massacres in Algeria." *Rationality and Society* 11 (3): 243–285.

———. 2005. "Warfare in Civil Wars." In *Rethinking the Nature of War*, edited by Isabelle Duyvesteyn and Jan Angstrom, 88–109. New York: Frank Cass.

———. 2006. *The Logic of Violence in Civil War*. New York: Cambridge University Press.

Karačić, Darko, Tamara Banjeglav, and Nataša Govedarica. 2012. *Re-vizija prošlosti: Službene politike sjećanja u Bosni i Hercegovini, Hrvatskoj i Srbiji od 1990. godine* [Re-vision of the past: The official politics of memory in Bosnia and Herzegovina, Croatia, and Serbia from 1990]. Sarajevo: Asocijacija Alumni Centra za interdisciplinarne postdiplomske studije and Friedrich-Ebert-Stiftung.

Karge, Heike. 2009. "Mediated Remembrance: Local Practices of Remembering the Second World War in Tito's Yugoslavia." *European Review of History* 16 (1): 49–62.

Kasapović, Mirjana. 2018. "Genocid u NDH: Umanjivanje, banaliziranje i poricanje zločina" [Genocide in NDH: Diminishing, banalizing, and denying crimes]. *Politička misao* 55 (1): 7–33.

Kasozi, A. B. K. 1994. *The Social Origins of Violence in Uganda, 1964–1985*. Montreal: McGill-Queen's University Press.

Katunarić, Vjeran. 2010. "(Un)avoidable War: Peace and Violent Conflict in Multiethnic Areas in Croatia." *Revija za sociologiju* 40 (1): 5–29.

Klasić, Hrvoje. 2012. *Jugoslavija i svijet 1968* [Yugoslavia and the world in 1968]. Zagreb: Ljevak.

Komnenović, Dora. 2014. "(Out)living the War: Anti-war Activism in Croatia in the Early 1990s and Beyond." *Journal on Ethnopolitics and Minority Issues in Europe* 13 (4): 111–128.

Kordić, Snježana. 2010. *Jezik i nacionalizam* [Language and nationalism]. Zagreb: Durieux.

Kuper, Leo. 1981. *Genocide: Its Political Use in the Twentieth Century*. New Haven, CT: Yale University Press.

Kutesa, Pecos. (2006) 2008. *Uganda's Revolution, 1979–1986: How I Saw It*. Kampala: Fountain.

Lampe, John R. 1996. *Yugoslavia as a History: Twice There Was a Country*. Reprint. New York: Cambridge University Press.

Lemarchand, Rene, and Maurice Niwese. 2007. "Mass Murder, the Politics of Memory and Post-genocide Reconstruction: The Cases of Rwanda and Burundi." In *After Mass Crime: Rebuilding States and Communities*, edited by Béatrice Pouligny, Simon Chesterman, and Albrecht Schnabel, 165–189. New York: United Nations University Press.

Lemkin, Raphael. 1933. "Acts Constituting a General (Transnational) Danger Considered as Offences against the Law of Nations." Prevent Genocide International website. Accessed December 4, 2018. http://www.preventgenocide.org/lemkin/madrid1933-english.htm.

———. 2012. *Lemkin on Genocide*. Edited by Steven Leonard Jacobs. Lanham, MD: Lexington Books.

Lešaja, Ante. 2012. *Knjigocid: Uništavanje knjiga u Hrvatskoj 1990-tih* [Librocide: Destruction of books in Croatia in the 1990s]. Zagreb: Profil.

Leutloff-Grandits, Carolin. 2013. "Srbi u Hrvatskoj deset godina nakon završetka rata" [Serbs in Croatia ten years after the end of the war]. In *Hrvatska od osamostaljenja: Rat, politika, društvo, vanjski odnosi* [Croatia since independence: War, politics, society, foreign relations], edited by Renéo Lukić, Sabrina P. Ramet, and Konrad Clewing, 133–157. Zagreb: Golden Marketing–Tehnička knjiga.

Magaš, Branka, and Ivo Žanić. 1999. *Rat u Hrvatskoj i Bosni i Hercegovini, 1991–1995* [War in Croatia and Bosnia and Herzegovina, 1991–1995]. London: Bosnian Institute.

Makdisi, Ussama, and Paul A. Silverstein. 2006. *Memory and Violence in the Middle East and North Africa*. Bloomington: Indiana University Press.

Malešević, Siniša. 2006. *Identity as Ideology: Understanding Ethnicity and Nationalism*. New York: Palgrave Macmillan.

Malkki, Liisa. 1995. *Purity and Exile: Violence, Memory, and National Cosmology among Hutu Refugees in Tanzania*. Chicago: University of Chicago Press.

Mamdani, Mahmood. 2001. *When Victims Become Killers: Colonialism, Nativism, and the Genocide in Rwanda*. Princeton, NJ: Princeton University Press.
Mann, Michael. 2005. *The Dark Side of Democracy: Explaining Ethnic Cleansing*. New York: Cambridge University Press.
Maynes, Mary Jo, Jennifer L. Pierce, and Barbara Laslett. 2008. *Telling Stories: The Use of Personal Narratives in the Social Sciences and History*. Ithaca, NY: Cornell University Press.
McAllister, Carlota. 2013. "Testimonial Truths and Revolutionary Mysteries." In *War by Other Means: Aftermath in Post-genocide Guatemala*, edited by Carlota McAllister and Diane M. Nelson, 93–115. Durham, NC: Duke University Press.
McAllister, Carlota, and Diane M. Nelson. 2013. "Introduction. Aftermath: Harvests of Violence and Histories of the Future." In *War by Other Means: Aftermath in Post-genocide Guatemala*, edited by Carlotta McAllister and Diane M. Nelson, 1–45. Durham, NC: Duke University Press.
Menchú, Rigoberta, and Elisabeth Burgos-Debray. (1983) 1994. *I, Rigoberta Menchú: An Indian Woman in Guatemala*. Translated by Ann Wright. 16th ed. New York: Verso.
Metelits, Claire. 2010. *Inside Insurgency: Violence, Civilians, and Revolutionary Group Behavior*. New York: New York University Press.
Mi, Yuni. 2009. "A West Nile Bandit in the City." In *Looking Back: Personal Memories of Uganda's Troubled Past, 1970–2000*, edited by Patricia Haward, 129–133. Kampala: Fountain Publishers.
Montejo, Victor. 1987. *Testimony: Death of a Guatemalan Village*. Willimantic, CT: Curbstone.
Mosley, Layna, ed. 2013. *Interview Research in Political Science*. Ithaca, NY: Cornell University Press.
Mutibwa, Henry. 2009. "Those Days in Luwero." In *Looking Back: Personal Memories of Uganda's Troubled Past, 1970–2000*, edited by Patricia Haward, 72–76. Kampala: Fountain Publishers.
Nazor, Ante. 2011. *Velikosrpska agresija na Hrvatsku 1990-tih* [Greater Serbian aggression on Croatia in the 1990s]. Zagreb: Hrvatski memorijalno-dokumentacijski centar Domovinskog rata.
Nelson, Diane M. 2009. *Reckoning: The Ends of War in Guatemala*. Durham, NC: Duke University Press.
———. 2015. *Who Counts? The Mathematics of Death and Life after Genocide*. Durham, NC: Duke University Press.
Nettelfield, Lara J. 2010. "Research and Repercussions of Death Tolls: The Case of the Bosnian Book of the Dead." In *Sex, Drugs, and Body Counts: The Politics of Numbers in Global Crime and Conflict*, edited by Peter Andreas and Kelly M. Greenhill, 159–187. Ithaca, NY: Cornell University Press.
Nora, Pierre. 1989. "Between Memory and History: Les Lieux de Memoire." In "Memory and Counter-memory," special issue, *Representations* 26:7–24.
Nsibambi, Apolo Robin. 2014. *National Integration in Uganda, 1962–2013*. Kampala: Fountain.
Pančić, Stjepan, Željko Cirba, Stjepan Milas, Tanja Paša, and Adam Rendulić. 2007. *Krvava istina: In memoriam* [The bloody truth: In memoriam]. Lovas, Croatia: Općinsko vijeće, Poglavarstvo općine Lovas.
Pandža Orkan, Ivica. 2012. *Vojska Krajine u Pounju i na Banovini: Zapisi komšija* [The Krajina army in the regions near the River Una and in Banovina: Neighbors' notes]. Sisak, Croatia: Agencija za istraživanje i dokumentaciju ratnih sukoba.

Parker, Kevin. 2006. *Report to the President: Death of Slobodan Milošević*. The Hague: ICTY, May 30, 2006. http://www.icty.org/x/cases/slobodan_milosevic/custom2/en/parkerreport.pdf.
Passerini, Luisa. (2007) 2014. *Memory and Utopia: The Primacy of Intersubjectivity*. First published 2007 by Equinox. New York: Routledge.
Pavlaković, Vjeran. 2008a. "Better the Grave than a Slave: Croatia and the International Criminal Tribunal for the Former Yugoslavia." In *Croatia since Independence: War, Politics, Society, Foreign Relations*, edited by Sabrina P. Ramet, Konrad Clewing, and Reneo Lukić, 447–483. Munich: R. Oldenbourgh Verlang.
———. 2008b. "Flirting with Fascism: The Ustaša Legacy and the Croatian Politics in the 1990s." In *The Shared History and the Second World War and National Question in Ex Yugoslavia*, edited by Darko Gavrilović, 115–143. Novi Sad, Serbia: Center for History, Democracy and Reconciliation.
———. 2008c. *Red Stars, Black Shirts: Symbols, Commemorations, and Contested Histories of World War Two in Croatia*. Washington, DC: National Council for Eurasian and East European Research.
———. 2010. "Croatia, the International Criminal Tribunal for the Former Yugoslavia and General Gotovina as a Political Symbol." *Europe-Asia Studies* 62 (10): 1707–1740.
———. 2011. "Sukob, komemoracije i promjene značenja: Meštrovićev paviljon kao prijeporno mjesto sjećanja" [Conflict, commemorations, and changes of meaning: The Meštrović Pavilion as a conflicting place of memory]. In *Kultura sjećanja: 1991. Povijesni lomovi i svladavanje prošlosti* [The culture of remembering: 1991. Historical destructions and overcoming the past], edited by Tihomir Cipek, 215–238. Zagreb: Disput.
———. 2013. "Symbols and the Culture of Memory in Republika Srpska Krajina." *Nationalities Papers* 41 (6): 893–909.
Pavlaković, Vjeran, Dario Brentin, and Davor Pauković. 2018. "The Controversial Commemoration: Transnational Approaches to Remembering Bleiburg." *Politička misao* 55 (2): 7–32.
Pelikan, Dragutin. 1997. *Slatina u vjetrovima povijesti* [Slatina in the winds of history]. Slatina, Romania: Gradsko poglavarstvo Slatina.
Perica, Vjekoslav. 2002. *Balkan Idols: Religion and Nationalism in Yugoslav States*. New York: Oxford University Press.
Petersen, Roger D. 2001. *Resistance and Rebellion: Lessons from Eastern Europe*. Studies in Rationality and Social Change. Cambridge: Cambridge University Press.
———. 2002. *Understanding Ethnic Violence: Fear, Hatred, and Resentment in Twentieth-Century Eastern Europe*. New York: Cambridge University Press.
———. 2005. "Memory and Cultural Schema: Linking Memory in Political Action." In *Memory and World War Two: An Ethnographic Approach*, edited by Francesca Cappelletto, 131–153. Oxford: Berg.
Portelli, Alessandro. 1991. *The Death of Luigi Trastulli and Other Stories: Form and Meaning in Oral History*. New York: State University of New York Press.
Posen, Barry. 1993. "The Security Dilemma and Ethnic Conflict." *Survival* 35 (1): 27–47.
Posner, Daniel N. 2004. "Measuring Ethnic Fractionalization in Africa." *American Journal of Political Science* 48 (4): 849–863.
Radstone, Susannah, and Bill Schwarz, eds. 2010. *Memory: Histories, Theories, Debates*. New York: Fordham University Press.
Ramet, Sabrina P. (1984) 1992. *Nationalism and Federalism in Yugoslavia, 1962–1991*. 2nd ed. Bloomington: Indiana University Press.
———. 1992. *Balkan Babel: Politics, Culture, and Religion in Yugoslavia*. Boulder, CO: Westview.

REMHI (Recuperación de la Memoria Histórica), Recovery of Historical Memory Project. 1999. *Guatemala Never Again! The Official Report of the Human Rights Office, Archdiocese of Guatemala*. Maryknoll, NY: Orbis Books.

Rihtman-Auguštin, Dunja. 2000. *Ulice moga grada* [My city's streets]. Belgrade: Biblioteka XX vek.

———. 2004. "The Monument in the Main City Square: Constructing and Erasing Memory in Contemporary Croatia." In *Balkan Identities: Nation and Memory*, edited by Maria Todorova, 180–196. New York: New York University Press.

Roginek, Igor, ed. 2011. *Rat, dokumentiranje i pravni status žrtve* [War, documenting, and legal status of victims]. Zagreb: Documenta, Centar za suočavanje s prošlošću.

Rothenberg, Daniel, ed. 2012. *Memory of Silence: The Guatemalan Truth Commission Report*. London: Palgrave Macmillan.

Rupić, Mate, ed. 2007. *Republika Hrvatska i Domovinski rat 1990.–1995., Dokumenti, Knjiga 2: Dokumenti institucija pobunjenih Srba u Republici Hrvatskoj (1990.–1991.)* [Republic of Croatia and the Homeland War 1990–1995, documents, book 2: Documents of the institutions of the Serbian rebels in the Republic of Croatia, 1990–1991]. Zagreb: Hrvatski memorijalno-dokumentacijski centar Domovinskog rata i Hrvatski institut za povijest.

Sanford, Victoria. 2009. "What Is an Anthropology of Genocide? Reflections on Field Research with Maya Survivors in Guatemala." In *Genocide: Truth, Memory, and Representation*, edited by Alexander Laban Hinton and Kevin Lewis O'Neill, 29–53. Durham, NC: Duke University Press.

Santa Cruz, Santiago Mendoza. (2004) 2006. *Insurgentes: Guatemala, la paz arrancada* [Insurgents: Guatemala, torn away]. Mexico City: Ediciones Era; Santiago: Lom Ediciones.

Savić, Gligorije-Glišo. 2007. *Prošlost koja se ponavlja: Bujavica, 1237–2004* [The past that repeats itself: Bujavica, 1237–2004]. Zagreb: Grafocentar.

Schatz, Edward, ed. 2009. *Political Ethnography: What Immersion Contributes to the Study of Power*. Chicago: University of Chicago Press.

Schäuble, Michaela. 2014. *Narrating Victimhood: Gender, Religion and the Making of Place in Post-war Croatia*. New York: Berghahn Books.

Schiemann, John. 2007. "Bizarre Beliefs and Rational Choices: A Behavioral Approach to Analytic Narratives." *Journal of Politics* 69 (2): 511–524.

Schirmer, Jennifer. 1998. *The Guatemalan Military Project: A Violence Called Democracy*. Philadelphia: University of Pennsylvania Press.

Schmitt, Carl. (1932) 2007. *The Concept of the Political*. Expanded ed. Chicago: University of Chicago Press.

Scott, James C. 1985. *Weapons of the Weak*. New Haven, CT: Yale University Press.

———. 2009. *The Art of Not Being Governed: An Anarchist History of Upland Southeast Asia*. New Haven, CT: Yale University Press.

Shaw, Martin. 2007. *What Is Genocide?* Malden, MA: Polity.

Short, Nicola. 2004. *The International Politics of Post-conflict Reconstruction in Guatemala*. London: Palgrave Macmillan.

Shoup, Paul. 2007. "The Disintegration of Yugoslavia and Western Foreign Policy in the 1980s." In *State Collapse in South-Eastern Europe: New Perspectives on Yugoslavia's Disintegration*, edited by Lenard J. Cohen and Jasna Dragović-Soso, 333–364. West Lafayette, IN: Purdue University Press.

Sieder, Rachel. 2001. "War, Peace, and the Politics of Memory in Guatemala." In *Burying the Past: Making Peace and Doing Justice after Civil Conflict*, edited by Nigel Biggar, 185–206. Washington, DC: Georgetown University Press.

Staniland, Paul. 2012. "States, Insurgents, and Wartime Political Order." *Perspectives on Politics* 10 (2): 243–264.
Staub, Ervin. 1989. *The Roots of Evil: The Origins of Genocide and Other Group Violence.* New York: Cambridge University Press.
——. 2001. "Individual and Group Identities in Genocide and Mass Killing." In *Social Identity, Intergroup Conflict, and Conflict Reduction*, edited by Richard D. Ashmore, Lee Jussim, and David Wilder, 159–186. New York: Oxford University Press.
Stoll, David. 1993. *Between Two Armies in the Ixil Towns of Guatemala.* New York: Columbia University Press.
Straus, Scott. 2007. "Second-Generation Comparative Research on Genocide." *World Politics* 59 (3): 476–501.
——. 2012. "Retreating from the Brink: Theorizing Mass Violence and the Dynamics of Restraint." *Perspective on Politics* 10 (2): 343–362.
——. 2015. *Making and Unmaking Nations: War, Leadership, and Genocide in Modern Africa.* Ithaca, NY: Cornell University Press.
Subotić, Jelena. 2009. *Hijacked Justice: Dealing with the Past in the Balkans.* Ithaca, NY: Cornell University Press.
——. 2013. "Remembrance, Public Narratives, and Obstacles to Justice in the Western Balkans." *Studies in Social Justice* 7 (2): 265–283.
Thompson, Paul. (1978) 2000. *The Voice of the Past: Oral History.* 3rd ed. Oxford: Oxford University Press.
Todorova, Maria. 2004. "Introduction: Learning Memory, Remembering Identity." In *Balkan Identities: Nation and Memory*, edited by Maria Todorova, 1–24. New York: New York University Press.
Trouillot, Michel-Rolph. 1995. *Silencing the Past: Power and the Production of History.* Boston: Beacon.
UNHCR (United Nations High Commissioner for Refugees) and Commissariat. 1996. *Registration of Refugees.* Belgrade: UNHCR and the Commissariat for Refugees of the Republic of Serbia.
Valentino, Benjamin, Paul Huth, and Dylan Balch-Lindsay. 2004. "'Draining the Sea': Mass Killing and Guerrilla Warfare." *International Organization* 58 (2): 375–407.
Varshney, Ashutosh. 2002. *Ethnic Conflict and Civic Life: Hindus and Muslims in India.* New Haven, CT: Yale University Press.
Verdery, Katherine. 1999. *The Political Lives of Dead Bodies: Reburial and Postsocialist Change.* New York: Columbia University Press.
Viterna, Jocelyn. 2013. *Women in War: The Micro-processes of Mobilization in El Salvador.* New York: Oxford University Press.
Waller, James. 2007. *Becoming Evil: How Ordinary People Commit Genocide and Mass Killing.* New York: Oxford University Press.
Waterston, Alisse, and Barbara Rylko-Bauer. 2006. "Out of the Shadows of History and Memory: Personal Family Narratives in Ethnographies of Rediscovery." *American Ethnologist* 33 (3): 397–412.
Wayenga, Masyale Sowedi. 2009. "Terror on the Road." In *Looking Back: Personal Memories of Uganda's Troubled Past, 1970–2000*, edited by Patricia Haward, 151–160. Kampala: Fountain Publishers.
Weber, Max. (1922) 1996. "Ethnic Groups." In *Theories of Ethnicity: A Classical Reader*, edited by Werner Sollors, 52–66. New York: New York University Press.
Wedeen, Lisa. 2009. "Ethnography as Interpretive Enterprise." In *Political Ethnography: What Immersion Contributes to the Study of Power*, edited by Edward Schatz, 75–93. Chicago: University of Chicago Press.

Weinstein, Jeremy M. 2007. *Inside Rebellion: The Politics of Insurgent Violence*. New York: Cambridge University Press.
Weitz, Eric D. 2003. *A Century of Genocide: Utopias of Race and Nation*. Princeton, NJ: Princeton University Press.
Weld, Kirsten. 2014. *Paper Cadavers: The Archives of Dictatorship in Guatemala*. Durham, NC: Duke University Press.
Wilmer, Franke. 2002. *The Social Construction of Man, the State and War: Identity, Conflict, and Violence in Former Yugoslavia*. New York: Routledge.
Wimmer, Andreas. 2001. *Nationalist Exclusion and Ethnic Conflict: Shadows of Modernity*. New York: Cambridge University Press.
———. 2013. *Waves of War: Nationalism, State Formation, and Ethnic Exclusion in the Modern World*. New York: Cambridge University Press.
Winter, Jay. 2010. "Sites of Memory." In *Memory: Histories, Theories, Debates*, edited by Susannah Radstone and Bill Schwarz, 312–324. New York: Fordham University Press.
Wolfgram, Mark. 2007. "The Process of Collective Memory Research: Methodological Solutions for Research Challenges." *German Politics and Society* 25 (1): 102–13.
Wood, Elizabeth Jean. 2003. *Insurgent Collective Action and Civil War in El Salvador*. Cambridge: Cambridge University Press.
Wood, Reed M. 2010. "Rebel Capability and Strategic Violence against Civilians." *Journal of Peace Research* 47 (5): 601–614.
Woodward, Susan L. 1995. *Balkan Tragedy: Chaos and Dissolution after the Cold War*. Washington, DC: Brookings Institution.
Woolf, Stuart. 2005. "Historians: Private, Collective and Public Memories of Violence and War Attrocities." In *Memory and World War II: An Ethnographic Approach*, edited by Francesca Cappalletto, 177–193. Oxford: Berg.
Zahar, Marie-Joelle. 2001. "Protégés, Clients, and Cannon Fodder: Civilians in the Calculus of Militias." In *Managing Armed Conflicts in the 21st Century*, edited by Dekeye Adebajo and Chandra Lekha Sriram, 107–129. London: Frank Cass.
Žarkov, Dubravka. 2007. *The Body of War: Media, Ethnicity, and Gender in the Break-Up of Yugoslavia*. Durham, NC: Duke University Press.
Zartman, I. William. 2005. *Cowardly Lions: Missed Opportunities to Prevent Deadly Conflict and State Collapse*. Boulder, CO: Lynne Rienner.
Žerjavić, Vladimir. 1992. *Opsesije i megalomanije oko Jasenovca i Bleiburga* [Obsessions and megalomanias surrounding Jasenovac and Bleiburg]. 2nd ed. Zagreb: Globus.
Žunec, Ozren. 2007. *Goli život: Societalne dimenzije pobune srba u Hrvatskoj* [Bare life: Social dimensions of the rebellion of the Serbs in Croatia]. Zagreb: Demetra.

Index

Note: The letter *t* following a page number denotes a table

Agamben, Giorgio, 27, 158n2
Alavanja, Goran, 9–10
amoral communities
    conditions favoring, 25–32, 143–144
    definition, 6, 19, 22, 27, 158n2
Anderson, Benedict, 25

Babić, Dragutin, 139
Baćin massacre, 123–124, 125
Balcells, Laia, 5, 24, 155n10, 172n1
banality of evil, 25
barricades, 59–60, 77–91
Bergholz, Max, 5, 66
Bermeo, Nancy, 30, 160n16
Bleiburg commemorations, 12, 105, 106
books, destruction of, 129, 175n52
borders, as mechanism for ethnicization, 77–91, 143–144
    in Croatia, 6, 12, 77–82, 85–89, 119
    in Guatemala, 83–85, 89–90
    methods, 20
    prevention of, 145–146
    in Uganda, 82–83, 89
Borovo Selo ambush, 57–58
Bulutgil, H. Zeynep, 159n9

Catholic Action, 64–65
Catholic *vs.* Orthodox, 53–54
Cederman, Lars-Erik, 4–5
celebrations and holidays, 53–54
Ćelije, 119
Central Croatia, 17t, 35, 39–40, 61, 67–68, 86–87, 110–111, 123–125
Čermak, Ivan, 127
Četniks, 11, 35, 107, 138
Četnik symbols, 57
children
    ethnicization among, 40–42
    as victims, 124
Christmas, 53–54
churches, destruction of, 129
church leaders, 11

civil patrols, 74–75, 136–137, 166n77, 176n75, 177n85
civil war/insurgency scholarship, 3–4, 118
Coalition of the Popular Compromise, 156n15
collective crimes
    concept, 5, 23–25
    context of, 19, 22
    prevention of, 142–146
collective intention, 158n6
collective memories, 93
colonialism, 43, 46, 113, 114
commemorations and monuments, 11–12, 101–107, 128–129, 174n49, 175n50
concentration camps, 11, 95, 96, 97, 98
constitution (Republic of Croatia), 10, 12, 110
counting of civilian victims, 1, 11–12, 15–17, 134, 156n17, 176n76
coworkers, ethnicization among, 39–40, 53, 61, 78, 82, 161n22
Croatian Cultural Center, 110, 128–129, 170n53
Croatian Defense Forces, 14
"Croatian silence," 99
culture, targeting of, 23, 31–32, 45, 128–129. *See also* symbols

Dalmatia, 17t, 35–36, 86–87, 105–106, 125–126, 147–153, 157n21
Danica concentration camp, 97, 98
Daruvar Agreement, 85–86
democracy, 26–27, 28, 159n10
Derrida, Jacques, 28
direct *vs.* indirect violence, 24
disappearances
    from communities, 45, 57, 62, 63, 67, 157n20
    from workplaces, 78, 82, 161n22
displacement/evacuation, 86–89, 119, 127, 139, 173n44
Dmitar Obradović, 68–69
Domobrani, 98, 99, 105
Dušan Silni, 120

INDEX

Eastern Slavonia, 52–53, 57–58, 69, 79, 100–101, 118–122, 157n17
Eck, Kristine, 24
elderly civilians, 87, 121, 123, 124, 174n45
elections, 8–9, 36, 44, 156n15
El Salvador, 63–64
"emergency" framing. *See* "state of exception" framing
emigration, 1–2
Erjavec, Tonči, 169n26
Esposito, Roberto, 160n13
ethnic groups
   definition, 155n11
   prewar lack of relevance of, 2–3, 7–9, 39, 78, 103
   solidarity across, 55, 97, 102–103, 140
ethnicization
   borders as mechanism for, 77–91, 143–144
   definition, 6
   of everyday life, 33, 39–43, 139–140
   exclusion of moderates as trigger for, 6, 73, 143–144
   identity creation, 23, 25, 30–32
   of memories, 100–110
   of statehood, 26–28, 33–34
   violence as contributor to, 73, 137–141, 145; Croatia, 57–62, 125, 126, 127, 173n43; Guatemala, 64–66, 133; Uganda, 63–64, 71, 131
   See also local-level ethnicization; political ethnicities; state-level ethnicization
evacuations/displacements, 86–89, 119, 127, 139, 173n44
exception, state of. *See* "state of exception" framing

families
   intergenerational narratives in, 93–100, 138
   multi-ethnic, 52, 55–56, 60–61, 68, 78–79, 102–103
fascism
   memories of, 37, 107
   targeting of antifascist symbols, 128, 174n49
flags, 42, 59–60
Foucault, Michel, 26–27
framing. *See* state-level ethnicization; "state of exception" framing

García, Lucas, 45, 133, 162n37
Garrard-Burnett, Virginia, 25
gendered experiences of war
   confiscation of food from women, 72

enforced recruitment of men, 55, 63–64, 65, 73, 90
mass arrests and killings of men, 130, 132, 174n45
rape of women, 132, 136
genocide
   concept, 23–24, 158n2
   Guatemalan violence as, 134–135
   modern states as enabling, 26–27
   scholarship on, 3–4, 66, 159n10
   state founding narratives and, 43
   See also war crimes trials
Gerardi, Juan, 134
Girard, Rene, 28
Goldstein, Ivo, 119, 156n17
Goldstein, Slavko, 94
Gornji Grahovljani, 103–105
Gorski Kotar, 17t, 37, 47–49, 50–51, 78, 107
Gospić massacre, 15, 126
Gotovina, Ante, 127
Guatemala
   border production in, 83–85, 89–90
   ethnicization in, 45–47
   memories of violence in, 109–110, 114
   moderates, exclusion of in, 64–66, 71–75
   research methodology, 18–19
   violence as political strategy in, 133–137, 143, 162n37, 163n41

Hadžić, Goran, 122
Haleem, Irm, 27
Harff, Barbara, 23
HDZ (Croatian Democratic Union), 8, 10, 35–36
Heberle, Rudolf, 30
historic factors, 20–21
holidays and celebrations, 53–54
Hultman, Lisa, 24
human shields, 59, 119–120, 132, 135

ICJ (International Court of Justice), 1, 155n1
ICRC (International Committee of the Red Cross), 16–17
ICTY (International Criminal Tribunal for the Former Yugoslavia), 69, 122–123, 126, 127–128
identities, creation of, 23, 25, 30–32. *See also* ethnicization; political ethnicities
imagined communities, 25
indirect *vs.* direct violence, 24
intentional *vs.* targeted violence, 23–24
interethnic cooperation, 55, 97, 102–103, 140
Ivanovo Selo, 101–103, 105

Jadovno concentration camp, 94, 95
Jasenovac concentration camp, 11, 95
JNA (Yugoslav National Army)
 arming of locals by, 50
 ethnic composition of, 156n16
 as Milošević's army, 9, 12
 proposed attack on, 51
 recruitment issues, 13
 violence by, 61, 119, 120–122, 125–26
Joševica massacre, 123, 124–125
"Just War Doctrine", 27

Kalyvas, Stathis, 118
Kashanku, Shaban, 69
kingship. See sovereigns
Krajina, Serbian Republic of. See RSK (Serbian Republic of Krajina); SAO Krajina

landmine massacre, 120–121
land ownership, 46
Lemkin, Raphael, 23
Lešaja, Ante, 129, 175n52
Levar, Milan, 69, 126
Lički Osik massacre, 125
Ličko-senjska, 17t
Lika, 17t, 61, 66–67, 125–126, 128, 157n21
literature, destruction of, 129, 175n52
local-level ethnicization
 conditions favoring, 29–32
 in everyday life, 33, 39–43, 139–140
 transformation from state-level, 19–20, 40, 50–52, 75–76, 143–144
 See also borders, as mechanism for ethnicization; moderates, exclusion of
Log Revolution, 9–10, 39–40
Lovas massacre, 120–121, 172n11

Mamdani, Mahmood, 31
Mann, Michael, 159n10
Marino Selo, 105, 106
Markač, Mladen, 127
Martić, Milan, 122, 125–126
media, 34–38, 53, 57–58, 138
memories
 activation of, 93
 ethnicization of, 100–110
 families, intergenerational narratives in, 93–100, 138
 in Guatemala, 109–110, 114
 instrumentalization of, 105, 107, 111–114, 116
 silencing of, 94, 99, 101, 116
 in Uganda, 108–109, 112–114

unclear links to Homeland War, 92–93, 99–100, 110, 115–116
methodology of study, 14–19, 157n21, 157n23, 158n24
military strategy, vs. political strategy, 6–7, 117–118
Milošević, Slobodan, 9, 12, 77, 122
minefield massacre, 120–121
mining companies, 46
Mitnica football club, 100–101
moderates, exclusion of, 50–76, 165n46
 by in-group policing, 66–69, 79, 85–88, 91, 124
 by killing: in Croatia, 51, 58–61, 66, 67, 68–69; in Guatemala, 64, 71–75; in Uganda, 63, 69–71, 131
 as mechanism for ethnicization, 6, 73, 143–144
 by ostracism, 52–56, 64–65, 163n41
 subnational variations, 50–52
 by threats, 52, 55, 56, 59, 60
 See also multi-ethnic families/individuals
monarchy. See sovereigns
Montt Efrain Ríos, José, 45, 73, 90, 133, 134, 162n40, 176n75
monuments and commemorations, 11–12, 101–107, 128–129, 174n49, 175n50
Mrkšić, Mile, 122
multi-ethnic families/individuals, 52, 55–56, 60–61, 68, 78–79, 102–103
Museveni, Yoweri, 44, 70, 108–109, 113–114

nationalism
 construction of threatening "others", 26–28, 33–36, 46–47, 159n9
 holidays/celebrations and, 53–54
 imagined communities, 25
 scholarship on, 3–4, 51–52, 159n9, 160n11
 in WWII and Homeland War, 112
NDH. See Ustaša (NDH)
Nelson, Diane M., 176n76
news programs. See media
Northwestern Croatia, 17t, 34–35, 60, 78, 97–99, 107
Novo Glinsko Selo massacre, 123, 125

Obote, Milton, 44–45, 108, 132–133
one-sided violence, 24
Operation Storm (Oluja), 13, 56, 86, 127–128, 174n45
oral vs. written history, 95
Orešković, Marko, 128
Orthodox vs. Catholic, 53–54
Ovčara farm, 122

Panda Gari, 130, 132
paramilitary units, 13–14
Partisans, 11, 12, 97–98, 100–102, 105–107, 169n26
Passerini, Luisa, 99
patriotic songs, 38, 59
peacekeeping systems, 146
Plitvice Bloody Easter, 12, 39, 61, 110
Podravina, 47–49
police
  attacks on stations of, 12, 68, 118–119
  at Christmas services, 53–54
  in Guatemala, 46
  killings of, 57–58
  replacement of, 35–36
political ethnicities
  concept, 23, 30, 160n14
  ethnicization of everyday life and, 33, 39–43
  exclusion of moderates as contributor to, 75–76
  formation of, 6, 19, 30–32
  in Uganda, 45
political science scholarship, 3–5, 51–52
political strategy
  military strategy *vs.*, 6–7, 117–118
  use of violence as, 4–5, 21, 31–32, 137–146; in Croatia, 118–129; in Guatemala, 133–137, 162n37; in Uganda, 130–133
politicide, 23

racialization, 31. *See also* ethnicization
Radić, Miroslav, 122
rape, 132, 136
Rašković, Jovan, 8
reconciliation, 103, 123, 128, 135, 138–139, 140, 145
Reihl-Kir, Josip, 51, 58
REMHI, 134
resources, and violence, 4, 46
revisionism, 11–12
RSK (Serbian Republic of Krajina)
  Gorski Kotar's rejection of, 78
  killings of Serbs by, 67
  mass displacement and, 87–89, 127, 174n46
  memories of WWII in, 107–108
  reinforcement of borders, 119–127
  rejection of Daruvar Agreement, 86
  See also SAO Krajina

SAO Krajina, 8, 12, 13. *See also* RSK (Serbian Republic of Krajina)
Savić, Gligorije-Glišo, 169n26
Schmitt, Carl, 28

schools, ethnicization at, 40–42
Scott, James C., 160n11
SDS (Serbian Democratic Party), 7, 9, 10, 35
Serbian Radical Party, 57
Serbian Republic of Krajina. *See* RSK (Serbian Republic of Krajina); SAO Krajina
Serbian Socialist Party, 37
Šešelj, Vojislav, 57, 77
Shaw, Martin, 159n10
Šibensko-kninska, 17t
silencing
  of crimes, 100
  of memories, 94, 99, 101, 116
Široka Kula massacre, 15, 125–126, 173n32
Sisačko-moslavačka, 17t
Sisak massacre, 119–120
Škabrnja massacre, 125–126
Slavonia, levels of violence in, 16–17, 17t. *See also* Eastern Slavonia; Western Slavonia
Šljivančanin, Veselin, 122
sovereigns, 28, 29, 44, 108, 113
Španovica, 169n26
SSSS symbol, 40, 41–42, 60
state-level ethnicization
  conditions favoring, 25–29
  national discourse, 34–38, 57–58, 61–62, 143, 145; barricades as aid to, 79, 82; in Guatemala, 46–47; violence as aid to, 125, 138
  transformation of to local-level, 19–20, 40, 50–52, 75–76, 143–144
"state of exception" framing
  conditions for, 26–29
  consequences of, 21, 140–141
  definition, 6
  in Guatemala, 45–47, 135–136
  as key element of amoral communities, 22, 25–26, 160n13
  national leaders, role of in, 33–34, 143–145
  in Uganda, 44–45, 132–133
statis, 158n2
statues. *See* monuments and commemorations
Stoll, David, 71–72
Straus, Scott, 43, 159n9
streets/public spaces, ethnicization of, 42–43
symbols
  antifascist, 128, 174n49
  Croatian national, 11, 35
  flags, 42, 59–60
  Guatemalan, 45
  monuments and commemorations, 11–12, 101–107, 128–129, 174n49, 175n50

patriotic music, 38, 59
Serbian national, 40, 41–42, 59–60
subnational variations in use of, 107–108
Yugoslavian, 42, 128, 174n49, 175n50

targeted *vs.* intentional violence, 23–24
Tito, Josip Broz, 128
TO (Territorial Defense), 13, 125–126, 169n26
trials. *See* war crimes trials
Tuđman, Franjo, 8, 35–37, 42, 57, 77

Uganda
border production in, 82–83, 89
ethnicization in, 43–45
memories of violence in, 108–109, 112–114
moderates, exclusion of in, 63–64, 69–71
research methodology, 18
violence as political strategy in, 130–133, 143
UN Convention on Genocide, 23
unemployment, 1–2
Ustaša (NDH)
civilian killings by, 169n26
"Croatian silence" and, 99
media on, 35, 105, 138
Nazi alliance of, 11
Partisans and, 12, 97–98, 100–101

violence, classifications of, 23–25
Viterna, Jocelyn, 63–64
Vukovar, mass violence in, 121–122
Vukovarsko-srijemska, 17t

war crimes trials
ICJ, 1
ICTY, 69, 122–123, 126, 127–128
of Montt, 134–135, 138–139
reconciliation and, 123, 128, 135, 138–139
weddings, 53
Western Slavonia, 78–82, 85–86, 101–105, 118
Wimmer, Andreas, 159n9
women. *See* gendered experiences of war
workplaces, ethnicization of, 39–40, 53, 61, 78, 82, 161n22
World War II
as context for local reactions, 37
discourse on, 10–12
in-group policing during, 66
memories of, 92–112
subnational variation of violence in, 17t
written *vs.* oral history, 95

Yugoslavia
dissolution of, 7, 12–13, 118–119
selective commemorations in, 107
silencing of crimes in, 100
targeting of symbols of, 42, 128, 174n49, 175n50
in WWII, 11

Zagreb-Balgrade highway, 86
Žarkov, Dubravka, 35
Zeynep Bulutgil, H. Zeynep, 4–5
ZNG (Croatian National Guard), 14, 59
Zomia, 160n11